PHILIP II. OF SPAIN.

BY

CHARLES GAYARRÉ,

AUTHOR OF "THE HISTORY OF LOUISIANA UNDER THE FRENCH, SPANISH, AND AMERICAN DOMINATION," ETC., ETC.

WITH AN INTRODUCTORY LETTER

BY

GEORGE BANCROFT.

NEW YORK:
W. J. WIDDLETON, PUBLISHER.
1866.

NEW YORK:
EDWARD O. JENKINS, PRINTER,
20 NORTH WILLIAM ST.

PREFATORY NOTE.

In the following work it has been the Author's intention, as the most general glance over its pages will discover to the reader, not to present a minute chronicle in regular narrative of the events of Philip's reign, but in a certain way a philosophical retrospect of what was most memorable in Spain during that period as it was shaped by the controlling mind at the head of affairs—such a deduction, in fact, as the modern student must needs draw for himself after he has exhausted the materials of that busy and important era. The book may, therefore, be regarded as an historical essay in its exhibition of results, while it really conveys to the reader the most noticeable facts upon which the various conclusions are established. The striking events both in the domestic and foreign policy of the reign are passed in review, while the constant working of Philip's irrepressible nature and activity are not for a moment lost sight of in his personal history. The work thus partakes of a biographical and historical interest, in which the former, perhaps, preponderates without injury to the latter.

INTRODUCTORY LETTER.

NEW YORK, *November* 17, 1866.

MY DEAR SIR,—Accept my thanks for giving me an opportunity of perusing the work of Mr. Gayarré on Philip the Second of Spain in advance. I am very glad that he has found a publisher in New York. We need a unity in the commonwealth of letters as well as in the commonwealth of States, and the development of the national mind would be imperfect if each part of the country did not contribute its stream to the great river of public opinion. Our literature, like our political life, should develop unity in diversity, and the more the minds of men in one part of the country are brought closely alongside the minds of men of other parts, the better will it be for national culture. Boston publishers recently brought out a new volume of Rives's Life of Madison, and it is the most valuable contribution of the last winter to the history of the American Constitution and Union. It supplies a want which has been very much felt. It traces the history of the Constitution from the point of view of the great statesmen of Virginia who took part in that immortal work. There are some things in the volume to which objections may lie; all analogies drawn from the Greek republics and applied to ours, are founded upon erroneous notions; for the Greek Republic and ours are as unlike as possible, the Greek republic being an absolute government and ours a limited government — the Greek republic asserting despotic authority for the State, and ours beginning by the assertion of the inalienable rights of individual man. I mention this in particular, because the inferences drawn from ancient examples and applied to our time have been as disastrous in their consequences as they have been wrong in their principle. Nor do I accept the statements of the distinguished author about republicanism and democracy. But differences of opinion and discussion lead to good, and it is no more than justice to say that Mr. Rives has treated his subject in a spirit of candor and impartiality. One of my friends on finishing the volume said to me that it had for him all the interest of a novel. It may certainly lay claim to be considered as one of the fairest and most complete histories, perhaps it can more justly be said that it is the best history, of the formation of the federal Constitution.

Mr. Gayarré has claims upon us of old. He is the author of a history of Louisiana which is the fruit of thorough research and takes a very high rank among the best histories of the several states. His present work is written with care and vivacity; with a mind superior to the influences of superstition, and comprehensive in its study of the causes and consequences of events. He has a quick eye for the picturesque, and a rapid movement in his narrative which, if sometimes too highly ornamented, is never languid; and he clearly portrays the social and political tendencies of the reign which he describes. The subject at the first blush might seem to be remote from our present interests, but it is not so. Spanish America from the mouth of the Colorado to the extreme South still languishes from the attempt continued through centuries to connect government and civil prosperity with the Church policy of Charles the Fifth and Philip the Second. So the volume of Mr. Gayarré, like that of Mr. Rives, has an important connection with the great questions which the mind of America is now engaged in solving. Both of them are indirectly the highest tributes to the incomparable excellency of our institutions, and are the most earnest admonitions in favor of their perpetuity. The lessons come with particular value and distinctness from Mr. Gayarré as he is of Spanish descent and is wholly free from even the suspicion of a bias unfavorable to Spain.

I hope in your career as a publisher you will go on as you have begun, introducing to the public the works of men from all parts of our great continental country; it is the only way to build up a truly national literature.

Respectfully yours,

GEORGE BANCROFT.

W. J. WIDDLETON, ESQ.

CONTENTS.

CHAPTER I.

CHAPTER II.

CHAPTER III.

CHAPTER IV.

CHAPTER V.

CHAPTER VI.

CHAPTER VII.

CHAPTER VIII.

CHAPTER IX.

CHAPTER X.

PHILIP II. OF SPAIN.

CHAPTER I.

It is impossible for one who knows anything of the life of Philip the Second, king of Spain, not to feel a strong curiosity to be truthfully informed how such a man died. Was there aught in the circumstances of his death which we may seize upon as a revelation throwing light on his dark and mysterious character? He of the iron will; he whose word, or sign-manual, had prematurely sent out of this world so many of his fellow-beings, how did he demean himself when tortures, a hundred-fold more terrible than any he had inflicted, racked his body for months, and when he found himself in the presence of a master and conqueror far more inexorable than he himself had been to any of his subjects or enemies? Prescott has left unfinished the history of the stern son of Charles the Fifth, and, to gratify a cherished companion of our solitude, who has lately been perusing with so much delight his immortal pages, and who has found in them a diversion from the pressure of daily anxieties, and from the apprehensions of impending dangers amidst the clash of arms, it is our purpose to penetrate into the Escorial, and to show Philip closing his earthly career. After depositing him in the tomb prepared by his pride, we shall condense, in a rapid review, the appreciation of the character and reign of one who presents so grand, so deep, so varied and so dramatic a subject to the study of the historian, the philosopher and the poet.

When the news spread that the monarch who had been surnamed the "Demon of the South" had retired, in his old age, from his capital, to pass his last fugitive days and expire, like his father, amidst Hyronimite Monks, in that gigantic architectural structure which he had been thirty-two years in erecting, and in which he had united a palace, a monastery and a mausoleum, the world, which he had so long agitated, drew a long breath and hoped for rest. Philip had been suffering from the gout for twenty years, and at last that disease had acquired an intolerable degree of intensity. During the two years which preceded his death, it had become complicated with a hectical fever, which had so completely exhausted his strength, that he had to be carried about in an arm-chair. That fever produced the dropsy; it tortured him with an unextinguishable thirst, which it was fatal to indulge, and which, to resist, was one of the torments attributed by the imagination to the reprobates of divine justice in the regions of eternal punishment. Eighteen months before he closed his eyes forever, the malignity of the humors into which his whole body seemed to be transforming itself, had produced sores in his right hand and foot, which gave him the most intense pains, particularly when coming into contact with the sheets of his bed.

It was in this condition that he had been transported to the Escorial, where had just arrived in great pomp, and been received with all the solemn ceremonies of the Catholic Church, a precious collection of sacred relics which he had procured from Germany, through the exertions of a Commission which had been sent to that country for that special purpose. On hearing of this religious festival, the infirm monarch seemed to revive, and, notwithstanding the advice of his physicians and the remonstrances of the members of his Council, insisted on his being taken to his favorite residence. "I wish," he said, "to be carried alive to the place of my sepulchre." It was impossible to disobey, and a chair was constructed in which he could almost lie down as if in bed. It was thus that he left Madrid on the 30th of June, 1598. The slightest jolt produced in the royal patient the most acute pains; the men, who carried him on their shoulders, had to walk with much precaution, and with such slow and measured steps, that the dismal procession was six days in traversing the twenty-four miles which separate the Escorial from Madrid. At the sight of the austere-looking building, for which he had always entertained the fondest predilection, Philip seemed to rally his spirits and to recover some bodily strength. He was received with the accustomed honors by the monks whom he had established there, and, on the next day, he was carried to the church, where he remained a long time in prayer. Afterward, and for several succeeding days, stretched in his arm-chair, and almost as motionless as a corpse, he was present at the ceremony of depositing the German relics in their destined places at the different altars of the church. Still upheld in his chair by the strong arms of his attendants, he visited the libraries, which were in the first and second stories of the edifice, and minutely inspected the vast pile in all its departments, examining all the objects of interest which it contained, like one who enjoyed the completion of his great work and wished to take final leave of all its magnificence.

But his fever increased, and assumed an intermittent character. The patient, with the complication of diseases under which he was sinking, became so weak that his physicians were much alarmed. It was a tertian fever, and although it was with much difficulty stopped for some time, it returned with more violence, with daily attacks, and within shortening intervals. At the end of a week, a malignant tumor manifested itself in his right knee, increased prodigiously, and produced the most intense pain. As the last resort, when all other modes of relief had been exhausted, the physicians resolved to open the tumor ; and, as it was feared that the patient, from his debility, would not be able to bear the operation, the physicians, with much precaution, communicated to him their apprehensions. He received this information with great fortitude, and prepared himself by a general confession for what might happen. He caused some relics to be brought to him, and, after having adored and kissed them with much devotion, he put his body at the disposal of his medical attendants. The operation was performed by the skillful surgeon, Juan de Vergara; it was a very painful one, and all those who were present were amazed at the patience and courage exhibited by Philip.

His condition, however, did not improve. The hand of God was upon him who had caused so many tears to be shed during his long life, and no human skill could avail when divine justice seemed bent to enforce its decree of retribution. Above the gash which the operator's knife had made, two large sores appeared, and from their hideous and ghastly lips there issued such a quantity of matter as hardly seems credible. To the consuming heat of fever, to the burning thirst of dropsy, were added the corroding itch of ulcers and the infection of the inexhaustible streams of putrid matter which gushed from his flesh. The stench around the powerful sovereign of Spain and the Indies was such as to be insupportable to the by-standers. Immersed in this filth, the body of the patient was so sore that it could be turned neither to the right nor to the left, and it was impossible to change his clothes or his bedding. So sensitive had he become, that the slightest touch produced the most intolerable agony; and the haughty ruler of millions of men remained helplessly stretched in a sty, and in a more pitiable condition than that of the most ragged beggar in his vast dominions. But his fortitude was greater than his sufferings ; not a word of complaint was heard to escape from his lips ; and the soul remained unsubdued by these terrible infirmities of the flesh. He had been thirty-five days embedded in this sink of corruption, when, in consequence of it, his whole back became but one sore from his neck downward ; so that, of him it might have been said with singular appropriateness of scriptural language, "that Satan had smote him with sore boils from the sole of his foot unto his crown," if, indeed, the prince of darkness could have been supposed to be so harsh toward one of whom he certainly had no cause to complain. On this occasion, it rather looked like the smiting of God.

It seemed scarcely possible to increase the afflictions of Philip, when a chicken broth sweetened with sugar, which was administered to him, gave rise to other accidents which added to the fetidness of his apartment, and which are represented, besides, as being of an extraordinary and horrible character. He became sleepless, with occasional short fits of lethargy ; and, as it were to complete this spectacle of human misery and degradation, the ulcers teemed with a prodigious quantity of worms, which reproduced themselves with such prolific abundance, that they defied all attempts to remove their indestructible swarms. In this condition he remained fifty-three days, without taking anything which could satisfactorily explain the prolongation of his existence. To some it seemed a miracle, but it certainly was a great lesson to the sufferer and to the world; for this man had been for nearly half a century called "majesty;" he had been considered as a thing august and sacred, as the representative of God on earth; so much so, that, being accidentally struck, when a boy, by one of his youthful companions, the unintentional offender was doomed to death, although the decree, through the entreaties of Philip himself to his father the Emperor, was not carried into execution. God was now showing to what a degree of abjection He could bring the haughty and sinful being who had always been above all human laws, and whom it had almost been a sacrilege to offend. So, at least, thought the folly of man.

In the midst of these excruciating sufferings, his whole body being but one leprous sore, his emaciation being such that his bones threatened to pierce through his skin, Philip maintained unimpaired the serenity of his mind and the wonderful fortitude which he had hitherto displayed. To religion alone, or what to him was religion, he looked for consolation. The walls of the small apartment in which he lay were covered with crucifixes, relics, and images of saints. From time to time he would call for one of them and apply it to his burning lips, or to one of his sores, with the utmost fervor and faith. In these days of trial, he made many pious donations, and appropriated large sums to the dotation of establishments for the relief of widows and orphans, and to the foundation of hospitals and sanctuaries. It is strange that, in the condition in which we have represented him to be, he could turn his attention to temporal affairs, and had sufficient strength of mind to dictate to his minister and confidential secretary, Cristoval de Mora, some of his views and intentions for the conduct of the government; or rather, it was not strange; for it was the ruling passion, strong in death. In old age and amidst such torments as appalled the world, Philip displayed the same tenacity of purpose and love of power which had characterized him, when flushed with the aspirations of youth and health, and subsequently when glorying in the strength and experience of manhood.

But the last act of the drama was to be performed, and the monarch felt that he must quit the stage where he had long acted so conspicuous a part. He begged the Nuncio of his Holiness to bestow upon him apostolic benediction in the name of the Supreme Pontiff. The request was granted, and a special messenger whom the Nuncio sent to Rome with information of what he had done, brought back the confirmation of the Pope before Philip had died. He next required, with a voice which was every moment becoming more feeble, the administration of the extreme unction, the ceremonial text of which he had previously desired his confessor to read to him from the Roman ritual. He sent for his son, the hereditary prince, that he might be present at this solemn religious act. The extreme unction was administered to him by the Archbishop of Toledo; on which occasion he said to his future successor: "I wished you, my son, to be present, that you might see in what way end all things in this world." After having given the prince much wholesome advice as to religion and the principles of good government, he dismissed him, much moved by a scene so full of tender and sad impressions. From that day the dying monarch gave up all thoughts of temporal affairs, to devote himself entirely to the salvation of his soul by preparing for a Christian death. He caused the coffin of the emperor, his father, to be opened, and the body to be examined, in order that his own should be dressed for its sepulture after the same fashion. He ordered two wax candles which his father had used in his last moments to be brought to him, and also the crucifix which Charles had held in his hands when expiring. He further requested that the crucifix be suspended to the curtains of his couch, in front of him, so that his eyes might rest on the image of the Comforter and Saviour. He had his coffin placed alongside of his bed, and directed that, before being deposited in it, his corpse be incased in a leaden box, as he well knew the state of putrefaction to which he had been doomed before death. These commands were issued with the utmost self-possession and the most tranquil precision, amidst agonies which it required superhuman courage to endure—in an atmosphere so fetid that it well-nigh stifled the most robust of his attendants—when rottenness was in the flesh and bones of him who spoke so calmly, and when myriads of worms were rioting on his carcass. At the sight of this triumph of the soul over perishing matter, admiration seeks to forget deeds, the memory of which must, however, live as long as the records of history shall last for the instruction of mankind and the terror of evil-doers.

On the 11th of September, two days before his death, he called the hereditary prince, his son, and the infanta, his daughter, to his bedside. He took leave of them in the most affectionate manner, and with a voice scarcely audible from exhaustion, he exhorted them to persevere in the true faith, and to conduct themselves with prudence in the government of those States which he would leave to them. He handed to his confessor the celebrated testamentary instructions bequeathed by St. Louis of France to the heir of his crown, and requested the priest to read them to the prince and princess, to whom he afterward extended his fleshless and ulcered hand to be kissed, giving them his blessing, and dismissing them melting into tears. On the next day, the physicians gave Cristoval de Mora the disagreeable mission of informing Philip that his last hour was rapidly approaching. The dying man received the information with his usual impassibility. He devoutly listened to the exhortations of the Archbishop of Toledo, made his profession of faith, and ordered that the passion of Christ from the Gospel of John be read to him. Shortly after, he was seized with such a fit that he was thought to be dead, and a covering was thrown over his face. But he was not long before coming again to his senses and opening his eyes. He took the crucifix, kissed it repeatedly, listened to the prayers for the souls of the departed which the Prior of the monastery was reading to him, and with a slight quivering passed away, at five o'clock in the morning, on the 13th of September, 1598. Philip had lived seventy-one years, three months and twenty-two days, and reigned forty-two years. Thus ended the career of this prince, in that place of retirement and meditation from which, with one stroke of the pen, he used to send dismay, dark intrigues, civil commotions, religious perturbations, and direful wars, into many regions of the Old and of the New World. Thus lay low and cold the head which had teemed with so many schemes fatal to Spain and to other countries. Thus was palsied forever the hand which had so long held the manifold threads of the complicated politics and interests of so many empires. The Christian Tiberius was no more.

What Philip had prescribed to be done with his corpse was faithfully executed. Don Cristoval de

Mora and Don Antonio de Toledo were the executors of his will. The body, after having been washed and cleansed from the impurities with which it was coated all over, was dressed in a linen garment, then wrapped in a modest and common winding-sheet, and deposited in a lead coffin, with an humble wooden cross hanging from the neck by a coarse rope. The monks paid such funeral honors as were due to the royal founder of their monastery, and to the liberal protector whom they had lost; after which the body of Philip the Second was laid with solemn ceremonies in the vault chosen by himself in the Pantheon which he had erected for the house of Austria.

No martyr ever died with more fortitude, more faith, and more religious hope, than Philip the Second. He seems to have had no remorse for the deeds he had done, and at the recollection of which it is hardly possible not to shudder. He was free from those terrors which haunted Louis the Eleventh of France, and other tyrants, on their death-bed. The spectres of Carlos, Orange, Egmont, Horn, Montigny, and other victims, did not rise, like Banquo's ghost, to shake their gory locks at the dying murderer. He expressed, for aught that we know, no regret, no repentance, no contrition for the shedding of those streams of human blood in which he had steeped himself to the lips, nor did he show the slightest disposition to make reparation to those whom the world thought he had wronged. He died with Christian meekness and serenity, and with his eyes fixed on the image of that Saviour against whose precepts his whole life had been a perpetual outrage. Surely, it is a moral phenomenon which requires explanation—a psychological mystery which demands a solution. This explanation and solution can be found only in the hypothesis, it seems to us, that Philip remained persuaded to the last hour of his life that he was right when he committed those acts which struck with horror his contemporaries, and are still execrated by posterity. The peculiar idiosyncrasy of the man, the ethics of the age in which he lived, the influence of the social and political atmosphere in which he breathed since his infancy, must be taken into consideration to do justice to his character. In his boyhood, as we have said before, he had been taught that to strike him, even involuntarily or accidentally, was a crime deserving death. He had grown up to consider himself, as king, the representative of God on earth ; his will was law, and he was subject to none. Bigoted as he was, he permitted no interference with his authority in temporal affairs, even from the head of the Catholic Church. He conceived himself to be as absolute in his dominions, as he acknowledged the Pope to be in spiritual matters and in such domains as had been granted to him for the support of his pontifical dignity.

It is not improbable that Philip conscientiously believed that any opposition to the king's will, either in religion or in matters of State, was the most heinous offence that could be committed. He was the temporal vicegerent of the Deity on earth; he drew his power from that source, and not from man. Therefore any attempt to restrain that power was a sacrilege, and death was but the deserved penalty, which he had the right to inflict, when, where, and how he pleased, whether by the stroke of the public executioner, by the secret dagger of the assassin, or by the slow but sure action of poison. What mattered the mode of death, if death was rightfully at his command? It was the justice of the king, not passion, not hatred, not revenge, which had struck the blow. He never was carried away by any sudden impulse; all his acts were the result of long meditation. He permitted no surprise of his judgment, no lashing of his blood into uncontrolled storms. The ebullitions of his heart never obscured with their hot fumes the icy chambers of his head. He never seemed to be aware of having committed a crime, and to seek, like many other bigots, to propitiate Heaven's indulgence, or to compromise with its wrath. He conceived himself to be the champion of royalty and of the Catholic faith; and which predominated in his mind as to importance may well remain a question. But both, as he thought, were necessary to their own reciprocal existence; they were twin-sisters, bound together by mysterious ligaments which could not be severed without fatal results to both. His mission was to keep the crown as sacred as the tiara; his duty was to protect the Catholic faith throughout the world; and, the better to accomplish it, he probably deemed it a holy purpose, not only to preserve intact his hereditary dominions, but also to extend his sway as far as possible for the destruction of heresy. The maintenance and extension of his power was but the maintenance and extension of the true Church, which had been specially established for the service and the glory of God. Hence any word which he pledged in his worldly wisdom to the enemies of the Church, and of the monarchy which his person represented, was null and void, unless it was subservient to the interests of that Church and of that monarchy. To break his promise under such circumstances was no deceit. To remove out of this world, by whatever means, any human being whom he conceived to be dangerous to Church and to royalty, was a meritorious act. This man was as much a fanatic in his appreciation of his kingly office as in matters of religion. Hence he, without compunction or hesitation, swept away Egmont, Horn, Orange, and so many others, like rubbish in the path of the two cherished objects of his veneration. Hence he once publicly said that, should his son be convicted of heresy, he would himself bring fagots to the burning pile into which he would order him to be thrown. We are afraid that there was a horrible but earnest sincerity in his crimes, an awful honesty of purpose in his villainy, a frightful delusion produced by the sophistry of iniquity, which assumed in his mind the form of the logic of rectitude.

These were probably the reasons why he took no pains to destroy, as he could easily have done, the proofs of many of his dark deeds. On the contrary, he seems to have been indifferent on the subject, if not solicitous about reducing to writing all that was required to bring them before posterity in their true colors, as if he did not care to carry the deception which he practiced beyond the time when it was necessary for the success of his political purposes. From these circumstances it might be concluded that he considered what he had done as legitimate and just, or at least as a warrantable exercise of the attributes of sovereignty. We do not believe that he was callous to shame and to the opinion of future ages. He was naturally, it is true, of a phlegmatic temperament, and he had no more heart than a marble statue. But if, during his whole life, he generally abstained from exhibiting any signs of grief, joy, anger, pity, or attachment, we do not attribute it altogether to insensibility. It may also have originated in his conviction that he was too far exalted above the common race of mortals to indulge becomingly in such feelings. It would have been beneath the dignity and the heavenly calling of the standard-bearer of the Church and of the grand apostle and missionary of royalty. This view of his character is the only one which to our conception accounts for the marvelous placidity and fortitude of his death. The singularity of such a self-deceiving hallucination is no argument against the possibility of its existence, and no refutation of the deductions which we have drawn. If they are correct, Philip was a monster, but a monster unconscious of the whole extent of his wickedness.

He had begun his reign as the most powerful sovereign of Europe by the vastness, variety and wealth of his dominions, as well as by his political and family connections. His marriage with Mary of England had given him, through her, considerable influence in that kingdom; and if he had not inherited the imperial sceptre of his father, he may have consoled himself with the reflection that it had fallen into the hands of his uncle, Ferdinand. Philip had always entertained the most profound veneration and admiration for his father, and felt for him all the love of which his nature was susceptible. The reproaches of filial ingratitude addressed to him by some historians are not correct, and it is now demonstrated that he seldom ceased to be guided by the advice of the hermit of Yuste, which he even frequently sought with due deference. The policy and designs of Charles were, after his death, fully adopted and continued by his son, but with such difference in the ways and means as necessarily resulted from their opposite characters. Both had talents of the highest order, a cool judgment, a far-reaching perspicacity, and a clear insight into men and things. Both constituted themselves the representatives of Catholicity and of religious unity. But here ended the resemblance ; if there was similarity of purpose, there was dissimilitude of action ; and it could not be otherwise. Charles was a native of Flanders, where he had been educated. As such, and in his habits, tastes and predilections, he was uncongenial to the Spaniards, whose language he did not even speak. By them he was looked upon as a foreigner, to whom, by the accident of birth, they unfortunately owed allegiance. He, on the other hand, did not love Spain ; like William of Orange, the Batavian restorer of the liberties of England in a later age, he never could divest himself of his Dutch partialities ; whilst Philip, who was as intensely Spanish as any of the most idolized heroes of Castile, where he was born, was disliked by his Flemish subjects, whose idiom he did not even condescend to know ; and yet Philip, although a Spaniard, was as cold-blooded and phlegmatic as any Fleming, whilst Charles, a Fleming, had all the vivacity and warm impulses of the Spanish temperament. It had the appearance of a capricious freak of nature, or it looked as if their cradles had been accidentally misplaced ; perhaps it was providential ; for if Philip had been like Charles, it is probable that the events which led to the independence of the Netherlands would not have taken place, at least under his reign. Charles would not have remained in Spain, like Philip, as motionless as an incrustation in the Escorial, when threatened with the loss of those provinces. He would have gone in person to remove their discontents. He was free, open, and captivating in his manners ; he adapted himself, when he chose, to localities and nationalities ; he was, as it were, a cosmopolite. Philip was repulsive, sombre, taciturn, fond of isolation, and destitute of human sympathies. Charles was a meteor which warmed the atmosphere through which it winged its course. Philip was an iceberg which would have congealed even the gentlest tropical waves. The Emperor was an ambulatory statesman, who seemed to draw inspiration from the perpetual motion in which he rejoiced ; the King, equally as politic, was a fixture in his own cabinet, and the sluggishness of his body seemed to impart more restless activity to his mind. Charles was indefatigable in all corporal exercises as befitted a fearless knight, a skillful warrior, who delighted in danger and in the clash of arms ; Philip, physically indolent, was so averse to the stern joys of martial life, that his courage was even suspected. Charles was ambitious of governing the world, and would have wished, if possible, to have been present at the same time in all its parts. He seemed to have thought that the imperial purple required of him the ubiquity of God. But if the father held the sword with the ever-ready hand of a hero, the son, who never drew one from its scabbard, and for whom it was a useless appendage, had a scribe's passion for wielding the pen, and aspired to rule Europe from the cell of a monastery. Charles dictated laws in person to every country in Europe which he had inherited or conquered ; Philip sent them from his writing-desk. The Emperor issued face to face with his enemies those mandates which intimidated them. They saw the flash of his eye, the motion of his lips ; they heard the deep intonations of the Cæsar's voice. The King, like one of the hideous idols of India, hidden from the sight of his subjects in a sanctuary, terrified the earth by decrees which came from an invisible source. The father was the lightning shooting from one extremity of the horizon to the other, and striking with Olympian power and majesty. The son was a grim-looking engine, riveted to one spot, but flinging afar its missiles of death. The father, like the gods of Homer, seemed in a few strides to overcome distance over land and sea. The son, relentless and fixed as fate, in the gloom of his half-royal and half-monkish residence, ran his finger over a map, and marked the spot where desolation was to alight. Wherever there was a grand public assembly in Europe, a Diet, a Congress, or a Council, there was Charles. Personating the genius of diplomacy, Philip sent abroad his ambassadors, and those agents of his subtle mind and iron will felt that their master, wrapped up in mystery and seclusion in his impenetrable retreat, knew more than they did of the business which they had to manage and of the men with whom they had to deal, notwithstanding the boasted knowledge and varied experience which they thought they had acquired in their constant contact with the world.

But, in our opinion, notwithstanding his natural and acquired qualifications, which are beyond dispute, notwithstanding his astuteness, his cultivated mind, his profound knowledge of men and of the secrets of courts, Philip was far from being a great statesman. He was inferior to Cardinal Ximenes, to his ancestor Ferdinand, the conqueror of Granada, to Richelieu, who ruled France in the beginning of the next century, and who was fully his match in cruelty, vindictiveness, and dissimulation. The vision of his intellect was like that of the lynx. He could see with wonderful distinctness through darkness, when crouching to spring upon the prey of vulgar ambition. But he had no soul to soar on its wings to that altitude where alone, in the full effulgence of the sun, a broad and comprehensive eagle-eyed view of the horizon can be taken. In one thing he excelled: it was in what was called, in those days, king-craft; and he was the perfection of incarnated despotism, without that genius in whose companionship its savage features sometimes lose their terrors, without those amiable or brilliant traits of character which seduce, and without the halo of those heroic achievements which dazzle into submission. Crafty, saturnine, atrabilious, always dissembling and suspecting, sombre and silent like night when brooding over the hatching storm, he lived shrunk within himself with the only fellowship of his gloomy thoughts and cruel resolves. His memory was prodigious; he never forgot a name which he had once heard, or a fact which had once come to his knowledge. His industry could not be surpassed; always at work, always ready to dispatch business, he was as attentive to the most insignificant as to the most important. Immovable in his convictions, never swerving from his designs, unscrupulous in the means of accomplishing his objects, indifferent to those pleasures which have charms for most men, free from all passions save one, or at least if he had any, holding them, like everything else, in a state of servitude to his will, dead to compassion, insensible to flattery, inaccessible to surprise, the paragon of caution, ever master of himself to be the master of others, as cautelous and wily as a Jesuit, as reticent of secrets as the priest is of the confessions of his penitents, as silent as a Carthusian Friar, this man could not but domineer over all who came within his reach, and be proof against any influence over his own mind or heart. Nature and education had destined him to be the impersonation of absolutism.

So absorbing was his love of power, so intense his distrust of others, that it made him accomplish prodigies to escape the necessity of being dependent on anybody but himself. He aspired to do everything; there were no details too trifling for him to descend to ; he would prescribe where capital letters were to be used in ministerial dispatches, correct the orthography and even alter the shape of a letter, so as to make it conform to his own taste in calligraphy. He would direct what ceremonial was to be adopted in written communications to individuals according to their rank, what type, and what ink, red, black, or blue, were proper for the printing of certain prayer-books, what habiliments were to be worn by priests on particular occasions. He would dwell on other minutiæ entirely unworthy of the attention of a great sovereign, whose time ought to be too precious to be frittered away on such fooleries, and who ought to remember that it is not in keeping with the majesty and attributes of Jupiter to be catching flies like an idle peasant-boy. But in his mania for ruling everywhere, in high and low places, and on all occasions, in his morbid love of power and of its exercise even about trifles, he could not refrain from displaying a ravenous appetite which would have disputed even dry bones with a dog. He reminds us of an eddy which with equal greediness swallows up the ponderous beam, and the hardly perceptible straw floating on the water. With such a disposition on the part of Philip, it may well be supposed that his ministers were mere clerks. True it is that he seldom came to any resolution without consulting them, and listening long and patiently to what they had to say. But after having submitted their thoughts to the process of a slow digestion, he elaborated them into resolves which were emphatically his own. It was his hand which worked the complicated machinery of the administration of his immense dominions in the Old and in the New World. No State business was transacted without undergoing the scrutiny of his ever vigilant and sleepless attention. The royal autographs are so numerous as to beggar belief; and one wonders how he could find time to give so much occupation to his pen. He made it a rule to read all the government dispatches, whether sent or received, and most of them were either corrected, modified, or copiously annotated by himself. He never moved from one place to another without being accompanied by a portfolio full of papers; and even with the private secretary who waited on his person he preferred communicating in writing, rather than verbally. It probably gave him time to reflect, and suited his cautious nature.

Philip had established a vast net-work of espionage, not only in his own dominions, but also over the whole of the civilized world. He knew the manœuvres, intrigues, interests, and plans of foreign courts, long before he was informed of them by his accredited ambassadors, and those very ambassadors who sent him minute dispatches about the influence which governed a cabinet, or about the weak side of the prince near whom they resided, were themselves the objects of confidential communications from other sources about their own doings, and about the accuracy or incorrectness of the information which they transmitted. He had agents, sub-agents, and counter-agents, innumerable spies unknown to each other, reporting on the same subject, and working like wheels within wheels. All those who watched for him were also closely watched. He was well acquainted with the personal affairs, the private interests, the virtues or vices, the inclinations, the aspirations and the plans of all the leaders of the insurrection in Flanders ; with the qualifications and resources of every pretender to the crown of France ; with the physical, moral and intellectual imperfections or perfections of every aspirant to the hand of Elizabeth of England ; with the qualities, foibles and circumstances of every cardinal, or of any one who exercised any influence at the court of Rome, and of all those who were to be members of a Council in which the affairs, or dogmas of the Catholic Church were to be discussed and settled. But his information was infinitely more varied, minute and extensive on many subjects of much less importance, and this searching inquisition on his part was carried so far that it can hardly be realized. Thus every applicant for office, even of inferior degree, was amazed to discover that he was thoroughly known to the King, and that juvenile errors which he thought to be secret, or long since forgotten, had found their way to him, and had not been dismissed from his tenacious memory. Like a gigantic spider, motionless and terrific in its apparent lethargy, Philip in his closet felt the slightest percussion which struck the extremities of any one of the threads of the web which he had spread to the four quarters of the globe. He seemed to be omniscient, to be all ears and eyes; and no man was ever more competent to avail himself of such an advantage, for the purpose of carrying into steady execution this favorite maxim of Machiavelian policy: "Divide in order to rule." He hoarded power with as much miserly avidity as Shylock did money, and, like the Jew of Venice, he did not scruple to exact, for its accumulation, the pound of flesh nearest the heart, both from his subjects and his enemies. Thus, as the supreme power was a thing which, with a man of his temperament, admitted of no partnership, he completed the destruction of the liberties of Spain which his father had already begun. Charles had reduced the Cortes to a mere matter of form and ceremony, to a delusive pageantry. Philip made them an object of contempt. Charles had prostrated at Villalar the ancient privileges, immunities and franchises of his subjects which Padilla had dared to advocate with arms in his hands. Philip extinguished them in the blood of Lanuza in Aragon. On that day, the axe of the executioner consecrated him absolute King of Spain and the Indies.

Philip used to abstain from presiding at the meetings of his Cabinet, in order that his presence should not check the unguarded manifestations of views or passions which might occasionally be elicited by the heat of discussion ; but the individual who happened to be commissioned to make an official report of the ministerial proceedings, would not unfrequently discover that the Prince was already informed of all that had occurred in the Council. When he chose to be present at their deliberations, he took an incredible quantity of notes, and when he was satisfied with the abundance of his materials, he withdrew without expressing either approbation or blame, or letting his councilors know which advice he was inclined to favor. His dissimulation was such that he would even dupe his ministers, and, for some purpose of deception best known to himself, would lay before them, at times, only garbled fragments of dispatches, suppressing what would have put in its proper light that which he presented to them ; or he would submit to their consideration certain documents which he had mutilated, or slyly altered to suit his views. Any man of common honesty and understanding would call it forgery, but it is probable that it went by another name in Philip's vocabulary. The leaders in his Cabinet were the Duke of Alva and Ruy Gomez, prince of Eboli. He liked to see them pitted against each other, and took care to encourage their fierce rivalry, raising and depressing them in turn, but cautious how he gave preponderance to one over the other. Thus, these grave and puissant personages were kept engaged at a play, which is the common amusement of children. Placed at each end of a board or plank, they moved alternately at see-saw up and down, according to the impulsion given by Philip. Sometimes, as shown by the correspondence of Antonio Perez with Escovedo, he would, in order to entrap suspected persons, authorize one of his ministers to feign to betray him, to communicate pretended State secrets, and even to write very abusively of his person. What a singular scene is offered to us when we see Antonio Perez reading to Philip letters in which he treated his royal master with very little respect, and that royal master writing in a marginal note, "*Good—very good*;" or, "*Something more pointed might be added to make the thing more effective!*" It was a peculiarity with him that he retained in office men who had long lost his confidence and whom he hated intensely. He disliked change in those whom he employed, and it was impossible for them to discover when they had forfeited his favor. None save one, and that was Antonio Perez, could cope with him in the courtly art of disguising feelings and thoughts; and the iron mask which he wore was proof against the penetration of his ministers and courtiers. It was when the tiger's paw was as smooth as velvet that the lacerating claws suddenly came out; it was when a smile was on the lips, when benignity was in the eye, when the apparently friendly hand rested on the trusty shoulder, that the fatal blow was struck which showed the long-cherished malignity of the heart. There is something terrific in the secrecy, dissimulation and dogged perseverance with which Philip would, during a series of years, meditate and prepare the destruction of one man, or of a whole population, and something still more awful in the icy indifference, the superhuman insensibility, the accumulated cold-blooded energy of hoarded-up vengeance with which, at the opportune moment, he would issue a dry sentence of extermination. Friend, brother, son, were empty and unmeaning words which imposed upon him no obligation of love or protection. Patiently, and, as it were, luxuriously chewing the cud of his resentment, he seemed to take pleasure in distilling, slowly and chemically, the poison which, Python-like, he darted at every object which he detested or feared, or which he considered an obstacle in his path. The minute instructions which, in his own handwriting, he sent to the hangman who was to strangle Montigny in his prison, and which were intended to make the death of that nobleman appear natural, produce in us a shivering of horror. A king teaching his trade to Jack of the gallows! The following laconic dispatch which he forwarded to another minister of his wrath, "Take Lanuza and promptly cut off his head," is another striking characteristic of the man, particularly when it is remembered that Lanuza had done nothing but his duty as a magistrate in attempting to resist the encroachments of the tyrant on the old constitutional liberties of his subjects.

CHAPTER II.

One of the grand objects of Philip's life, as he professed, was the suppression of heresy; but he did not pursue it with the zealous disinterestedness of a missionary working solely for the salvation of the converted, or with the candid fervor of an apostle of truth. His purpose was entirely selfish. He proceeded in his assumed mission with the cold calculations of a mathematician. Catholicity was the lever of Archimedes with which he intended to raise the world from its foundations, and make it assume the position which he chose. He took care, however, that the service of God should lead to the aggrandizement of his dominions, and that religious fanaticism should never be permitted to work to the detriment of his temporal power. He was ready to extirpate the heresy which agitated Europe, by helping everywhere the Catholics against the Protestants; but it was to become the master of both Protestants and Catholics. The unity of religious faith was to be first imposed, in order to arrive at the unity of political authority. He had constituted himself the defender of the Roman Church, and as long as the Pope would favor his designs, he was profuse in blandishments, and professed to be his dutiful son. But whenever the Pontiff ceased to be a pliant tool, Philip treated him with great harshness, and seemed to approve and enjoy the insults which his ambassadors and generals heaped on the Vicar of Christ. Papal displeasure and Papal excommunications had no terrors for him, although he wished them to be dreaded by others; and he was willing to support the encroachments of the Holy See against every sovereign except himself. His first war, on his ascending the throne, was against the Pope, after his having fortified his conscience by the decision of a body of theologians and of jurists from his several Councils. Some years afterward, in 1578, he wrote as follows to the Marquis of Las Navas, his ambassador at Rome: "You will give His Holiness to understand that, according to the opinion of our councilors and canonists, who have put my conscience at rest on that point, the Prince is not obliged to conform to the mandates of the Pope in temporal affairs, and that His Holiness, in thus travelling out of his spiritual jurisdiction, exposes the Holy Apostolic See to be treated with little respect, which, in these days and under present circumstances, should be carefully avoided by His Holiness." The fact is, that the temporal power of the sovereign, as Philip understood it, was always sure to conflict with the spiritual rights of the Pope whenever it suited Philip's policy. For instance, he was inflexible in not permitting any pontifical bull to be published in his kingdom of Naples and Sicily, and in his Duchy of Milan, much less in Spain, without being examined and approved by him. The Pope would remonstrate, and maintain that those bulls only concerned ecclesiastical affairs; but Philip, with a pertinacity which was always successful in the end, would contend that there was some point in those ecclesiastical affairs which touched the temporal, and threw the whole, as being inseparably blended, within his own jurisdiction. The "rights of the crown" (*las regalias de la corona*), as he conceived them, were rather of unlimited length, breadth and depth, and armed with so keen an edge, that they never failed to clip and shorten the long fingers of the Church whenever they came in contact. At times he would even lecture the successor of St. Peter with the asperity of a disciple of Luther; for when the Pope wished to establish in Spain the military order of St. Lazarus, with extraordinary privileges and immunities, Philip wrote to Don Luis de Requesens, his ambassador in Rome, a communication which was to be shown to the Pope, and in which he said: "that the creation and multiplication of so many religious orders had been already an odious thing in the Church, and was reproved by the old canons; that if this was true in relation to the ordinary monastic and other ecclesiastical orders, it was still truer in application to those of a military character; that the baleful consequence of it was to withdraw individuals from the regular jurisdiction of the civil and ecclesiastical laws which governed the community at large ; that the object of such creations was the making of money by selling privileges, immunities and exemptions ; that such a course was unworthy of the Holy See ; that it was the scandal of the world ; that such policy was rotten in its very roots, and therefore no wholesome fruit could be expected from it ; that it was not within the legitimate authority of the Holy See to withdraw from the jurisdiction of princes such of their subjects as it might choose ; that those princes could not, in reason, permit it ; that there was neither justice nor honesty in such proceedings ; and that religion, on such occasions, was a mere pretext to serve other purposes." When the Council of Trent, which had been adjourned, was to meet again, the Pope insisted on its being a new convocation. Philip wanted it to be called a "continuation" of the Council. It gave rise to long discussions, during which Philip treated the Pope so rudely that the Holy Father was frightened into a compliance with the King's wishes.

He had a passion and a veneration for monks ; he liked to be surrounded by them, but he never failed to have them strangled if they threw any obstacle in his way. Although a most zealous advocate and supporter of the interests of the Clergy, he did not scruple to take one half of their revenues whenever it was required by his wants. It pleased him to keep up in that Clergy a spirit of opposition to the pretensions of the Holy See, and he generally promoted those who had been the warmest in that opposition; so that, whenever he was at variance with Rome, he was sure of being supported by his own clergy, of whom he may be said to have been the head, much more than the Pope. It is one of the inconsistencies of this man's character, that, fond of monks as he was, he was opposed to the increase of religious communities or associations; that he considered them as in conflict with the true spirit and ends of the Church; and that, far from being in favor of their augmentation, he desired their reduction to the old and primitive number. He used to say that piety throughout the world diminished in proportion to the increase of religious orders. He made strenuous efforts to curtail those that were in existence, and to make them conform to the severity of the ancient by-laws and regulations. He was a rigid censor of the morals of the clergy, and, assisted by his prodigious memory, he succeeded in keeping himself accurately informed, not only of the names and circumstances, but also of the deportment and capacity of every member of that numerous clergy who was in a position to pretend to preferments and dignities, which he made it a rule to grant to virtue and learning rather than to birth or favoritism. He had established an Argus-like police, which made him acquainted with the delinquencies and faults of the sacerdotal order, much to the dismay of those who knew that they were subjected to this unsparing ordeal. An individual had been repeatedly and strongly recommended to him for an ecclesiastical dignity. On those occasions the King had listened with a darker shade of moroseness on his face than usual, and had remained silent. At last, on being pressed, he replied with a withering sneer: "If we make him a bishop, which of his two natural sons will inherit the dignity after his death?" On another occasion, the Count of Chinchon, for whom he professed much esteem, was urging the claim of an aspirant to an Episcopal See. "I want you first," said the king, "to tell me what your candidate has done with that son he had when a student in the College of Salamanca." It may well be imagined that it was not without some degree of apprehension that he was approached for office when the applicant was received with such home-thrusts.

Although Philip kept his priesthood well bridled, and never permitted them, in the pulpit or elsewhere, to interfere beyond what he thought proper with the affairs of State, he allowed them occasionally to take more personal liberties with him than he vouchsafed to any other of his subjects. His High Almoner, Don Luis Manrique, once wrote to him in the following bold strain: "Your Majesty's subjects everywhere complain of your manner of doing business—sitting all day long over your papers, from your desire, as they intimate, to seclude yourself from the world, and from a want of confidence in your ministers. Hence such interminable delays as fill the soul of every suitor with despair. Your subjects are discontented, because you refuse to take your seat in the Council of State. The Almighty does not send kings into the world to spend their days in reading or writing, or even in meditation and prayer, but to serve as public oracles to which all may resort for answers. If any sovereign has received this grace, it is your Majesty; and therefore the greater the sin, if you do not give free access to all." Philip bore patiently with this lecture on his royal duties, and it is the more remarkable from the circumstance, that, from his boyhood, he had shown a disposition to wince under the administering of any rebuke from those preceptors to whose care his education had been intrusted, as we see by an admirable letter written to him by the emperor his father in support of old Zuñiga, who used to speak his mind too frankly for the taste of his pupil. "If he deals plainly with you," wrote Charles to Philip, "it is for the love he bears you. If he were to flatter you, and be only solicitous to minister to your wishes, he would be like all the rest of the world, and you would have no one near you to tell you the truth; and a worse thing cannot happen to any man, old or young, but most of all to the young, from their want of experience, which prevents them from discerning truth from error." The natural haughtiness of Philip's temper was such that there was very little chance of his profiting by this paternal admonition. A striking proof of this disposition was given by him at Augsburg, in Germany, during his father's life, as related by Prescott. "When Charles returned to his palace, escorted, as he usually was, by a train of nobles and princes of the empire, he would courteously take them by the hand, and raised his hat as he parted with them. But Philip, it was observed, on like occasions, walked directly into the palace, without so much as turning round, or condescending, in any way, to notice the courtiers who had accompanied him. This was taking higher ground than even his father had done. In fact, it was said of him that he considered himself greater than his father, inasmuch as the son of an Emperor was greater than the son of a King." Such a man was not apt to listen meekly to any unpalatable truths, or to be patient of control, or even of guidance, from whatever source it was offered, unless at rare intervals, probably for effect, or, perhaps, to serve some purpose of his own, if it was not because, among the cloying dishes which flattery served up to him daily, it was a relish for him to find one occasionally seasoned with a few grains of pungent truth.

Lafuente, the Spanish historian, says, probably with truth, that Philip would have invented the Inquisition if he had not found it already in existence. He made that bloody tribunal his right arm, and he patronized inquisitors, provided they understood that they were to be his humble and obedient ministers. To their jurisdiction he found it convenient to turn over all those whose ruin he could not accomplish with as much ease by the exercise of secular or civil authority. They had nets which no hunted game, whatever it was, could hardly hope to escape. This terrific institution, in the hands of Philip, reminds us of those cells in Venetian prisons, the lateral walls and the vaults of which were said to be so constructed that they daily closed tighter round a doomed victim, gradually depriving him of air and space, until they finally came together and crushed his body to death. But whenever the Inquisition endeavored to emancipate itself from the leading-strings in which it was put, a gentle paternal slap from the monarch was an admonition which warned the tool to remain what it was, and not to presume to be the head or even the hand. Thus, in 1574, the Inquisition had resolved to establish in several of the most important provinces of Spain a military Order, under the name of "St. Mary of the White Sword." This Order was to be composed exclusively of men whose genealogy, after the most severe and scrupulous examination, would show them descended from many generations of Christians who had never deviated from the old Catholic faith, who had never been soiled by the impurities of new-fangled doctrines, and whose veins had never been contaminated by the admixture of any Moorish, heretic, or Jewish blood. This militia was to be governed by the Inquisitor-General, and to be the Pretorian guard of the State religion, and its members were to be exempt from any other jurisdiction, either civil or royal. Many scions of the most influential and noblest families of Spain had already entered the Order, and a petition had been laid before the Sovereign for the confirmation of its constitution and privileges, when Philip, to use a homely but expressive and well-known figurative saying, "smelt a rat," and immediately crushed this insidious conspiracy against his authority. He ordered all the papers of the embryo Order to be seized; he commanded that, for the future, a profound and perpetual silence be observed in relation to the contemplated institution; and he addressed to all religious and secular corporations a circular, in which he recommended to them not to make themselves uneasy about the safety and purity of the true faith, because it was his duty, in the post in which God had placed him, to look to these matters, giving them the assurance, at the same time, that he would fulfill his obligations in that respect without any officious assistance which he did not need. If he was satisfied with this exhibition of displeasure, and did not inflict actual punishment, it is probably because he did not choose to weaken an instrument which he found so useful to his purposes.

Time has explained some of the acts of that mysterious man, which for so many years had remained puzzling riddles for those who studied his reign. For instance, his contemporaries were amazed that a young and ambitious sovereign, after the battles of St. Quentin and Gravelines, when France lay at his feet, was so anxious for peace as to assure one of his negotiators, the Prince of Orange, "that the greatest service he could render him in this world was to make peace, and that he desired to have it at any price whatever, so eager was he to return to Spain." To another envoy he had said: "O ambassador, I wish for peace on any terms, and if the King of France had not sued for it, I would have begged for it myself." Charles the Fifth, in his retreat of Yuste, was convulsed with rage when he learned that his son had lost the opportunity to march to Paris after the victory of St. Quentin. The world was taken by surprise, and wondered why the King of Spain, in the midst of his triumphs, was so clamorous for a cessation of hostilities. We know now that it was because Philip's head was full of a scheme by which he was to prevail upon the King of France to massacre all the Protestants in his dominions, at the same time when he, Philip, should do the same butcher's work in the Netherlands. Hence he had been most anxious to propitiate his royal brother of France by an unexpectedly advantageous treaty of peace, and he gained his object, since Henry the Second agreed to the proposed wholesale assassination, which was defeated only by accidental circumstances, and postponed to take place a few years later, under the reign of Charles the Ninth. Thus Philip stands revealed to posterity as the real author of the St. Bartholomew. To him belongs the original idea, and he cannot justly be deprived of a copyright so authentically and in due form registered in the records and under the great seal of Hell.

The sudden termination of the war with the Pope was of the same nature. By his order the victorious Duke of Alva, under the weight of whose iron hand Rome had tottered to its foundations, fell at the feet of the Pope, and begged his absolution for having beaten his troops and insulted his person. It was in vain that Alva bitterly exclaimed that the treaty of peace which he was instructed to grant "seemed to have been dictated by the vanquished rather than by the victor." It was in vain that the haughty Duke consoled himself with this remark: "Were I the king, His Holiness would be ordered to send one of his nephews to ask for my pardon, instead of my General suing for his." It was in vain that Charles V. at Yuste, when he heard of what he thought to be so disgracfel to the King, was beside himself with mortification; it was in vain that the recluse Emperor swore with the coarse energy of a trooper. No pride or vain-glory could have induced Philip, at any time of his life, to step one line beyond that point to which, and no further, he thought necessary to carry that policy or design which he had at heart. On the occasion to which I have referred, he had shown that he could be driven into the painful necessity of flagellating, after the fashion of savage tribes, the idol before which he knelt, whenever that idol should become troublesome, or deaf to his pressing entreaties. That was enough ; this practical warning had answered his purpose ; and he would go no further. He was not the man to weaken the Papacy, when the main object of his life, and, we may say, his fixed and dominant idea, was to hunt Protestantism out of this world with all the hounds which he could muster to his assistance.

We believe that Philip was sincere, when he asseverated that he would lose a hundred lives, if he had them, rather than compromise with heresy. We believe that he was equally sincere when he affirmed that he would lose all his dominions rather than suffer them to be tainted with Protestantism, and his conduct in relation to the Netherlands proves, we think, that sincerity ; for he would have secured the allegiance of all those provinces, if he had made concessions in matters of religion. We believe that he was sincere when he wrote to the Emperor of Germany, who had remonstrated with him on his treatment of the Netherlands, that "he had seen with the deepest sorrow that his Imperial Majesty wished to persuade him in religious matters to proceed with mildness. The Emperor ought to be aware," added Philip, "that no human consideration, no regard for his realms, nothing in the world which could be represented to him, or risked by him, would cause him to swerve a single hair's breadth from his path on the subject of religion.

This path was the same through all his kin
He had ever trod in it faithfully, and he m
keep in it perpetually. He would admit n
counsel nor persuasion to the contrary, and v
take it ill if counsel or persuasion should be c
ed. He could not but consider the terms of t
instructions given to the Archduke * as exceedin
the limits of amicable suggestion. They, in fact, amounted to a menace, and he was astonished that a menace should be employed, because with princes constituted like himself such means could have but little success.†

Motley, in his admirable History of the Rise of the Dutch Republic, raises doubts on the earnestness of Philip's fanaticism and on the sincerity of his religious convictions, because that monarch, as he maintains, was willing to purchase his election to the imperial throne of Germany, which his father had occupied, by abjuring what were supposed to be his most cherished principles. "Philip of Spain," he says, "whose mission was to extirpate heresy throughout his realms, and who, in pursuance of that mission, had already perpetrated more crimes, and waded more deeply in the blood of his subjects than monarch had ever done before; Philip, for whom his apologists have never found any defence, save that he believed it his duty to God rather to de-

* One of the Archdukes of the German Empire had been sent on a special mission to Philip.

† Motley's Rise of the Dutch Republic, p. 272, vol. II.

;e his territories than to permit a single within their limits, now entered into secret ations with the Princes of the Empire. He ,ed himself, if they would confer the crown ı him, that he would withdraw the Spaniards om the Netherlands; that he would tolerate in hose provinces the exercise of the reformed religion; that he would recognize their union with the rest of the German Empire, and their consequent claim to the benefits of the Passau treaty; that he would restore the Prince of Orange and 'all his accomplices' to their former possessions, dignities and condition, and that he would cause to be observed, throughout every realm incorporated with the Empire, all the edicts and ordinances which had been constructed to secure religious freedom in Germany. In brief, Philip was willing, in case the crown of Charlemagne should be promised him, to undo the work of his life, to reinstate the arch-rebel whom he had hunted and proscribed, and to bow before that Reformation whose disciples he had so long burned and butchered. So much extent and no more had that religious conviction by which he had for years the effrontery to excuse the enormities practiced in the Netherlands. God would never forgive him so long as one heretic remained unburned in the Provinces; yet give him the imperial sceptre, and every heretic, without forswearing his heresy, should be purged with hyssop and become whiter than snow."

In the facts here related we certainly see abundant evidence of Philip's unbounded duplicity, but none of his being a hypocrite in his manifestations of religious faith. We therefore respectfully dissent from the conclusions of the distinguished historian. He himself has too deeply studied Philip's character not to be convinced that, had the champion of Catholicity been elected to the throne of the Cæsars like his father, he would have violated all the engagements which he had taken to secure the coveted object of his ambition, and would have made use of the increase of his power to quarter, disembowel and burn Protestants with renewed energy and on a larger field of operation. He would, no doubt, as Emperor, have given terrible proofs of the genuine earnestness of his fanaticism, instead of "bowing before the Reformation," as the illustrious author we have quoted affects to think. It was the very essence of his system of ethics to keep no faith with the enemies of God. There was merit in the breach, and sin in the observance. No covenant with Satan and Satan's offspring could be binding upon a true son of the Holy Catholic Church, which, as he believed, permitted such dealings with the "accursed vermin" of Protestantism, only as praiseworthy snares to entrap the disciples of the arch-enemy. It was the general impression in those times, when universal deception was the order of the day among the rulers of the earth, that Philip, notwithstanding all the promises he might make and all the oaths he might take, would not, in reality, compromise in matters of religion, and that he and toleration of heresy were two things which could not exist in the same atmosphere. The Prince of Orange and all the Electoral Princes of the Empire knew but too well that Philip would not "undo the work of his life," but would have grimly smiled at their stupendous credulity, if they had been such fools as to put any faith in his word. Therefore not a moment's consideration was given to assurances which must have been regarded as insults to the intellect of those to whom they were addressed. Hence the Electors took very good care to withhold the imperial mantle from the shoulders of him who, as a bigoted Catholic, hated heresy with an intensity not to be exceeded by the fiercest of the Popes, and who, as a sovereign and a statesman, looked upon religious reformation as a pretext for civil revolutions, which he also abhorred as much as heresy, "with all his heart, with all his soul, with all his strength and with all his mind."

It appears to have been a part of Philip's policy to make his most faithful servants and most powerful nobles feel that he could exalt and depress them at will, according as he needed, or not, their services, and that they were entirely dependent on him for their worldly honors and prosperity. Thus he used them like implements, dismissed them, and recalled them again with a degree of indifference which was peculiar to his nature, and what is still more extraordinary, with a cool conviction that they would be at hand whenever wanted, or whistled for. The haughty Duke of Alva, to whom he was but too much indebted for the fidelity with which his tyrannical orders were executed in Flanders, was exiled from court for a slight cause of displeasure, and, a short time after, he was put, as if nothing had happened, and without one soothing word of conciliation, at the head of the army destined to invade Portugal. He raised Espinosa from nothing to be president of the Council of Castile and Italy, to be Grand Inquisitor and Cardinal; and without any sufficient motive that we can discover, he struck at his favorite a blow which broke his heart and brought him to the grave. His confidential minister and agent, Antonio Perez, whom he had intrusted with so many dark secrets, he did not fear to persecute at last with relentless fury. So it was with others. His own sister, Margaret of Austria, who, as regent of the Netherlands, had suffered much for his sake, he filled with disgust, as soon as she ceased to answer his purposes, and he superseded her by the Duke of Alva in a manner which wounded her feelings and was highly offensive to her dignity. The Duke met with the same fate in his turn. It is not necessary to pursue any further this enumeration. They were blind indeed, who, in serving him, did not see that, although things of life, real men of flesh and blood, they were used by Philip like chessmen on a chess-board.

Whoever excited Philip's fear or jealousy did not usually live any length of time, when within reach of his arm, and that arm was a long one. It will be sufficient to mention three instances in which death, whether brought by accident, or by the subtle means which he always had at his disposal, served opportunely what was supposed to be the secret desire of his heart. Thus, Philip was still in the full vigor of manhood, when his son and heir, Don Carlos, had reached his twenty-third year. This, in itself, was an untoward circumstance for a man of Philip's temperament, for reasons which we shall mention. Besides, that prince was the very opposite of his father. A creature of ungovernable passions, and of a violence so extreme that it must be attributed to insanity, he was so free, so open, or so imprudent that he never could conceal one single feeling or thought. He was of a fiery, martial disposition, and knew no fear. Capriciously generous or cruel, headstrong, obstinate and reckless, rushing blindly like an infuriated bull on any obstacle to his will, he recalled to mind, with exaggerated and distorted features, his kinsman and namesake, Charles the Bold of Burgundy. These were sufficient causes of dislike in a man of Philip's nature, and he treated Carlos with such studied coldness, if not persecuting aversion, that he drove him into a sort of frantic despair. The partially mad prince wished to be something in the State ; he desired to be initiated to business, to have the command of armies, and his father gave him to understand that he was to remain a cipher. He had been affianced to the beautiful Isabelle of France; his father took her for himself. Exasperated by this outrage and by what he conceived to be the uniformly and systematically bad treatment to which he was subjected, the Prince loudly complained. He uttered words of savage passion against the King and his ministers. He breathed vengeance against his enemies. He criticised the policy pursued by the Government in the Netherlands. He determined to go himself to that country and look into the causes of discontent. Dagger in hand, he made an assault upon the Duke of Alva for having accepted the command which he, the Hereditary Prince, wished to have. Several eligible matches had been proposed for Carlos, but the King had always defeated them. He seemed to be anxious that his son should never marry. He probably thought that it would have strengthened the position of the Prince. At last the unfortunate Carlos resolved to fly from the Kingdom. He communicated his intention to his uncle, Don John of Austria, whom he loved and trusted, and who in vain remonstrated on the folly of such a scheme. Don John thought it his duty to report the fact to the King; and the Prince, on suspecting it, gave way to one of his ungovernable fits of passion, and attacked his uncle sword in hand. There was something still worse: it was suspected that the Prince was tainted with heresy. Otherwise, he could not sympathize as he did with the insurrectionists of the Netherlands. Be this true or not, the time had evidently arrived when the heir apparent was to be a thorn in the King's side. It was probable that, like most heirs apparent, he would soon become a centre of opposition, a focus of dangerous intrigues, a rallying-point for all malcontents, a pole-star toward which would be directed hopes and aspirations, if not actual plots and rebellions, and therefore that he would turn out to be a source of anxieties to the ruler of the realm. That ruler was Philip, who, as we may reasonably suppose, trembled at the prospect of a long and dangerous struggle with so fierce and unmanageable a character as Don Carlos. It might become necessary to conciliate, to make concessions, and even to part with some fragment of power. In one of the gloomy cells of the Escorial, Philip, on this occasion as on many others, deliberately pondered, slowly made up his mind, and decreed that his son be arrested and never again restored to liberty. The Prince, soon after his incarceration, as was to be expected, sickened, lingered, and died.

We know in history of no scene so dramatically horrible, and at the same time so contemptible, so cowardly and so ruffianly as is presented by Philip, with armor over his clothes and a helmet on his head, stealing at midnight on the slumbers of his son, through a door whose boltings and fastenings he had ordered a skillful mechanic to make secretly insecure, advancing like a thief and a murderer, tremblingly and cautiously, preceded by six of the great lords of his Councils, and by twelve men of his body-guard, who were to seize his victim in his bed and remove all possibility of danger, before he ventured into the chamber. The Prince had long suspected an attempt against his life, or liberty. He therefore always wore arms on his person, and slept with weapons under his pillow. But on this occasion, the Grandees of Spain whom Philip had converted into alguazils crept as stealthily as wild Indians, and pinioned Carlos before he was awake. Now the worst fears of the victim were but too sadly realized. "Your majesty," said Carlos to Philip, "had better kill me than keep me a prisoner. It will be a great scandal to the Kingdom. If you do not kill me, I will make away with myself." "You will do no such thing," replied the King, "for that would be the act of a madman." "Your majesty," continued Carlos, "treats me so ill that you force me to this extremity. I am not mad, but you drive me to despair." The prisoner's words, relates Prescott, became so broken by sobs as to be scarcely audible. But Philip was no more moved than the steel cuirass he wore over his breast. He quietly completed his arrangements for the safe-keeping of his son, took with his own royal hands a coffer which contained the papers of Carlos, and withdrew with it from the apartment of the miserable being who was doubly miserable from having such a father. Shortly after, the prince was no more, and Philip slept better.

The death of Carlos was attended with a circumstance in which there seems to be a degree of impious mockery and diabolical hypocrisy which reaches the sublime. We mention the anecdote, because in it the whole of Philip's nature stands revealed. It paints to the life, like one of Rembrandt's finishing strokes of the brush, or rather it is like a photograph taken by the lurid light of a flame shot out from Pandemonium. If some doubt that Philip killed his son, none doubt that he cherished against him the most deep-rooted aversion; and yet look at this scene! Here lies the Prince on his bed, dying, if not from poison, at least from despair produced by his father's treatment. He is insensible, or he sleeps for a little while, before sleeping forever. Philip steals softly behind the Prince of Eboli and the High Prior, Antonio de Toledo, who are watching over the last agonies of the victim. He stretches out his hand toward the bed, and, making the sign of the cross, gives a parting benediction to his dying son. Was Philip in earnest? Was this the blessing of a kind parent, after the sentence of a just and inexorable judge? Was there some kind of sophistry by which Philip persuaded himself that he had fulfilled the duties of both? If not, we wonder if the arch dissembler thought that he deceived by the stage effect of this grand piece of acting his accomplices who stood by, or hoped that their report of it would dupe the world?

There is a figure which projects in bright relief

from the dark canvas of Philip's reign, with a lambent glory sporting around its head. It is that of Don John of Austria, who was the natural son of Charles V., but who, if barred from the patrimony which went to the legitimate offspring, had inherited all the grand and heroic qualities which his father had possessed. He was born a hero, a paladin of romance. The beauty of his person was equal to the excellence of his mind and heart. He seemed to have been intended by nature as a satire on his royal brother. He served that brother faithfully, gained victories for him, and ought to have been the pride of the house of Austria, by which he aspired to be acknowledged as if he had been born in wedlock. As a reward for all he had done, he begged to be raised to the rank of infante, or member of the royal family, by a formal decree, but this boon Philip never granted. Don John found it more easy to be the conqueror of the Moors in the Alpujarras, and of the Turks at Lepanto, and to be the idol of Christendom, than to possess himself of one particle of his brother's affection. Others, with the bar sinister in their shields, had ascended thrones, and he also wished, with his good sword and with the sanction of the Pope, to conquer a kingdom for himself. Philip took care to prevent it. Don John aspired to the hand of Mary Stuart, of Elizabeth of England, and other royal dames. He probably thought that his glory was too dazzling to permit the defect in his birth to be seen. But Philip was determined that his bastard brother should not become a king like himself. Besides, it looks as if it had been settled in his mind that Don John should not contract any matrimonial alliance whatever. It was sufficiently bitter to be eclipsed by his subject, and it was a consolation that he could thwart, oppress, humiliate and crush, at will, the object of his envy. To permit him to become independent was a thought not to be endured. Would he allow Don John the opportunity to show himself as superior to him in the capacity of a king, as he had proved himself to be by his personal exploits, his brilliant valor, and other moral qualities? Unfortunately, Antonio Perez, the only man, perhaps, who, for many years, succeeded in thoroughly deceiving Philip, and in slyly leading him into the paths in which the skillful minister wished him to tread, convinced the tyrant, who listened but too greedily to such suggestions, that Don John not only schemed to encircle his brow with a foreign crown, but also nourished designs which might be fatal to the royal authority at home. Philip began to fear. That was enough. Escovedo, the secretary and friend of the Prince, who was suspected of encouraging his ambitious aspirations, was assassinated by Philip's order. Don John's noble heart was broken with grief by this event and by the King's suspicions of his fidelity, combined with various causes of despondency emanating from other sources. Although still redolent with youth, he sickened and died in the

Netherlands, where he had been governing, fighting, negotiating, and pining away in the service of his brother. Livid spots appeared on his body after death. The multitude, and particularly his companions-in-arms, who composed the funeral procession, shed a profusion of tears, but did not venture to whisper the suspicions that were in their minds. The finger of caution was raised to the lips to give warning, and to close them against any unguarded expression. The king might hear. To be impartial, it must be admitted that Philip had shown, on repeated occasions, more affection for his brother, and more solicitude for the preservation of his life, than could be expected from his cold-blooded temperament; nor is there any proof that Don John's death was not natural, or if it was caused by poison, that Philip was accessary to that crime. Be it as it may, however, Don John's ambition had become troublesome, and he ceased to live at an opportune moment for Philip's peace of mind.

William of Nassau, prince of Orange, the Washington of the Netherlands, was one of the men whom Philip hated the most intensely, and no man ever knew Philip better than William. He was not to be cajoled and entrapped like Egmont and Horn. He was proof against all of Philip's oaths, arts, flatteries and deceptions. Philip never made a move on the chess-board which had not been guessed at and anticipated by William. It is really interesting to see these two wary antagonists keenly watching each other's combinations, plotting and counter-plotting, mining and undermining, and trying to outmanœuvre each other. Philip the taciturn had found his match in William the silent. If the King's perseverance equaled that of the Prince; in diplomacy and in fertility of resources the Prince surpassed the King. Philip's generals could beat William in the field, but hardly had one army been destroyed, when he created another. It was Antæus rising from the ground with more energy and desperate resolve, each time after he had been prostrated on his mother earth, and Philip was no Hercules to lift him up and crush him whilst struggling in the vacant air. The Catholic King got tired, at last, of the exhausting game he had been playing so long against the champion of Protestantism, and, one day, the world heard with horror that the Prince of Orange had died by an assassin's shot.

Philip did not possess that valuable art which some sovereigns have of saying gracious or soul-stirring things which live forever in the memory of him to whom they are addressed, which soften disappointment and double the value of a favor. He could not, like his contemporary, Henry IV. of France, utter those sentences which take forcible possession of a man's heart; which make the greatest sacrifices light and even acceptable to him from whom they are expected; which cause toils, privations and dangers to be forgotten, and send one bounding over a battery of cannon with as much alacrity as if going to a wedding feast. There was one occasion, however, on which Philip was so moved that he was betrayed into paying a compliment with the dignity of a Sovereign and the sensibility of a man. It was when, after the battle of St. Quentin, the Duke of Savoy, laying at his feet the banners and other trophies conquered over the French, and kneeling down, would have kissed his hand. The King raised him from the ground, embraced him, and said that "the acknowledgments were due from himself to the captain who had won such a victory." But we believe that, as a general rule, it was his intention, as it was his nature, to be impassive, and that he was resolved to permit himself, as seldom as possible, to be warmed into any exhibition of feeling. He seems to have taken pleasure in reversing the celebrated saying, "*Homo sum; humani nihil a me alienum puto*," and to have adopted as his motto, "I am not a man, and what concerns man is foreign to me." Thus his policy was to appear to be a stranger to human affections and sentiments, and to be impervious to grief and joy. When he heard of the disaster of the Invincible Armada, his countenance did not change, and he contented himself with saying, "That he had sent his ships to contend against men and not against the elements." The glorious triumph of Lepanto was received with the same apparent indifference. Such impassiveness was easily attained by a man who had no heart. It is to be regretted that he was not dissected after his death, for the special purpose of examining the place where that organ should have been. Even Alva felt for the widow and children of Egmont. He informed Philip that they were reduced to the most horrible destitution, and begged him to have pity on them. The reply was: "I will think of it, and let you know my determination." This was all that could be obtained, and they would have starved if Alva had not, out of his own private fortune, granted a pension to Egmont's widow and Egmont's children. How bitter must have been to them the bread proceeding from such a source!

One of the singularities of Philip's character was the anxiety which he frequently showed concerning the future life of his victims in a better world. He seemed to be extremely desirous that they should die like Christians, and that their souls should be saved, as in the case of Egmont, Horn, Montigny and others. This feeling was exhibited in secret and confidential letters; it must, therefore, be accepted as sincere, and cannot be presumed to have been intended for effect. But the mystery which shrouded so many of his acts was one of the distinctive features of his reign. The death of Montigny, of Don John, of Escovedo, of Don Carlos, the persecution of Antonio Perez, the incarceration of the Princess of Eboli, and other deeds equally dark, were enigmas which excited, at the time, the most intense curiosity, and which the world still attempts to solve. Light has fallen upon them in the course of years, but yet there are in them obscurities which remain impenetrable. Much is unexplained as to the causes and circumstances of those events which glide before us with an iron mask on their faces like the celebrated prisoner of the age of Louis XIV. But those mysteries give a sort of painful attraction to the reign of Philip. To them he is indebted for a great part of his fame and for the effect which he produces on the imagination. It is due to their influence that he has become a favorite study, a rich theme, not only for the historian, but also for the philosopher and the poet. Seen through deep mists and frowning clouds, by the imperfect glimpses of the fugitive lightning leaping from the bosom of the howling storm, the figure of Philip assumes colossal proportions. Like one of those gigantic peaks which, at the North Pole, overhang the angry waves of tempestuous seas in a sunless atmosphere, it derives its majesty from the terrors with which it is surrounded.

Patience is said to have been the great virtue of Philip. That virtue was, probably, due to his temperament. We think that he carried it to an excess, and that it became a defect. It is an important art to know how to wait, but there is something like waiting too long. He used to boast that "he and time were a match for any two." But he deceived himself; time was not always his ally. Time favors genius and virtue; to the latter it renders tardy justice, and to the former it tenders golden opportunities, which must be snatched with a ready grasp. Time, like tide and wind, waits for no man; and Philip, progressing at the slow and measured step of an Iberian mule, frequently arrived too late to co-operate with time. His faith in its agency, however, remained unshaken, and it betrayed him into the adoption of a system of procrastination. It grew into an unconquerable habit, which, by his example, he seems to have made a national one, and to have bequeathed to all the subsequent governments of Spain. It drove his officers and ministers into fits of despair, and they were constantly complaining of his dilatoriness. Whilst he was deliberating, the moment for action had passed away. During the time which it took him to write long dispatches, in which he equivocated to his heart's content, and sedulously abstained from meeting those difficult questions on which his answer was anxiously expected, his father, Charles V., would have conquered a province. Many of the important decisions and measures into which he was at last driven were too late. If he had been prompt on those occasions, more than one success would have been secured, and more than one reverse avoided. Philip was too prudent, too cautious. He was ambitious to acquire, but he had too much to lose to be bold and adventurous. Like Cæsar, he would not have trusted to the cast of a die. It is true that he was not Cæsar, and was not of a temperament to do violence to fortune. The mole, which gropes laboriously under ground, would not be true to its nature, and would act unwisely, if it hung its destiny on the wing of an eagle. Philip could hardly have been surpassed as head of the Order of the Jesuits, as chief of the Inquisition, as minister of police, or as a wily ambassador. Considering his indefatigable industry and his peculiar qualifications, we even think that he might have united in his person all these different characters and cumulated their functions, without fear of suffering from comparison with anybody distinguished for exalted merit in any one of those positions. But Providence had destined him to be a king, and we deem that, as such, he had many superiors.

There is a wonderful monument, in the architecture of which the character of Philip is typified. It is the Escorial. The vow which he had made to erect this prodigious structure, if he won the battle of St. Quentin, was probably but an occasion for him to carry into execution a conception which was already in his mind. It may have suggested, however, the whimsical idea of dedicating it to St. Lawrence, the patron saint of the day on which that event took place, and of adopting for the plan of the building the shape of the gridiron on which the saint is said to have suffered martyrdom. Great monarchs had bequeathed to posterity architectural creations, as the manifestations of the power and taste which they had possessed. It is to be supposed that Philip had the same ambition, and the Escorial arose in its massive proportions to astonish the world. It was with Philip a labor of love during many long years, and he spent in its construction six millions of ducats—a sum which, considering the difference in the value of coin between that epoch and ours, may be set down as equivalent to almost thirty millions of dollars. Within a few miles of Madrid, in a region which seems to have been calcined by the fiery wrath of heaven, where the winds howl with fury, or moan in a piteous tone during the greater portion of the year, there is a chain of mountains whose heads are white with snow even at the end of July. Those mountains are bare of vegetation and are of an ashy color, as if their cheeks were pale with affright at the scene of desolation in which they are placed. This was the spot selected by Philip for the monument which was to commemorate his reign. It is a palace, a cloister and a tomb. God and the King in Philip's mind were intimately associated—they could not be separated. God, it is true, might be where the King was not, but where the King was, there was God bound to be. In such close alliance with the Deity, the King felt secure. He could do no wrong, and nothing could be attempted against the majesty of earth, without its being also an attempt against the majesty of Heaven. The blending of the two was to strike with awe all mortal eyes. He seems to have thought that he was in a sort of mystical copartnership with God and His Church, and that he was entitled to most of the profits of the association. If as the omnipotent representative of divine power—as king—he violated any of the commandments of the Decalogue, provided he conscientiously thought it was for the benefit, first of the throne, and next of the Church, he felt sure that the hand of God was extended over his head for absolution. Thus one part of the Escorial was a palace for himself, and another a temple for God. To each his share. It was also to be a mausoleum for his race—the tomb, side by side with the throne—which is not to be wondered at—for from the insane Joanna who gave birth to his royal line down to the idiotic Charles the Second who closed it, there seems to have been in the family a strange disposition to keep up a kind of mournful dalliance with the grave, and to entertain a wild curiosity to peep into its secrets.

It is impossible to see the Escorial without coming to the conclusion that it is the fittest abode on earth for monastic austerity, ascetic devotion and penitential remorse. The very stones seem to pray. There stands revealed at one glance the whole spirit of Christianity—not of Christianity smiling with hopes, but convulsed with terror, prostrated at the feet of an angry God, and listening to the trumpet which announces the day of judgment. The blood freezes in the veins; the very soul shivers with cold and awe. The Escorial is a Biblical monument, and one is almost tempted to fancy that it was planned by Moses under the inspiration of his Egyptian recollections. He who enters its sombre walls feels a creeping of the flesh, as if he was conscious of standing in the invisible presence of Jehovah. He imagines, with a French writer, that he hears the thunders of Sinai and the lamentations of the prophets. He has a vision of Asia, of Jerusalem, of the temple of Nineveh, of the feast of Belshazzar. The whole of the Old Testament is before him. He shudders as he advances under those gloomy vaults, when suddenly the cross of the Saviour meets his eyes, and the Calvary and Mount Tabor rise before him, the one with all the sublimity of its sufferings, and the other with all its hopes, its consoling promises and its final glorification. This is the religious aspect of the building, but it has also its political physiognomy.

It has been said with some felicity of expression that the Escorial was the capitol of the Inquisition. To some imaginations it may look like a jail, out of which the genius of progress, if once incarcerated in it, could never escape ; or it may be taken with its frowning towers for a fortress, into which Philip hoped that new ideas and innovations would not venture to penetrate, and which even the whirlwind of revolutions would not dare to assail. It certainly has the stamp, and might be accepted as the type of the immutability of the Catholic Church. Perhaps Philip persuaded himself that the one hundred and thirty monks whom he had established so near his bed-chamber, who prayed for him and did penance night and day on his behalf, might be expiatory victims sufficient to atone for his sins. Who knows that he may not have thought that he could thus strike a balance-sheet between Heaven and himself, in which much might remain to his credit, and Heaven turn out to be his debtor? Be it as it may, the Escorial is singularly emblematical of Philip and of the country over which he ruled. Spain, Philip, and the Escorial so naturally harmonize together, that it is hardly possible to conceive their separate existence.

CHAPTER III.

Philip had a cultivated mind and a pure taste in the fine arts. He was considered a good judge of Latin compositions, and was sometimes consulted by authors in that language on questions of prosody and on the propriety of certain idiomatic expressions, although perhaps it was but artful flattery on their part. He was acquainted with several modern languages, and was fond of books, as is evidenced by his formation of the magnificent library of the Escorial. He was no mean connoisseur in painting and architecture. A daub would not have been palmed upon him under the prestige of a celebrated name. He corresponded with men who had made themselves illustrious by their science, and he professed much esteem for erudition in general. But, nevertheless, he issued an edict by which he condemned to perpetual exile, or to the loss of all their earthly possessions, any of his subjects who should leave the realm to pursue their studies in the colleges, universities or schools of other kingdoms. He was afraid of the infiltration of foreign ideas into Spain. He patronized science and literature on condition that they should be well used to the bit and whip, like docile and thoroughly trained horses, fattened and groomed in his stables to pull his coach with a stately and decorous step on State occasions. Poetry might tune its lyre as it pleased, to sing the loves of piping shepherds and fugitive nymphs, or describe the social manners of the age, or of former times, in comedies and novels. The imagination was permitted to take its flight according to the strength of its wings, but it was bound not to alight on any ground which might possibly fall within the domain of State affairs, or of the Catholic Church. The philosopher, the theologian, the astronomer, the jurist, the geologist, the student, or explorer in whatever field of science, were still more restricted than the poet. How could it be otherwise, when no man could publish one single idea without putting this question to himself: What will the King or the Inquisition think of it? Approbation might bring no reward, and disapprobation was sure to send a victim to the dungeon, the stake, or the scaffold. Philip may be said to have loved science after the fashion of the Sultan in the Arabian Tales, who caused to be strangled in the morning the Sultana of the preceding night. He embraced Science as long as she ministered to his purposes and served him as a willing slave, in the glimmering dawn of the intellectual atmosphere which he liked, but as soon as the light which is inherent in her threatened to break out into an illumination, the axe of the executioner extinguished it in blood.

The person of Philip has been as variously described by historians and chroniclers as his character.' To some he is Hyperion, to others a satyr—half beast, half man. The truth is between the two representations. As he stands before posterity, brought again into life by the pencil of Titian, when the bloom of youth had not yet faded before the sallow tints of disease, and before the smooth brow had been wrinkled by age, by care and thought, he is not destitute of comeliness. The light yellow of his hair and beard, his fair and delicate complexion, would remind us of his German extraction, even without the assistance of the famous thick underlip of his Austrian race, which mars the symmetry of his lineaments. Another defect was the protrusion of his lower jaw, which was more marked than in his father's face, to which his own bore a strong resemblance, although having a less intellectual cast. It gave him a heavier and duller look, and partook more of animalism. His eyebrows approached each other too closely over the root of his nose, but that nose was thin and aquiline. Behind the cold, pensive and even sad expression of his blue eyes as they settle in fixed repose on him who gazes on the monarch's portrait, there seems to lurk something sinister, which sends a chilling sensation to the blood. His forehead was finely developed, and gave the assurance of high intellectual powers. His stature was below the middle size; his figure was slight and spare, but in his limbs there was beauty of proportion and shape. He was scrupulously neat in his dress, which was rich and elegant, although of a sable color that seemed to be in harmony with the complexion of his thoughts. It always consisted of black satin or velvet, of which his shoes were also made. The only ornament which he generally wore was the superb collar of the Golden Fleece, which hung from his neck to his breast. A black cap with feathers covered his head and completed his costume. In this dark livery, amidst the gorgeous train of his nobles resplendent with jewels and all the colors of the rainbow, he, with his moody brow, looked like the picture of night followed by the starry host of Heaven.

The boy in Philip had prognosticated what the man would be. There were in the sapling clear indications of the strength and vast proportions of the future oak. It might, perhaps, be more proper to say that Philip never was young. If youth was in his body, it never was in his soul. A boy, slow of speech, frigid in his demeanor, without any of the occasional sallies of his age, saturnine like a misanthrope, reserved like a diplomatist, so self-possessed as to be rarely off his guard, is a portentous anomaly. He may be said to be prematurely old, and a sort of moral prodigy to be wondered at and pitied. With such a temper, with the ambition which he had, with his fierce love of power, it may readily be supposed that he was, as his father wished, easily trained to business, for which, besides, he had a strong natural disposition. Furthermore, he had the good fortune to have in his imperial parent the best of guides, under whom he served, if I may use the expression, the apprenticeship of kingcraft. With a view, no doubt, of initiating his son to the art of governing, Charles, on leaving Spain for one of his last continental expeditions, had made him regent in his absence. By a short extract from one of the admonitory letters of Charles to Philip, we can judge of the excellence of the tuition administered by the father to the son: "The Duke of Alva," wrote Charles, "is the ablest statesman and the best soldier I have in my dominions. Consult him, above all, in military affairs; but do not depend on him entirely in these or in any other matters. Depend on no one but yourself. The Grandees will be but too prompt to secure your favor, and through you to govern the land. But if you are thus governed, it will be your ruin. The mere suspicion of it will do you infinite prejudice. Make use of all; but lean exclusively on none. In your perplexities, ever trust in your Maker. Have no care but for Him." One can hardly study the life of Philip, without being satisfied that he bettered some of these instructions. He certainly depended "on none but himself," although fond of consulting others. But if in his perplexities he "trusted in his Maker," he no less trusted in himself, in the public executioner, in the fagots of the Inquisition, in the secret blow of the dagger, and in the withering effects of the poisonous cup. "Have no care but for Him alone," wrote Charles. Philip obeyed, but modified the precept. He had no care but for God, save the King; and if, throughout life, the King persuaded himself, as we think he did, that he served only the cause of God, and fought none but His battles, it was, it must be admitted, by incasing himself in a panoply furnished by the armory of the powers of darkness.

In that same letter of paternal advice, the Emperor cautioned Philip against yielding to the blandishments of libertinism, which, syren-like, would lead him to perdition by emasculating his body and putting the seal of reprobation on his soul. This highly moral instruction, although coming from a source which Philip respected more than any other, did not save him from the contamination of more than one vicious amour and adulterous connection; but, unlike the monarchs of the epoch, he threw a decorous veil over his frailties. No woman ever exercised any real influence over him, and his dalliance with beauty was attended with the same mystery which shrouded his other actions. Philip sedulously guarded his name against the pollution of any amorous scandal as unbefitting the uniformly religious color which he wished to give to his life; and as derogating from his kingly dignity. Although in gallantries he may have sinned more than his father, yet he would not, like him, have blazoned out to the world any foibles of the kind and acknowledged a natural son, had that son been a hero like Don John of Austria. Philip was not the man to be driven by the logic of contrition, or any impulse of the heart, into the public confession of an error, and to make amends for it. He was too much of a royal Grandison, with a dash of Joseph Surface. No Falstaff could have been his boon companion, and could have induced him, in the intoxication of wit and mirth, to perpetrate any of the follies of the Prince of Wales. In his youth he had been one of those well-behaved lads who give to old spinster aunts the infallible promise of a virtuous and rectangular life, and Charles had written to him after the fashion of most fathers who have decent boys: "On the whole, I will admit I have much reason to be satisfied with your conduct. But I would have you perfect; and, to speak frankly, whatever other persons may tell you, you have some things to mend yet. Your confessor and old preceptor, the Bishop of Carthagena, is a good man, as all the world knows; but I hope that he will take better care of your conscience than he did of your studies, and that he will not show quite as accommodating a temper in regard to the former as he did to the latter." We beg leave, with the utmost respect, to differ with the Emperor in this matter. We think that the proficiency of Philip in his studies was, for a royal pupil, creditable enough to the old bishop. As to the education which that ecclesiastic gave to the conscience which he had under his care, the world knows the results. We fancy that Philip always held his eccentric and peculiarly constituted conscience in his own keeping, and that his priestly preceptor found him more refractory on that subject than in learning his lessons in Latin prosody.

Philip was but little over sixteen years old when he married Mary of Portugal, who died shortly after giving birth to the unfortunate Don Carlos. He cared very little for Mary of England, his second wife, who doted on him ; but he seems to have been, as far as it was in such a nature, a good and indulgent husband to Isabel of France and to Anne of Austria. The writers of fiction have wronged Philip when representing him as the Blue Beard of the nursery tale. He has too many real crimes to answer for, without being charged with imaginary guilt. All his wives were exemplary, as such ; and the supposed amours of Isabel and Don Carlos, which are acceptable themes to poetry, must be rejected by the truth-loving justice of history. It may seem strange that such an unlovable character as Philip should have secured the sincere attachment of his connubial partners, but such is the fact. It is related that, on his being once dangerously ill, his fourth and last wife, Anne of Austria, implored the Almighty to spare a life so important to the welfare of the Kingdom and of the Church, and, instead of it, to accept the sacrifice of her own. "Heaven," says the chronicler, "listened to her prayer. The King recovered, and the Queen fell ill of a disorder which, in a few days, terminated fatally." Isabel of France, his third wife, had been looked upon by the country of her adoption as an angelic being, as perfection on earth, and she was literally adored by the Spaniards. The soft emanations of her gentle heart seemed to warm the icy atmosphere of Philip's court. When the sun hangs on the confines of the Western horizon, a light, rosy cloud oft comes down from heaven and diffuses itself round the snow-capped diadem of the monarch of the Alps. The Titan is lulled to repose, and smooths his rugged features into celestial loveliness. But soon the vaporous light disappears, and nothing is left but increasing darkness, with the terrors of the glacier and the avalanche. The benighted traveler shudders, and his heart grows cold. Thus felt Spain when Isabel died, and when, on his exalted and isolated throne above his subjects, Philip loomed up an object of deeper gloom and more terrific aspect.

It may easily be conceived that such a man as Philip could not have favorites like the effete Henry III. of France, or friends like the magnanimous Henry IV., the white-plumed hero of Navarre, both his contemporaries. He had none but fawning courtiers around his person, for whom his will was law in all matters, with the exception of the haughty and iron Duke of Alva. The subtlest of them all was one of the ministers, Ruy Gomez, prince of Eboli, who from his boyhood to his death after a long career, had been the companion of Philip, whom he had studied to the very marrow of his bones, whose humors he thoroughly understood, and whose favor he retained to the last. But Ruy Gomez was neither a favorite nor a friend. He was a most skillful clerk, a convenient tool, a discreet and able adviser, a safe confidant, a pleasant attendant, whose time-piece was always so set as to strike the hour which the King desired to be marked on the dial. It is probable, however, that he was really liked by Philip, for he never was dismissed from office with one of those withering smiles which that Prince was known to keep in reserve for those who had long appeared to enjoy his confidence and patronage—a smile which killed as surely as the far-famed poison of the Borgias. It is true that the wife of Gomez, the Princess of Eboli, may have been the lightning-rod which warded off the thunderbolt from her husband's breast. But her subsequent misfortunes, inflicted by her royal paramour, leave it in doubt to decide whether Philip's love and Philip's hatred were not twin-sister furies, not easily distinguished from each other, and whose embrace was equally fatal.

In very few acts of his life did Philip ever forget his exalted station. The king and the man in him were seldom found apart from each other, and the man had a kind of fanatical reverence for the king. Therefore, although personally of a frugal and unostentatious disposition, he deemed that his royal dignity required a household clothed in splendor, and his was constituted on a scale of stateliness and magnificence which far surpassed any other in Europe. It amounted in the number of retainers to no less than fifteen hundred persons. The most rigid and pompous etiquette was established. Forty pages, sons of the most illustrious houses of Castile, waited on his person. Dukes, whose pedigree went back to Hercules and the demi-gods of fabulous antiquity, were his major-domos and gentlemen of the bed-chamber. The chief muleteer and a host of officers with menial titles were nobles and cavaliers of gentle blood. The establishment of the Queen was in the same gorgeous style, and she was always attended by a train of no less than twenty-six ladies in waiting. All this display was probably the result of calculation rather than of taste, and was, in Philip's estimation, the necessary appendage to one who aspired to be King of Kings.

Always clad from head to foot in an armor of impenetrable and chilling reserve, Philip had too much respect for himself to be overbearing, capricious, or impatient with his servants. It is said that he was kind and liberal to them, and that there was more than one occasion on which he showed himself with them a good-natured gentleman. For instance, once he had been writing late through the night some important dispatch to be sent in the morning. Exhausted by fatigue, his Secretary had fallen into a doze ; and when Philip handed the document to him, with a request to throw sand over it, this functionary, in the confusion of the moment, emptied the inkstand on the royal manuscript. Philip coolly remarked: 'It would have been better to have used the sand;" and, without one word of complaint or impatience, betook himself to rewriting the whole of the letter. Nevertheless, we cannot but imagine that his servants were not much at ease under the eye of such a master. One of them, we are sure, must have remembered to the last day of his life the message which Philip sent to him, on discovering that he had disturbed the methodical arrangement in which papers had been left in the royal closet. "Tell him," said Philip to an attendant, "that were it not in consideration of the services of his uncle, who has placed him near my person, I would have ordered his head to be cut off." This anecdote offsets the other. Here the lion, there the lamb. On another occasion, when on the return to Spain of Don John of Austria, after the battle of Lepanto, Philip had conducted him to the apartment of the Queen to be welcomed home by her, it happened that the sword of the Prince, on his bowing low to her Majesty, was by that motion of his body suddenly pushed back in such a way as violently to strike the King, who stood behind him, right on the forehead above the eye. The blow was such as to stun and fell him to the ground. The consternation was indescribable. Don John was beside himself, and profuse in his expressions of deep regret and sorrow. "There is no cause for such concern on your part," observed the King, with his usual phlegmatic demeanor; "it is an accident for which you are not responsible." "O, sire," exclaimed Don John, "if it had been worse, I would have thrown myself out of the window." "And why? it would not have remedied anything," replied King Statue, with the same cold and metallic tone of voice.

Philip was exceedingly methodical, systematic and precise. So carefully set in order were all his voluminous papers, that he could at any time indicate where any one of them was to be found. It was a rule which he rigidly enforced—that there should be a place for everything, and that everything should be in its place. He fully understood the value of time, and economized it as a miser does his money. His occupations and even his pleasures were regulated with the utmost precision. The festive table had no attraction for him. He was prudent and abstemious in his diet. After the slight repast which constituted his dinner, he gave audience to his subjects and received their memorials. On those occasions he attempted to be gracious; but graciousness sat awkwardly on Philip. It was an unnatural conjunction—a ray of the sun imprisoned in an icicle. He listened patiently, it is true; but his countenance was so exceedingly grave, that the boldest was abashed, and felt as if the ground was giving way under his feet. The hand of the supplicant trembled on his delivering his petition, his tongue faltered in pressing his suit, and the chilling tone with which

Philip said : " Compose yourself," increased his confusion. It was as if a marble statue had spoken, and the suitor was glad to back out of the presence of petrified royalty, and to retreat where something like the intonations of the human voice were heard, and human sympathies expressed. Even a Papal Nuncio forgot in his presence what he had to say ; and although Philip kindly said, " If you will bring it in writing, I will read it myself, and expedite your business," it is not improbable that the representative of the Pope thought this defender of the faith and dutiful son of the Church as grim-looking a personage as any of those dreaded beings whom she was occasionally called upon to exorcise with bell, book, and holy water.

Philip was said to be indolent because he had a horror of locomotion and could seldom be prevailed upon to travel, even when it was required by the most pressing exigencies of State. But this indolence of the body was combined with the most restless activity of the mind. He toiled day and night, and never was known to utter an exclamation of weariness. He seemed to delight in the multitude of business, as a lion-hearted warrior grows more fierce when the battle thickens upon him. Perhaps Philip, who boasted that, without moving from his closet, he shook the world with a scrap of paper, was pleased with the idea that he personated Fate immutably seated on a rock, whilst weaving the web of human destinies. As he advanced in age, he became less easy of access and more averse to motion. His public audiences were infrequent, and, in the beginning of summer, he would escape from them by retreating to one of his country palaces, particularly to the Escorial, his beloved creation ; not, however, to admire the beauties of nature, but to be more free from the contact of man. When in Madrid, he shrank from the eye of the public as from that of a basilisk, commonly went out in a close carriage, and waited for the congenial shades of night to return to his palace with the silent wings of an ill-omened bird of darkness.

The Cortes made it a matter of complaint that he withdrew from the eyes of his subjects, and would have been well pleased if he had occasionally appeared in different parts of Spain, to judge for himself of the resources and wants of the country. But he paid no more attention to the representations of the Cortes on this subject, than he generally did to every other on which they addressed him. He was willing that they should remonstrate humbly and respectfully, provided it was understood by them to be a mere ceremony. It was a sort of arrangement with which he was even gratified ; for it kept up an appearance of liberty on the side of the people, and of benevolent condescension on his part. He continued, however, to make himself more and more invisible, and contented himself with being felt. As a recreation and exercise, he would sometimes go to one of his country-seats near Madrid, where he would shoot with a gun or a cross-bow at the game which was driven to his presence. Even on those occasions Philip, who always carried with him a mass of papers, would soon turn away from the sport, to examine into some serious or intricate matters of State. He was too mighty and too keen a hunter of men to find any relish in the less exciting pursuit of the wild beasts of the forest. But there was one amusement for which Philip had a real passion. It was one which the Inquisition, who knew well the royal inclinations, took care to afford him on days of extraordinary rejoicings, such as the celebration of his marriages, the birth of his children, or any thanksgiving for some unusual blessing. That entertainment was the burning of heretics. The rank and qualifications of the victims, with other circumstances, were generally such as to enhance the interest of the lurid scene, and there were in all the details of the offered feast an appropriate selection and magnificence of horrors which did credit to the dramatic skill of the Inquisition, and which were intended to produce the desired impression on the royal spectator. If Philip felt any emotion whatever on witnessing such exhibitions, his countenance did not allow the secret to transpire. There he sat in conspicuous pre-eminence, the observed of all, stern, silent, almost motionless, and to all appearances with his usual stony impassiveness. We imagine that his satisfaction must have diffused itself inwardly, and must have derived additional zest from the conviction that, on these occasions, pleasure and duty went hand-in-hand together like a loving married couple returning from the parish church. It is this perfect accord of his conscience and his taste which perhaps recommended these spectacles to his preference. Who knows but he may have thought that those victims, sacrificed to Jehovah and snatched from the perdition of heresy, would rise with the white robes of innocence from the purifying flames, and would attend him as a body-guard when he should appear before the judgment-seat of the Eternal, circling in serried ranks round his sins as a protective phalanx of expiation? Be it as it may, when with the mind's eye we see Philip presiding at these holocausts of fanaticism, we cannot but fancy that there stands before our dismayed vision one of those horrible Mexican deities of his own dominions, whose nostrils were regaled with the fumes of blood, and whose sight was rejoiced with the offering of warm and still palpitating hearts, torn by priestly hands from living breasts.

The Marquis of Custine, in his work entitled "Spain Under Ferdinand VII.," says in relation to Philip: "This King, who used his power on earth to prepare for himself a seat in Heaven, may have often deceived himself, but in his errors there was at least nothing that was mean. If he was cruel, it was after the fashion of one who performs a duty. Therefore the terror with which I am inspired by his name will not be unmixed with pity, as long as it is not fully proved to me that he ever committed a crime which did not mainly originate in a scruple of conscience." If this be true, it would solve the enigma of the virtuous tranquillity and magnificent fortitude of his death. We may be permitted, however, to exclaim: What a terrible conscience that man had! From some preceding remarks it may be seen, that we are not disposed to reject altogether the view taken by the French author of Philip's character. In some of his acts, crimsoned with blood as they are, Philip may have been guided by his conscience. It must be remembered that he more than once asseverated that he would surrender his kingdoms—nay—life itself, rather than reign over heretics; and if he put Don Carlos to death, he may really have thought with his apologist, the priest Salazar de Mendoza, blasphemous as the sentiment is, that "in making a sacrifice of his son, he rivaled in sublimity that of Isaac by Abraham, and even of Jesus Christ by the Almighty." This would be a remarkable aberration of the intellect, but it is not inexplicable in Philip, when it is kept in mind that his royal line sprang from insanity in the person of his grandmother, Joanna of Castile, and that it ended as it had begun—in the idiotic madness of the wretched Charles the Second, the last scion of the House of Austria on the throne of Spain.

The memory of Philip is more popular in Spain than that of Charles V., although his reign is far less brilliant. The reason of this is, that the Spaniards have always considered Philip as one of them, and Charles as a foreigner, as one not identified with their interests, their language, their feelings, their prejudices, their habits and their morals; whilst Philip was emphatically a production of their country—one to the manner born—and the embodiment of their nationality. Charles was rather the Emperor of Germany than the King of Spain; whilst the crown inherited from Ferdinand and Isabel was more precious in Philip's estimation than all the other kingdoms of the earth. Spain was for Charles no more than one of the gems of his imperial jewel-box; for Philip it was the principal gem, and far more valuable than the jewel-box itself, with all the rest of its contents. His reign was absolutely and exclusively Spanish. Neither in his Court nor in his councils did he allow the influence of foreigners to prevail. His father had done the reverse. So identified was Philip with Spain, that he could hardly breathe and live when not within its hallowed frontiers. When he went beyond them, which happened but rarely, he seemed out of his element, and hastened to return, frequently at the sacrifice of important interests, to the congenial atmosphere for which he panted. When reading his history, we see what powerful reasons united at times to call him out of Spain, and what pressing and incessant solicitations added their force to the influence of these reasons. We know what promises he made to yield to them, and we also know that he never could summon resolution enough to keep those engagements and to lose sight of his beloved Escorial. Charles, on the contrary, felt uncomfortable in Spain, and never was more cheerful than when rushing to his Flemish or German dominions. In the language of a Spanish historian, if Philip had subjugated Europe, he would have made it Spanish, whilst Charles would have made it German. Under the reign of Charles, the blood and wealth of Spain were lavished to support German or other foreign interests, and in furtherance of the personal or family ambition of the Sovereign. Spain occupied a subordinate position in the plans of the great Emperor. In Philip's head and heart Spain was paramount to everything else. It is the consciousness of this fact which has almost endeared the memory of Philip to every Spaniard, notwithstanding his crimes and the terror attached to his name. Spaniards will easily forgive many sins in one whom they consider so intensely Spanish. Hence they complain that Philip is treated with undue severity by foreign writers. They say that his general character was at least no worse than that of most of the Sovereigns of the epoch. They point to Henry VIII. of England, who, with the same pen with which he wrote against Luther, issued a decree by which he adopted his doctrines, made them the religious creed of the State, and gave himself to his subjects the example of the abjuration of a former faith, not because he had changed his convictions conscientiously, but because the Pope had refused to sanction his divorce from a virtuous wife. Henry VIII.!—who successively sent to the scaffold the objects of his insatiable lust, and who, with impartial ferocity, condemned to the stake seventy thousand Catholics and Protestants. They ask if Cardinal Fisher and the illustrious Thomas More and many other victims were not as guiltless as Horn and Egmont. They ask if Cardinal Wolsey was not truer to Henry than Antonio Perez to Philip, and if the King of England was a better man than the King of Spain? What of bloody Mary? Did she not send her sister Elizabeth to a dungeon, and threaten her life? What became of Lady Grey, of her father and husband? What became of Warwick, of Piat and of Bishop Cranmer? Are they less to be pitied than Montigny? Were not hundreds of her subjects burned without mercy? Had she not organized an army of hangmen whose standard was the gallows? Had not, under her reign, the axe of the public executioner become the sceptre of England? What of Scotland? Were her rulers more tender-hearted? Were not adultery and murder seated on her throne, whilst round it the weird sisters, with their choppy fingers on their lips, led their hideous dance? Was not the great Elizabeth as perfidious as Philip, and far more licentious? Was she not as cruel, she whom poetry represents as a "fair vestal throned by the West," but whom history brands as "the mistress of nine acknowledged lovers ?" Her father beheaded his wives. Was she less infamous and heartless when doing the same office to her paramours ? Philip despotically struck off the head of the patriot Lanuza. Was Elizabeth less arbitrary in many of her acts ? What account has she to render of Norfolk, of Essex, of Raleigh, and of so many other illustrious magnates who had adorned her court and basked in her smiles ? When Philip offered a reward for the head of Orange, one of his rebellious subjects, was he more criminal than Elizabeth, when, under the hypocritical appearance of a trial, she, with feigned tears, murdered her kinswoman, who was her guest, and a crowned head like herself? Had not the two heroes, Alexander Farnese and Don John of Austria, entertained the full conviction, founded on what they considered undeniable proofs, that she had bribed assassins to take away their lives in the Netherlands ? *

Turning to France, the Spanish historians inquire if her chivalrous Francis I. had not many crimes to answer for. Was not his ceaseless persecution of the Constable of Bourbon merely to serve the vengeance of the rejected love of his mother, as reprehensible as it was fatal to France ? Did he not, to meet the expenses occasioned by his extravagant tastes and unrestrained passions, put up the royal favors at auction, even in the distribution of judicial

* History of Spain, by Modesto de Lafuente.

offices? Did he not convert his Court into a place of shameless prostitution? Did he not, when Diana of Poitiers, the wife of one of his most devoted nobles, knelt at his feet to beg for the life of her father, make adultery the condition of the solicited pardon? Did Philip ever do anything more basely horrible? Was Francis less imperious than the Spanish Sovereign, when he said to his Parliament: "I consent to your addressing remonstrances to me; but when I do not choose to defer to them, I want instant obedience? This warning ought to suffice. Remember that you derive your authority from me. Do not imagine yourselves to be the Roman Senate." Did not Francis, whilst he was keeping up a correspondence with Melancthon and inviting him to establish his domicile in France, whilst he was forming treaties of alliance with the Sultan and the Protestant Princes of Germany against Catholic powers, have six Protestants burned in his presence in Paris with refinements of cruelty unknown in Madrid, and after having exhibited himself in a farcical procession surrounded with all sorts of relics in which he certainly did not believe like the fanatic Philip; for he had once threatened the Pope to become a Protestant like his "dear brother" Henry VIII. of England? Did he not declare on that occasion, as Philip did afterward in imitation of such a precedent, that "he would treat his children in the same manner, if they became tainted with heresy?" Did he not declare that those who should not denounce heretics should also be burned? Did he not grant to the denunciators of those who should swerve from the Catholic faith one-fourth of all the property of the accused in case of conviction? Was not the Count of Montecuculli horribly tortured and then quartered on mere suspicions? Was Francis a faithful observer of his plighted word? Was he bound by the most solemn oath? Did he not die at last the victim of his crapulous amours? Did Philip ever give to society such examples of demoralization? Was it not of Francis that a French historian has said: "France will long remember his reign stained with all the vices which disgrace those inconstant, credulous, and vain monarchs who are incapable of acquiring experience or the knowledge of men?"* What of Henry II. and of his horrible edicts against the Protestants of France? What of their wholesale massacre which he had planned? What of his morals? What of the infernal Catherine de Medici? What of Charles IX. with his St Bartholomew? What of the famous window from which he amused himself with firing at his subjects as if they had been lawful game for his carbine? What of Henry III., whom his own countrymen had surnamed "Herod?" What of his impurities? What of his assassination of the Duke of Guise and of the Cardinal of Lorraine? Passing in review the other Sovereigns of Europe at that time, the apolo-

* Velly. Histoire de France, p. 147, vol. VII.

gists of Philip come to the conclusion that he was not so pre-eminently wicked as to justly concentrate upon himself all the hatred of mankind, and deserve a severer judgment from history than all the rest of his royal brothers. They seem to contend that bad example and the spirit of the age must in part be answerable for the crimes of Philip. All this may be true, but there is this difference between Philip and those personages whom we have enumerated. We remain conscious, when reading their history, that they may have been carried away by passion, and that their guilt is not incapable of remorse, of repentance, of atonement, of self-condemnation. We feel that there is flesh and blood in them ; they are criminal after the fashion of human beings ; Philip, after the fashion of a demon who has nothing in common with our race in his cool and scientific premeditation. That man is surrounded with mysterious horrors like something unearthly. There is in him no soul, no heart, no feeling ; all is dead. The vampire is no longer fabulous, but stands before us ; and our awe increases when we see him gorged with blood, reposing in the lap of crime with the self-approbation of the performance of duty, the complacency of fancied righteousness, and the sweet tranquillity of conscious innocence.

Another reason for the popularity of Philip's memory in Spain is the recollection that, during his reign, the preponderance of that country in Europe reached its climax. For the first time since the fall of the dynasty of Rhoderic the Goth, the Iberian Peninsula had been united under one sceptre—a consummation which had been long desired, and which to this day is the aspiration nearest the heart of every Spanish statesman. Besides, by her arms and her literature the influence of Spain had become supreme over the civilized world. After having added to her immense colonial acquisitions the vast possessions of Portugal in Asia, Africa, and America, well might she boast that the sun never set in her dominions. So great had been the power of Philip at one time, that it was apprehended he might realize the dream of a universal monarchy. Twice his armies had marched to the capital of France, which he used to designate as "his beautiful city of Paris," and which he had once garrisoned with his troops. All eyes for years had been turned with fear toward Madrid. Spain was then what France became under Louis the Fourteenth, and under Napoleon the Great in the 19th century—a colossus before whom the world trembled. With a handful of men she had performed exploits and accomplished conquests which staggered belief, and threw into the shade the most fabulous achievements of the heroes of antiquity. Not only had she expelled the infidels from her bosom after eight hundred years of indefatigable and incessant wars, but she had become the bulwark of Christianity at Lepanto, at Malta, in Hungary, wherever the Crescent had threatened the Cross. The Pactolus of mythology literally flowed at her feet from the mountains of Peru and Mexico. Her fleets lorded over the seas. The heavy weight of the Spanish heel had been felt everywhere, like that of the Roman in the days of Augustus, and the tone of command of Spanish chiefs had sounded as haughty as any which had ever issued from the Eternal City. Besides, the superiority of her statesmanship and of her literature was universally acknowledged. She gave the tone to Europe. Her language was the one which had spread the most. Her manners, her costumes, her fashions, her tastes, her ideas preponderated in the saloons of diplomacy, in the mansions of the noble and wealthy, in the humble dwellings of the poor, in the studio of the artist, in the attics of the poet, in the theatres, and in all the fields of literature. Even now, in many of the cities of France, the traces of Spanish dominion are still visible in the architecture which meets the eye of the traveler. At that epoch, the power and the glory of Spain had reached their meridian splendor, to be obscured ever since in their rapid decline, until lately arrested. Philip's reign had been the culminating point at which her fortune, like a dazzling meteor, had rested awhile before sliding downward, to her mortification, into the morasses and quagmires of national debility and decay. Hence Spaniards cling to the recollections of that reign with patriotic tenacity, and seem anxious to ward off from its escutcheon all that might dim its lustre. We sympathize with what is praiseworthy in this feeling ; but, guided by the impartiality and the love of truth which ought to be the main characteristics of the historian, we shall now take a brief view of the long reign of Philip, and ascertain what amount of commendation and censure it deserves at our hands.

Broken down by infirmities, defeated in most of his ambitious schemes, Charles V. had abdicated the imperial crown, and delivered into the younger hands of Philip the sceptre of Spain. Charles, when he ascended the throne of Ferdinand and Isabel, had found that country in a state of transformation and transition. All the small Christian kingdoms which had divided the Peninsula for centuries, and had been so long waging war against each other, had been absorbed into one. The last of the Moslem principalities had fallen with Granada. The sword of Chivalry, in a struggle which for its duration was without a precedent, had reconquered for the Cross one of the most beautiful parts of Europe, from the Pyrenees to the banks of the Tagus, and to the rock of Gibraltar. Unknown seas had been explored ; unknown countries had been discovered ; unknown kingdoms, the hereditary domains of powerful princes, had been subdued in a new world, and millions of infidels, either converted to the Christian faith, or driven away from the bloody altars of their idols, when not crushed into destruction under the iron-clad foot of their conquerors. A steady stream of gold, broad and deep, was flowing into the lap of

Spain, as the guerdon for her valor and enterprise. Impatient of repose, bursting as it were with exuberant strength, she had leaped over the Pyrenees, and fought France on her own territory with signal success. She had crossed the Mediterranean, subjugated Sicily, invaded Italy, and although confronted there by the intrepidity and skill of French legions, she had proved irresistible, and the kingdom of Naples had remained the trophy of her prowess. She had landed in Africa in pursuit of the dismayed Moors; the battle-cry of the Christian knight had been shouted on the ruins of Carthaginian splendor, and the flag of Castile raised over the soil which had given birth to Hannibal. At Rome, in the Vatican, her desires were beginning to assume the shape of orders, and she had taught the Pope that the kingdoms of the earth were no longer fiefs of the Tiara. Europe was taken by surprise and amazed at the sudden apparition of the Power that had so abruptly started into active life from behind those gigantic ribs of the earth which Providence seems to have extended, like a massive fortification, from the Mediterranean shore to the Atlantic, with some special purpose of protection to a chosen people. If Spain was not Pallas, springing from the disrupted brow of Jupiter, and received by Olympus and admiring nations, as the acknowledged goddess of wisdom in the panoply of war, she certainly was the heroine of Christianity, wielding in her robust faith the lance of Ithuriel, sallying in the romantic spirit of true chivalry in quest of adventures for the honor of the Mother of God, wearing her colors as those of the proclaimed Lady of her love and allegiance, and believing, like the Hebrews, in the special and constant interposition of Heaven. Such was the appearance which she presented externally, and well might Europe be struck with admiration and fear. It was no mean champion who had entered the arena, and flung down his gauntlet in the contest of national ambition and supremacy.

Internally, Charles had found royal authority stronger than it had been for centuries, and reposing on a solid basis—that of an undisputed hereditary succession rooted in the affection and veneration of a loyal and enthusiastic people. God and the King might be said to be the motto of every true Spaniard. A turbulent, proud and wealthy nobility no longer overshadowed the throne, but, curbed into respectful and devoted allegiance, had become the Corinthian pillars of social architecture, instead of being its battering-rams. The clergy, among whom salutary reforms had taken place, and who had virtuous, enlightened and devout men at their head, were working in strict subordination to the Crown, and actively engaged in propagating the Catholic faith, in reforming the people, and in striving to convert the recently conquered Moslem, although after having committed the fatal and unchristian error of seducing the pious Isabel into establishing the Inquisition. That institution was, however, in its infancy, and had not, therefore, begun to display the terrific vigor which afterward struck the world with terror. The Commons were possessed of privileges, franchises and liberties which existed nowhere else at the time, save, perhaps, in the Netherlands and Switzerland ; the peasantry were as brave, as courteous, as punctilious on the code of honor as the most high-born and polished knight, and as proud and dignified in their humble station as any Cæsar who ever wore the purple mantle. In the interior of the land as on the sea-shore, in the cultivated field as in the depth of the forest, on the mountain as on the river bank, in villages as in cities, there had sprung up a spirit of industry and enterprise which had been unknown for many ages. The sword of the warrior, it is true, was still of primary importance and an object of special admiration, but the loom of the artisan and the plow of the husbandman had at last attracted the attention of the rulers of the land. Commerce, trade and manufactures were rising to no slight degree of consideration. In a country hitherto convulsed with the shock of arms and irrigated with blood for centuries, a national literature had suddenly sprung up, vigorous in its infancy, and full of promises of future and lasting glory. The fine arts, better appreciated than those of the mechanic order, had made their welcome appearance, had been received not only as beloved and admired guests, but had also been presented with letters of naturalization, and were shedding their benign and humanizing influence on the former scenes of protracted wars. Spaniards were no longer to be looked upon as divided into petty tribes, temporarily associated in bands of rude cut-throats—now engaged in an insane mutuality of slaughter—now uniting in a holy league to endeavor to drive out of their native soil the invaders who had, from the remotest antiquity, so long threatened them with entire annihilation. They had aggregated themselves into a single, powerful and polished nation, although dwelling in distant Kingdoms and Provinces which had retained their own peculiar laws and characteristics. It was rather a Confederacy of Sovereignties under one ruler, than a consolidated Government. There was unity in the head, it is true, but there was plurality and individuality in the limbs, organs and features of the associated and welded bodies. All the elements of a vigorous nationality were at hand—a territory capable of uniting on its surface almost all the productions of the earth, teeming in its entrails with all the metals required by the industry of man, indented with an extraordinary number of magnificent harbors, and inclosed by seas and lofty mountains which protect it against the hostility of the rest of mankind; an immemorial community of sufferings and of triumphs, of humiliation and glory, of traditional and historical lore, of hatred for the foreign foe, and a vast fund of that melancholy experience which results from the evils of fratricidal struggles; an intense love for old customs and habits, which does not exclude those innovations demanded by the march of civilization, but which, venerating the past as the tomb of a cherished ancestry, secures thereby to future generations prosperity at home, respect abroad, and a long life in the land ; a spirit of chivalry carried even to excess, but beautiful in its aberrations ; the sacred importance of family ties and the worship of the Household Gods taught from the cradle, without which the social order is destitute of stability and loses its most amiable charms ; an innate spirit of religion, deeply imbedded in every heart and almost incarnated in every Spaniard ; strong local attachments made sacred by the most tender and cherished recollections, and invigorated by the possession of much valued franchises and immunities ; some of the provinces enjoying liberties as great as now exist, in the nineteenth century, in Great Britain, or in any country on the face of the earth ; tribunals of justice performing their functions with regularity and impartiality ; a civil and political administration operating with enlightened economy, accommodating itself to local immunities, customs and prejudices, but necessarily imperfect, and founded on the erroneous ideas of the age ; public education patronized by the throne and in a state of remarkable progressiveness ; universities and schools, recently established, but already celebrated, and in which men, and even women of the most illustrious birth, lectured with becoming pride and distinguished ability ; a legislation, not uniform, it is true, throughout the whole monarchy, but having powerful elements of assimilation, as it derived its main principles and features from the jurisprudence of Rome, and the laws of the Goths which had been gathered into a code, and which, translated into old Castilian, had been disseminated through Spain, although with manifold modifications to suit the wants, wishes and interests of the former petty Kingdoms into which the country had been subdivided. When looking at all the advantages showered upon Spain by a bounteous Providence, it seems as if it would be impossible to the imbecility or wickedness of man to prevent them from having their natural effects, and from elevating the people dwelling in that favored region to the most enviable position among the nations of the world.

Under such circumstances, what was the mission of Charles V., if properly understood? It was to avail himself of all these resources, and of all the elements of national prosperity which presented themselves to his hand. It was to harmonize and to perfect all the parts of that society which he found already created and established, but which, being lately regenerated under the genial influence of virtue and genius, demanded all the progressive ameliorations which such a condition required. By all the means which an enlightened, humane and artful policy might have suggested, he had to reconcile to their fate the Moorish and the Arab population of the Southern and Eastern provinces of Spain, who by their skill in agriculture and in the mechanic arts constituted an important portion of the wealth of that country. He had to entice them into adopting the religion, laws, customs and usages of the conquerors by a well-imagined system of blandishments, rewards, and protection. In this way a fusion might have been operated, in the course of time, between the hostile races. To attempt it would at least have been statesmanlike; it would have been time enough to fall back on the cruel measures of compulsion, or even expulsion, if the work of conciliation and fusion had been found impossible, and if the continued existence of a heterogeneous element had been deemed dangerous to the safety of the State. It should have been the aim of Charles to have kept in co-ordinate and healthful action the principles of liberty and of legitimate authority which he found co-existent in the land; to have given uniformity to the civil legislation whilst ameliorating it in all its ramifications, and to have imparted a durable unity to the former distinct Kingdoms of the Iberian Peninsula, whilst avoiding the perils of too much centralization; and in particular to have bent all his diplomacy, or his military power, toward reuniting to Spain the Kingdom of Portugal, which had been torn from it, and which was like a branch violently separated from the trunk of the majestic oak on which nature had intended it to grow. It should have been his policy to stimulate industry in all its pursuits, to facilitate the intellectual growth which had begun in the country; to encourage the arts and literature; to expand the wings of commerce; to establish manufactures; to open canals and roads, and make all those internal improvements which were so much needed; to organize the immense colonial possessions of Spain, give them the kind of government best adapted to their wants, put in friendly connection the inhabitants of the two hemispheres, and civilize by a paternal administration and a beneficial commercial intercourse between the Old and the New World, the numerous population of her American domains. It was a vast and magnificent field for a man whose brain and heart had been equal to the task, or for a prince like Peter the Great. Charles had seen what commerce and the mechanic arts had done for his native Flanders. He ought to have profited by that practical example of political economy, and his ambition should have been to have introduced into Spain the blessings of such a state of things. Then she would have known how to use the new market which Providence had given her in America. Agriculture, commerce, the arts, and industry in all its branches, could not but have had a languid existence in a country in which war had been the normal condition of society during eight hundred years, and when, every day, the national existence of that country, its language, its religion, its freedom, had been exposed to be lost forever. What did Charles? He began with destroying the public liberties which he found flourishing, and with reducing to the insignificance of imbecility the Cortes, who, before his reign, had been full of life, energy and action, and a time-honored part of the Government. He established a political and religious despotism in Spain, in order to use her like a well-sharpened sword to carve his way to the glittering bauble of imperial domination. She was in his estimation nothing but a war-horse, which could serve no better purpose than to enable him to ride rough-shod over Kingdoms and Principalities. As Neptune is represented by the poets of antiquity stirring in his fury the depths of the ocean with his trident, convulsing its waves with tempestuous winds, and lining its coasts with shipwrecks, thus Charles, in his mad ambition, wielded the sceptre of Spain with no other object than to strike with it the bosom of Europe, from which, at his bidding, issued forth desolating wars and unspeakable miseries to the human race. What did Spain gain by it? It is true that he made more refulgent the halo of glory which was round her head, but he paralyzed in it the organ of thought; he robbed her of liberty,—the soul of her body; and that body, bleeding at every pore, he laid prostrate like an exhausted knight, covering with a gorgeous heap of laurels the wounds which he had inflcted on its breast and the chains which he had riveted to its limbs. So much for the reign of Charles. That of Philip was but its continuation, with a still more fatal termination.

CHAPTER IV.

On the abdication of Charles V., Philip found himself the greatest monarch in the world, although the Imperial Crown had not descended to him. He might, however, have consoled himself with the reflection that it had not departed from his family, and had become the possession of his uncle Ferdinand. What remained to him seemed, indeed, ample enough to satisfy the most craving ambition; for the whole Iberian Peninsula with the exception of Portugal, the provinces of Roussillon and Franche Comté in France, the Kingdoms of Naples and Sicily, the Balearic Islands and Sardinia, the Duchy of Milan, the wealthy and populous Netherlands, were his hereditary dominions in Europe. He owned in Africa the Canary Islands, and his authority was acknowledged in the Cape de Verd Islands, in Oran, Bougiah and Tunis. In Asia he possessed the Philippine Islands, and a part of the Moluccas, or Spice Islands. In America he was the Lord of the Kingdoms of Mexico and Peru, of Chili and other boundless territories, as well as of Cuba, Hispaniola and other islands of the New World. Besides, his marriage with the Queen of England had put under his indirect control all the strength and all the resources of that Kingdom. Well might it be said that such a Sovereign could hardly turn to the right or to the left in his bed without exciting the anxious attention of mankind. We may take this as literally true, when we consider what influence sleep or digestion may have on the resolves of man, and a philosophical mind may well think with concern of the effect which may be produced on the fate of millions of our fellow-creatures by a more or less healthy secretion of bile, in a being possessing the power and temper which Providence had given to Philip.

When he ascended the throne, a temporary peace had been granted to Europe by the truce of Vaucelles, agreed upon by the rival houses of Austria and France, represented by Charles V. and Henry II. It is a singular circumstance, that the Pope should have been the first Power to provoke Philip into breaking the truce, and to compel the proclaimed champion of the Papacy to wage war against the Holy See. The mad Pontiff, Paul the Fourth, invited the King of France to invade the Spanish possessions in Italy, ill treated the Spaniards in Rome, and, among others, Garcilasso de la Vega, the Envoy of Spain, excommunicated the Colonnas and other Italian partisans of Philip, and was so blinded by his hatred for the house of Austria as to perpetrate the folly of summoning his Catholic Majesty to appear before him and a consistory of Cardinals, to be tried as a vassal of the Church for the Kingdom of Naples, and to be deprived of that crown which he was alleged to have forfeited in consequence of having failed in his loyalty to the Holy See, and for other reasons specified in the extraordinary judicial document by which the monarch was arraigned. Charles, from his retreat at Yuste, encouraged his son in adopting the proper means to bring the Pope to his senses, and Philip, after consulting a body of Spanish theologians who justified him in making war against the vicar of Christ, acted with prompt energy. The Viceroy of Naples, Duke of Alva, was soon at the gates of Rome, after having taken possession of the cities and fortresses of the domains of the Church, in the name, as he declared, of the Sacred College, and until the election of another Pope. These words were ominous, and the Pontiff hastened to propose terms of peace which led to a suspension of hostilities for forty days granted by Alva, who knew how averse the King was to a conflict with Rome. But, on receiving assistance from France, the Pope perfidiously changed his tone and his course, and became as hostile as ever. Philip, who was then in Flanders, was not slow in picking up the gauntlet which France had flung at his feet. He was, at that time, in all the vigor of youth, and showed on that occasion more decision and activity than he ever did afterward. He seemed desirous of proving to Europe that he was worthy of the heritage of Charles, and would know how to defend it with becoming spirit. He sent his best captains to Hungary and Germany to raise bodies of cavalry and infantry ; he called to arms his Flemish and Spanish subjects ; he made all the necessary preparations for a vigorous war, and went in person to England to prevail upon his wife, Queen Mary, to assist him with the force of her Kingdom. He returned in three months to Brussels, with the satisfaction of having succeeded in his mission and of having obtained eight thousand English auxiliaries, commanded by the Earl of Pembroke. Philip, who during his long life, was destined to show as much aversion to witnessing a battle as his father had shown partiality for it, remained in the background under the pretext of organizing his forces and sending them to the scene of action, and appointed the Duke of Savoy commander-in-chief of his army. The splendid victory of St. Quentin was gained, and then Philip made his appearance among his victorious troops. The Duke of Savoy proposed to march rapidly to Paris, which remained defenceless. Philip refused, and Charles, at Yuste. when he heard of his son's prudence, could not dissemble his vexation. Intimidated by the triumph of Philip over the forces of France, the Pope again sued for peace, which was granted, as we have said before, on terms which seemed to imply that the victor in appearance was the defeated in reality. The Pope renounced his alliance with France, it is true, but carried his point in everything else. The royal dignity was, on that occasion, held very cheap by Philip, much to the mortification of the Duke of Alva, who, by the command of his master, had to kneel as a suppliant before the Pope and beg his pardon for having whipped his troops and treated his holy person with arrogance. This treaty of peace was so derogatory to the majesty of the King of Spain, and so advantageous to the Pope, who seemed rather rewarded than punished for his perfidiousness and insolence, that Charles could hardly believe it at first, and, when no doubt could any longer be entertained on the subject, gave way to an uncontrollable fit of indignant rage. This was not all. Philip ceded the principality of Sienna, acquired by his father, to the Duke of Tuscany, as an equivalent for a certain sum of money due to him, and in consideration of a promise made by that Prince to defend the other Spanish possessions in Italy against any attack, from whatever quarter it might come. On the part of one who possessed the mines of Peru and Mexico, with so many other resources, and for a monarch so powerful as Philip, it certainly was a striking specimen of undignified statesmanship to give away a portion of his patrimony to pay a debt, and to secure the military assistance of a Duke of Tuscany! His forbearance toward the Pope is susceptible of an easier explanation, as it was not his policy to weaken a power which he intended to use as an engine to serve his purposes.

But Philip was not so accommodating to the

French. After a second victory—that of Gravelines—a treaty of peace took place at Cateau Cambresis, which is the most advantageous that Philip made during his whole reign. A French writer observes, that the King of Spain could not have dictated in Paris conditions more onerous and fatal to France, who lost in one day what it had cost her thirty years to acquire. Suffice it to say, that she gave up one hundred and ninety-eight cities and fortresses in exchange for three: Ham, Le Catelet, and St. Quentin. Besides, by a secret agreement, it appears that Henry II. had promised to massacre all the Protestants in his Kingdom—"a consummation most devoutly to be wished" by Philip, who then departed to seat himself on the throne which had been surrendered to him by his father. Round his brow were the laurels of St. Quentin and Gravelines. It is true that he was indebted for them to his generals, but he might claim as his own the merits of the two treaties of peace which he had made and which had been concluded according to his wishes and directions; for he certainly was able to lead his negotiators, if not his armies. In his war with the Pope he had been successful and magnanimous; in that with France, triumphant to an eminent degree. He had humbled her, greatly curtailed her power, and secured as his bride the beautiful Isabel of Valois. Europe gave him credit for moderation and profound statesmanship. He had gloriously inaugurated his reign. The worthy scion of a noble line was presumed capable of surpassing his imperial sire. His prestige and influence at that time were perhaps greater than they ever were afterward. Much was expected of him at home and abroad. How were these expectations realized? We have already mentioned the extent and wealth of his immense dominions. To protect or to increase them he had not only the untold gold of his American possessions, but he had also the best disciplined and most experienced troops in the world, commanded by heroic and skillful captains. The combined fleets of Spain and Flanders far exceeded the naval armaments of any other power, and assured to him the supremacy of the seas. Save in the Low Countries, which had retained some show of independence and liberty, his will was undisputed in all his dominions, and no Cæsar had ever been more absolute. Place in such a position such a man as the glorious rebel, William the Silent, his hated subject, and what would he not have done for his fame and the welfare of the millions intrusted to his paternal care! Place on the throne which Philip occupied such a monarch as his contemporary Henry IV. of France, and he might have established that universal monarchy of which Philip is said to have dreamed—such a universal monarchy as Heaven might have smiled upon, for he would, no doubt, have attempted to do for it what he aimed at on behalf of France, which was, in his own words, that "the poorest of his subjects should have a chicken in his pot every Sunday."

But what did Philip accomplish with all his mighty means of execution? His repeated wars with France and his manifold intrigues with the factions which desolated that Kingdom were equally fruitless as to their final results. He plotted and bribed, and spent millions, year after year, to put his daughter Isabel on the throne of St. Louis to the exclusion of the heretic Henry of Navarre, and after having exhausted his diplomacy, his treasury and the skill of his generals, he signally failed in his cherished schemes. He had long fought and negotiated to have the Protestants exterminated in France, and yet by the Edict of Nantz, the Protestants obtained in the end the protection and security which they desired. One of his other favorite plans, if he could not make his daughter Queen of that Kingdom, was to weaken or dismember it, so as to secure the supremacy of Spain over that neighboring rival, and yet when he died, France was much less exhausted than Spain. Under the wise administration of her gallant Henry, she was rapidly passing into a healthy and recuperative condition, whilst her once dreaded and powerful antagonist was falling into a state of consumptive prostration, from which she is but now recovering after a lapse of nearly three centuries. In his attempts against England he was still more strikingly foiled. The sympathy which he professed for Mary Stuart and his endeavors to assist her contributed to send to the scaffold that unfortunate pretender to the crown of Elizabeth. In his vain efforts to invade the fa anchored island he wrecked his whole navy, and England soon became what Spain had been—the mistress of the seas, over which swarmed her bold seamen who appropriated to themselves the treasures sent to Philip from the New World, swept over the coasts of his American dominions which they repeatedly plundered, and even took and sacked Cadiz under the leadership of the Earl of Essex, whose ships returned in triumph to England with a booty of more than twenty millions of ducats. At the close of his career, his Catholic Majesty must, to his mortification, have been conscious that Protestant England was as much in the ascendant under Elizabeth as France was under the seemingly converted Henry to the faith of Rome.

The champion of Christianity had not known how to avail himself of the victory of Lepanto, so as to crush forever the maritime power of the Infidels, and toward the end of his reign he had the humiliation of seeing the shores of his Italian dominions devastated by the piratical incursions of turbaned corsairs. Even the city of Reggio was sacked by those miscreants, whilst Hungary, the hereditary possession of his nephew, the Emperor Rodolph, was still threatened by the Mahomedan hosts. Worse than that, he had not been able to retain in Africa the important city of Tunis and the celebrated fortress called the Goleta, the acquisition of which had cost so much Spanish blood and treasure.

During a long portion of his long reign he quarrelled with the Court of Rome, although he professed to care for the Papacy next to God. He had, however, the satisfaction of dying on good terms with Clement VIII. In relation to Rome and religious matters, his great achievement was the reconvocation of the Council of Trent, which had been suspended so often, and which had encountered so many difficulties in the accomplishment of the object of its meeting. The labors, however, of the two hundred and fifty-five learned prelates who composed that Council terminated harmoniously, much to the satisfaction of Philip, and the articles of faith for all Catholics were at last clearly and definitely settled, although the disciplinary rules established by that body were rejected in France as contrary to the privileges and liberties of the Gallican Church, and as hostile to the rights of the Crown. This, if we consider the nature of the subject, the importance and duration of its wide-spread results, was perhaps the greatest success obtained by Philip, without whose exertions it may well be doubted whether the Council of Trent would not have been an abortion, and whether the Catholic world would have enjoyed its present unity. That event, fraught with such incalculable consequences, must therefore be justly traced up to Philip as its chief promoter. But, nevertheless, in his cherished scheme of crushing Protestantism he was far from being as successful as he desired. He had, it is true, consolidated and invigorated the Catholic Church, but he had neither weakened, nor circumscribed within a smaller area, nor materially damaged its youthful antagonist. Wielding the terrific engine of the Inquisition, he had smothered heresy in Spain, but it was still defiant in every other part of Europe where it had taken a foothold, and when the Monarch closed his eyes forever, it must have been with the painful consciousness that the disciples of Luther had even wrested from his grasp some of his own provinces, and secured forever their political and religious independence.

Henry of Navarre had seated himself on the throne of France by his activity, his heroism, and his making opportunely the religious concession required by the majority of his subjects. Philip lost his fat provinces of the Netherlands by his unbending fanaticism, by his invincible sluggishness, and by the near-sighted jealousy which prompted him to thwart successively the administration of his sister Margaret, and particularly of Don John of Austria and of Alexander of Parma, who, if permitted to act according to their own plans, and granted the supplies in men and money which they needed, would, according to such probable conjectures as we can draw from historical evidence, have won back, partly by force, and partly by management, the revolted provinces.

The only real acquisition made by Philip was that of Portugal and her immense colonies. Considering the geographical situation of that Kingdom, it was of far more importance to Spain than the distant Low Countries, from which she had derived but few, if any advantages. But Philip, by the arrogant and injudicious administration which he gave to his conquest, had sowed in it those seeds of discontent which grew up under his weak successor into a revolution, and again disunited the Iberian Peninsula. In conclusion, after reviewing Philip's external relations, it is difficult not to admit that they were less satisfactory at the end of his reign than at its beginning, and that, when he descended into the tomb, he was less powerful as a monarch, and less influential as a statesman in the Councils of Europe, than he had been when ascending the throne. It is probably for these reasons that several historians, and among others, Voltaire, have unjustly, we think, denied him the talents which he really possessed, and have looked upon him as a mere mischief maker, a royal busy-body, who, for nearly half a century, kept Europe in a constant state of agitation, without results worthy of his ambition, and commensurate with the extent of his gigantic power, the subtlety and multiplicity of his intrigues, and the darkness of his crimes.

Let us now see how he conducted the administration of his internal affairs, which he found in no flattering condition when he took in hand the reins of government. Commerce and industry were paralyzed, almost dead, the population was greatly diminished, the public debt enormous, the revenues of the State much reduced, and its financial, if not other resources, exhausted by improvident management. What did Philip to remedy these evils? France, which had been brought down to a similar state of distress by its civil wars, found a Sully, who, with the friendly and enlightened protection of Henry IV., substituted order for chaos and wealth and abundance for penury and famine. Such was not the fate of Spain. The deficit for the ordinary expenses of the Kingdom was 197,182,000 of maravedis in 1557. Philip and his ministerial advisers imagined, in their wisdom, to replenish the empty and beggarly coffers of the Government by selling one thousand titles of nobility, without taking into consideration, in order to facilitate the sale, any flaw in the lineage of the purchasers, or even any stain which might rest on their escutcheons. With a view not to depreciate the value of this commodity by throwing too much of it at once into the market, it was resolved to part at first with only one hundred and fifty titles of nobility, at the price of five thousand ducats each, reserving the rest for successive sales equally advantageous. To alienate in perpetuity the rights of administering justice, and to extend in the same way, for money, certain jurisdictions, was another contrivance which was thought as felicitous as the former. Municipal, notarial and manifold other offices were put at auction, as it were; "this, no doubt," said the

Council, and the saying found approbation in the royal breast, "will bring a good round sum of ducats." Some revenues derived from the Clergy and which had not been paid for two years were remitted in consideration of a much smaller amount furnished without delay. The commons of villages, towns and cities, were offered for sale, leaving only what was barely indispensable. Forced loans were resorted to, payable in annual pensions on the Royal Treasury and "in vassals," or sale of human beings, and so evidently forced were those loans, that the Bishop of Cordova being invited to offer two hundred thousand ducats, the King said to one of his agents: "You will give him to understand that if he does not do it voluntarily, we shall be compelled to enforce our request; and should he continue to excuse himself, let means of rigor, but with the greatest possible decorum and propriety, be employed to obtain the sum required." The Archbishop of Toledo received the same broad hint and for the same amount. The Archbishop of Seville was put down for 150,000 ducats on the list of the Royal borrower. The Priors and members of the Tribunal of Commerce of that city and of Burgos were taxed at 70,000, and the Archbishop of Saragoza at 60,000. The towns of Estepa and Montemolin were sold to the Counts of Ureña and Puebla. A contract made with the Pope for the supply of certain mineral salts which were to be procured from the domains of the Holy See was shamefully violated and was adjudicated to the highest bidder. The people were made to contribute large sums, which were to be received in satisfaction of future taxes, and the creditors of the State had to content themselves with promises to pay contained in bonds which stipulated increased interest. Other equally absurd and tyrannical measures were adopted. Far from disapproving them when presented to his sanction by his Council, Philip ordered that they should be executed "instantly and without any kind of consideration for anybody." He even pithily recommended "that more be taken from those who should not readily comply." One of his own suggestions was, to appropriate for his benefit one-half of the revenues of the whole Clergy. This had been temporarily granted by the Pope, Julius III., to Charles V., to enable him to carry on war against the Protestants of Germany. This concession had been since revoked, but a body of theologians was convoked by Philip to examine into this matter, and they declared that the Pope could not recall a bull which had been once received and ratified by the Kingdom; for which reason they concluded that the King had the undoubted right to collect the same tax from the Clergy. Philip accepted this conclusion as very logical, and acted accordingly, with an untroubled conscience. Besides, the sending of money to Rome was prohibited anew under the severest penalty, such as death and confiscation of property for all those not in Holy Orders, and for ecclesiastics the sequestration of their rents and temporalities, and exile from the Kingdom.

To collect the forced loans decreed by the Council, the King sent commissioners to the provinces, with instructions to proceed with the utmost severity. The prelacy, the high and inferior nobility, and all the men of property, had a hard time of it. The Archbishop of Saragoza had been taxed by the Council at 60,000 ducats. He proposed to compromise for 20,000. It turned out badly for the Archbishop. "Tell him," said Philip to one of his messengers, "that I, the King, have put him down for 100,000 ducats." The other Archbishops attempted to elude the Royal pressure under manifold pleas and excuses, but the inexorable master ordered that "a rigid and scrupulous estimate" of their rents and other sources of wealth should be made, to establish their ability to yield what was demanded, and showed them that he understood the grinding process as well as any miller in his Kingdom. This pious and decorum-loving King, who pretended to care so much for the morals of the Clergy, did not blush to offer to legitimate the sons of priests for money, and even to publish that he would ennoble them "at a moderate price," which measure, however, did not produce the expected results; "for the Clergy," wrote an illustrious Princess to Philip, "choose to keep their money, as they have other ways and means to obtain what they desire for their bastards." The Government went so far as to take at discretion from merchants and traders what it needed, offering them in payment very high interests, and pensions on the Treasury. Notwithstanding all these exactions, its most pressing wants were very far from being met. The vast and ravenous maw of the Royal Exchequer still cried for more substance to be devoured; and yet, the year before, the enormous sum of more than fifteen hundred and forty-nine millions of maravedis had been received from the mines of the New World. Not satisfied with this, the Government had at last run into the habit of seizing all the gold and silver coming from America for the account of individuals, taking for itself, under divers pretexts, the lion's share, and leaving nothing, or very little, to the legitimate owners. It was worse than black-mail levied by His Catholic Majesty; it was downright wholesale robbery.

The Cortes who assembled in 1558 remonstrated against these outrages, and suggested many measures, reforms and ameliorations which, if adopted by the King, would have done much good, but that body was no longer what it had been. The authority of the Representatives of the nation had been reduced to a shadow; that of the King was but too stern a reality. Formerly, when the Cortes petitioned for anything, the common formula used by the Monarchs in their answer was: "Let it be done as you desire," or some other phrase of acquiescence. Under Charles V. those petitions had begun to be disregarded, and in the very first years of the reign of Philip they hardly ever elicited a categorical concession, or an explicitly favorable answer. This would not have suited the despotic, reserved and mysterious character of the Monarch. His replies on such occasions were always ambiguous like the very nature of his mind. They usually ran as follows: "We shall order this matter to be examined;" or "We shall remember what you say in order to provide for it in the manner most conducive to our interest;" or "We shall order the members of our Council to consult together on what may be best to be done, and report to us accordingly." This was the phraseology of his most benign answers. Generally they were unfavorable, and couched in these terms: "For the present it is not proper to make any innovations in this matter."

Charles had written with fierce zeal to his son, exhorting him to give no quarter to the heresy which had penetrated into Spain, and declaring that, notwithstanding his infirmities, he would leave his retreat at Yuste to crush the monster, if proper measures were not soon taken to secure its extermination. Philip needed no such stimulation, and had Charles lived a little longer, he would have seen the heretics treated to his heart's content. He would perhaps have been amazed at witnessing the ferocious impartiality with which the Inquisition proceeded against so many personages illustrious for their science, their services to the State, their birth, or their official position. He would have seen archbishops, bishops, abbots, monks, priests, nuns, marquises and other great lords, delicate women of the most exalted rank, magistrates, professors at universities, artisans, mechanics, servants, and other small fry, democratically driven pell-mell to judgment under the levelling rod of the same prosecution. The Inquisition must be given its due ; it was no respecter of persons. The highest and the lowest had to bend equally under its red hot sceptre, and lucky was he who had only his beard singed. The Archbishops of Granada and Santiago, the Bishops of Lugo, of Leon, of Almeria, with far-famed theologians who were the boast of Spain and the pride of the Catholic Church, and who had figured conspicuously as members of the Council of Trent, were arraigned at the bar of a tribunal as grim as Tartarus, and with all its flames and apparatus of torments at its command, The very Primate of the Church of Spain, the Archbishop of Toledo, who had been the confessor of Philip, and who had administered the last consolations of religion to the Emperor on his death-bed at Yuste, was accused of heresy, and dragged before judges far more terrible than any mythological Minos, Eacus and Rhadamanthe. His crime was to have written certain commentaries on "the Church's Catechism of the Christian Doctrine," Many prelates and theologians had given their approbation to these commentaries. Hence they were also enveloped in the same prosecution. Who could feel safe, when such men were not? Hardly had Philip returned from Flanders, to begin his royal administration in 1559, when autos-de-fè were inaugurated, to greet him with special honor; and the burning piles to consume heretics, or pretended heretics, threw their lurid light all over Spain. On one occasion, the bones of an old woman were disinterred, and those bones, together with a statue made to represent her, were reduced to ashes in the presence of Philip, with, alas! many other victims whose living flesh was not, like that vain image, proof against the agonies of the inflicted torture. These exhibitions were known to afford keen satisfaction to Philip, and one may suppose, without any great stretch of fancy, that when the flames crackled round the bodies of his subjects, the phlegmatic Monarch extended with glee his cold-blooded hands to meet the genial heat which they diffused. Those autos-de-fè, or acts of faith, as they were called, were to continue to be one of the characteristic features of his reign, and were not the least of the potent causes of the decline of Spain. The genius of evil was seated on her throne in the person of Philip, and the curse of God had settled on her majestic mountains and her lovely valleys.

In the beginning of his reign he issued a most extraordinary decree, strikingly in keeping with the spirit which animated the Inquisition and its supporters. That document is a signal revelation of the policy which Philip adopted as the very soul of his

Government. Determined to stop, by all imaginable means the infiltration into Spain of the doctrines of the religious reformation which agitated Europe, it seems that he planned to isolate her intellect from that of the rest of the world. On the other side of the Pyrenees the human mind was in motion, and ran onward, as it ever will, like a magnificent stream, sometimes lashed into fury by tempestuous winds and sinking the precious freight floating on its bosom, sometimes reflecting gently the hues of Heaven, the radiancy of the sun, and gracefully swelling under the keel of the thrifty bark of commerce, or the gilded boat of pleasure, now overleaping its banks with swollen and angry waves and carrying desolation far and wide; now spreading fertility, abundance and joy, but always keeping its steady course toward its goal, and always, notwithstanding its rapids, its shoals, its eddies and the other dangers of its navigation, continuing to be a priceless channel of intercourse between nations and an instrument of civilization. This was no grateful spectacle to Philip. The brain of Spain, at least, was in his iron grasp, and should work only in harmony with his own. He would not permit her intellect to be like an ocean heaving under vivifying gales and rolling its vast volume of water to distant shores in a sublime continuity of measureless expansion. It was to be like the Dead Sea, contracted, dreary, motionless, lifeless, useless. For this purpose he ordered that none of his subjects, without any exception whatever, should leave the Kingdom "to learn, or to teach, or to read anything," or even "reside" in any of the universities, colleges or schools established in foreign parts. To those who were thus engaged he prescribed that they should return home within four months. Any ecclesiastic violating this decree was to be denationalized and lose all his temporalities; any layman was to be punished with the confiscation of his property and perpetual exile. Thus a sort of Chinese legislation and policy was adopted for Spain. There was to be on her frontiers a line of custom-houses through which the thought of man could not pass without examination. No Spaniard was to receive or to communicate one idea without the leave of Philip. Truly this was despotism carried to the height of sublimity. That man must have snuffed on the breeze the parturition of future revolutions, and would have stopped, if possible, the circulation of air across mountains and seas to the doomed theatre of his tyranny. Spain was to be fossilized, to be mummified in the swaddling-bands of unprogressive ignorance, in order that Philip might slumber in peace under the sombre vaults of the Escorial. With such facts staring us in the face, we cannot but wonder that some Spanish historians have claimed for this bird of darkness, this extinguisher of the intellect, the merit of having been the lover and patron of literature and the arts, after the fashion of Francis the First of France.

In 1560, the Cortes of Castile had their second

meeting under the reign of Philip. Don Carlos was acknowledged as legitimate heir to the throne with great solemnity, on his swearing to observe and maintain the privileges and laws of the kingdom. The Cortes presented to Philip one hundred and eleven petitions, some of which deserve to be mentioned, as specimens of the political economy and of the statesmanship prevalent at the epoch. These were, that the Sovereign should visit the principal cities of his Kingdom, in order that he might know personally those whose services he might require; that there be a sumptuary reform in dresses, equipages and the general way of living, his Majesty being the first to give the example; that the sale of the domains of the Crown be suspended; that the work of making a digest of the law be continued without interruption; that the King cease to pay such high interests on his debts; that he persist not in taking for himself the gold and silver coming from America for individuals; that these precious metals be not permitted to be carried out of Spain; that no butcher's meat and no grains be exported from Castile to the kingdoms of Portugal, Aragon and Valencia; that nothing be plated with gold or silver, except such articles as were required for the use of Churches; that the custom-houses between Castile and Portugal be suppressed; that the delinquencies committed by the soldiers against the peasantry be cognizable by the ordinary tribunals of the country, and that the accused in such cases be not allowed to shelter themselves behind their military franchises or privileges; that no officer of the Government be permitted to trade; that the Moors of Granada be prohibited from purchasing black slaves; that vagrants be prosecuted; that thieves be branded on the arm; that the Grandees be compelled to reduce the number of their lacqueys, because the attraction of the livery deprived agriculture of too many of those laborers which it needed; and that it be not lawful for anybody, whatever be his rank, to have on his table more than four dishes and four different kinds of fruit; that the cities on the sea shore be fortified, and proper means be taken to check the depredations of the Moslem corsairs who made the navigation of the Mediterranean so insecure, and who, by their incessant landings on the coasts of Spain, had caused the lands, from Perpignan in Roussillon to the frontiers of Portugal, to be abandoned and to remain uncultivated as far as twelve or fifteen miles in the interior. Philip paid but very little attention to most of these requests, except the last, which induced him to make an unsuccessful attempt to possess himself of Tripoli, Oran, Mazelquevir, and some other points on the African coast. To those petitions which aimed at something practicable and judicious he gave some of his usual evasive answers, but he granted very readily those which were absurd. For instance, he promulgated sumptuary ordinances which were ridiculous, and which could not possibly have any salutary effects. He also published decrees which were restrictive of commerce, and prohibited the exportation of gold, silver, grains, cattle and other products of the soil, or of the manufacturing industry of the country. Three years after, in 1563, the Cortes of Castile having remonstrated against the practice of alienating real estate in mortmain to the Clergy, and represented that religious corporations, if not checked, would in the end possess themselves of the whole of Spain, the King replied, in his favorite phraseology, that "it did not seem expedient to him to make any innovation in this matter;" and the Cortes of Aragon having complained of the encroachments of the Tribunal of the Inquisition, which was gradually usurping jurisdiction to the detriment of the ordinary courts of the country, the King vouchsafed no other answer than that "he would talk about it to the Grand Inquisitor General."

In the mean time, the financial condition of the Kingdom was rapidly growing worse, and the deficit resulting from the inequality of expenditure and revenue was assuming the most alarming proportions. All the ordinary and extraordinary means and resources had been exhausted. Philip, instead of remedying the evil by a prudent and wise economy, gave the example of extravagance in the royal household. The sum annually granted to the Queen had in two years been raised from 60,000 to 80,000 ducats, and the allowance to Don Carlos and to Don John of Austria, from 32,000 to 50,000 each, so that the expenses of the Royal family amounted, in 1562, to 415,000 ducats a year, a sum equal to about $2,000,000 in our days, whilst some of the highest officers of the realm had to content themselves with the comparatively pitiful salary of 400 ducats. With such aberrations in political economy and such a wasteful administration, it is not astonishing that the personal debts of the Monarch and those of the Kingdom should have been frightfully on the increase; and yet, on an average, Philip received annually from his American Dominions alone more than one million two hundred thousand ducats—which was at least equivalent to six millions of dollars at the present epoch. The Council of Finances, or Hacienda, after consulting with Philip, could not devise anything else, to get out of difficulty, than to resort again to the sale of titles of nobility, the sale of vassals and other Royal property, the alienation of certain rights, and the concession of privileges. This was but a sad way to stop the holes in a sinking ship, and fatal as were the measures to relieve the pressing necessities of the moment, they were rendered still more so by the manner in which they were carried into execution; for the King was informed by one of his ministerial advisers, that in order to realize 500,000 ducats, it would be imperative to alienate property worth fully 700,000, on account of necessary deductions which would have to be made, and which he enumerated. It is difficult to give an idea of the wretched administration which had been introduced in Spain, and of those abuses which, like venomous leeches, preyed upon her vita. Suffice it to say that in Castile, for instance, according to a census made in 1541, there was a population of near 800,000 souls, and that out of every eight men there was one who was noble and exempt from taxation, thereby increasing the weight of the burden on the shoulders of the rest; and as if this evil was not already unbearable, Philip was selling profusely letters patent of nobility. One is tempted to suppose that the wreckless Royal spendthrift cared very little what became of Spain after he had closed his mad career of visionary ambition and selfish gratification.

In these conjunctures, Philip, who had shown, on all occasions, that he preferred residing in Madrid than anywhere else in Spain, determined to make that city the permanent seat of the Court and of the Supreme Government, and therefore the capital of the Monarchy. That barren and insalubrious locality presented but one advantage, if it be one of much value, that of being a central point. Its disadvantages were manifold and glaring, and are felt to this day. Such a selection redounds very little to the credit of Philip. It has been severely censured by his own countrymen, and justifies inferences unfavorable to the reputation of that Monarch for judgment, discretion and foresight. Reason and common sense condemned it from the beginning, and their verdict has been confirmed by time and experience.

Shortly after having selected Madrid as his capital, Philip had laid with his own hands, in the vicinity of that city, the first stone of the foundations of the Escorial, that eighth marvel of the world, as it is called by the Spaniards, and it was when superintending the erection of that edifice, which he intended as an eternal monument of his piety, that he attempted to introduce the Inquisition in his provinces of the Low Countries, and inaugurated that system of tyrannical vexations by which he goaded faithful subjects into insurrection. It was when thus engaged that he found leisure to negotiate with France the cession and translation to Spain of the bones of the martyr St. Eugene, who had been the first Archbishop of Toledo, and whose body had, for centuries, reposed in the famous abbey of St. Denis, near Paris. The King of France readily granted the favor desired by Philip, but the Cardinal of Lorraine, who was Abbot of St. Denis, stoutly refused to part with the canonized treasure. This difficulty almost produced a collision between the two Kingdoms. Fortunately the Gordian knot was cut by having the dead saint secretly taken out of his place of rest, and conveyed to Bordeaux, after having obtained from Philip the solemn assurance that he would, in return, compensate the Cathedral of St. Denis for its loss by a donation of a similar nature and value. The body of the saint was received in Toledo with the most gorgeous ceremony. The whole Court was present ; Philip and Austrian

Archdukes who happened to be on a visit to Spa. assisted by the highest Grandees of the land, carried the body on their shoulders to the doors of the Cathedral of Toledo, where it was received by the Clergy and deposited in the most sacred part of the edifice. A Monarch who had thus bent reverently under the weight of the coffin which contained the remains of a saint could not but feel, or pretend to feel, great concern at the dissoluteness which had penetrated into many religious Orders, and profaned the sacred walls of Convents and other such holy asylums. He accordingly published decrees remedying the evil, and put an end to the liberty which female recluses had taken to come out of their monastic abodes at will—which liberty had been fraught with peril to their virtue, and had been the cause of much scandal. He proposed to the Pope several measures, the object of which was to restore the antique purity of the cloister, and he took care as usual, that His Holiness should not long resist his views. He particularly insisted on the abolition of the Order of the Piemonstratenses, or Norbertines. "They are all idiots," he said, "without literary or doctrinal education. There is no preacher among them, and in several of their houses there is not even a pulpit. Besides their being idiots, they have very loose morals, whereby they give a bad example; for they neither keep themselves confined to their monasteries, nor observe any of the regulations of their Order." In this matter, Philip had y readily listened to the representations of the Cortes, who, having assembled at Madrid, in 1567, had petitioned against the abuses and scandal which resulted from the visits of monks to the convents of nuns, proposing that they should not be permitted to enter such establishments, but instructed on the contrary never to hold any conversations with such female recluses, except at the hole of the turning-box, or at the iron gratings of the common parlor. The Monarch did not, however, lend to them so favorable an ear, when they repeated the prayer of former Cortes, that Monasteries, Churches, and ecclesiastics individually, be prohibited from purchasing real estates, and be declared incapable of acquiring them either through inheritance, or donation. The same answer was returned as on preceding occasions: "It is not expedient to make any innovation." Hardly any other answer could have been expected from a Prince, who had just entailed on the monastery of the Escorial which he was then constructing enormous rents and other dotations.

The Pope Pius V., seeing Philip in such good disposition, requested him, in return for favors granted, no longer to forbid the publication of the Bulls of the Holy See, unless they had the Royal Exequatur. But the King showed himself very stubborn on this subject, and replied that he desired to live in the utmost harmony with the Holy Roman Catholic and Apostolic Church, provided he was not expected to sacrifice any of the authority which had inherited from the most pious of Princes. He expressed his astonishment that the Pope should find fault with him for using his royal privileges, when His Holiness knew that the same course had been pursued by his ancestors, who had conferred so many benefits on the Church, by which their great services to religion had always been acknowledged. The Pope prudently yielded, but not without bitter complaints. It was, however, a compensation for the Court of Rome, that Philip was bent upon establishing the Inquisition in the Low Countries. Already those Provinces were in a state of insurrection, and the heads of Egmont and Horn had fallen on the scaffold. In connection with this tragical event, we will mention as strikingly characteristic of Philip what he wrote to the Duke of Alva, the ruthless Minister of his bloody policy: "It has grieved me exceedingly that the delinquencies of the Counts have been so grave as to deserve the sentence which was executed on their persons. But since that sentence was so just and so well grounded, we have nothing more to say than to recommend their souls to God." This letter never was intended for publicity, and has but recently come to light. Was Philip playing the hypocrite, even when confidentially addressing such a man as Alva?

These same Cortes of 1567, to whose proceedings we have already referred, had petitioned the King put an end to bull fights, on account of the serious accidents which resulted from this favorite, popular pastime, and to replace it by useful military and knightly exercises which would instruct the people in the art of war, and the better qualify them to serve His Majesty. The King replied that, as to the accidents mentioned, it was the business of those who presided at those festivals to prevent them, and he had no doubt they did their duty in that respect, as well and as efficaciously as could be expected; and as to the nature of the amusement itself, that it was a very antique and general custom which could not be changed, unless after much deliberation; and therefore, for the present, that he "did not see any reason for innovation." Although such a hater of innovations, Philip was very fond of such as suited his purposes. For instance, not satisfied with having provoked an insurrection among his Flemish subjects by having infringed some of their cherished laws, privileges, customs and usages, he was driving into rebellion the conquered Moors of the Kingdom of Granada by the same course of absurd and tyrannical legislation—a legislation which aimed at suddenly changing the nature of those miserable beings, and transforming them at once into full-blooded Spaniards. He seems to have exhausted his imagination to make life intolerable to that unfortunate race. It was not enough that they should have been compelled to abjure their relligon; it was not enough that they had undergone every sort of oppression ; they were at last forbidden to use their own native language, and ordered to speak Spanish only, whether they knew it or not, under the most terrible penalties. They were also commanded to deliver up all the Arabic books which they might have in their possession. Moreover, they had to renounce their usages, ceremonies, customs, dresses, and even their family names. Their ablutions for the sake of religion or cleanliness were to be abandoned ; their ordinary as well as medicinal baths were to be destroyed. They were instructed to keep their houses opened, and their women were to show themselves unveiled in the streets. In one word, they were to lose the very consciousness of their former identity ; they were, in every act of their life from the most important to the most trifling, to relinquish what they cherished, and to adopt what they abhorred. It would have been no wonder that such a decree had maddened men of less fiery temper than the Moors. On its promulgation, they flew to such weapons as they had kept concealed, for they had previously been disarmed as completely as possible, and, in their uncontrollable fury, they committed the wildest atrocities. This was a pretext for retaliation and plunder, and a war of extermination began against those who had been driven into those excesses by the very Government which had assumed their punishment.

Whilst the increasing troubles and perturbations

in Flanders and the new horrors of a fanatical war in the Kingdom of Granada were filling Spain with mourning and with anxiety for the future, the arrest and secret trial of the hereditary Prince, Don Carlos, for causes which have remained unknown to this day, and his subsequent mysterious death, threw a funereal pall over the face of the whole country. But, when a few months after, it became known that the beautiful and beloved Queen, Isabel of Valois, had, at the age of twenty-two, departed this life, not without suspicions of foul play at the time, although historians admit that they were unfounded, the loyalty of the Spaniards, proof as it was against all assaults, melted into tears and shuddered with terror. The marriage of Philip with Anne of Austria, who had also been destined to his son, Don Carlos, although celebrated with much pomp, did not afford much consolation to the heavily taxed and much afflicted subjects of the despot. The festivals which took place on that occasion contributed to empty the Royal purse, and, when after having captured Harlem, the Spanish soldiers mutinied for the want of pay, it was with the utmost difficulty that, to satisfy in part their just demands, the Sovereign of so many Kingdoms and Provinces could raise 400,000 ducats, on agreeing to exorbitantly usurious interest. And yet he had just put to death Montigny and confiscated his estates, together with those of many other Magnates of the Netherlands, and he had taxed and plundered those rich Provinces with the utmost ingenuity and without mercy. But the more he robbed and oppressed, the poorer he became. His exactions were fruitless; they could not replenish his exchequer. It was like pouring water into a bottomless tub.

Philip, in his proceedings against the Moors of the Kingdom of Granada, had probably two objects in view—the one, was to establish in it religious unity, as well as in the Low Countries, and the other, to fill up his Royal coffers by wholesale confiscation and all the other arts of spoliation. He consulted learned prelates and laymen to know whether the prisoners in that war could be reduced to slavery. The majority of his advisers decided in the affirmative; excepting only from servitude boys under ten years and girls under eleven, who were to be intrusted to certain administrations by which they were to be educated in the Christian faith. Therefore, such of the captives as were not permitted to become the share of the soldiers were sold for the benefit of his Catholic Majesty, and the fifth of all the spoils that were taken from the sacked dwellings of the Moors was also reserved for the Monarch; and that those spoils were not trifling we may easily conceive, when we reflect that many of the Moors were rich, and when a contemporary Spanish historian declares, that most of the soldiery engaged in hunting the rebels from their cities, and even from the caves and mountain recesses where they had sought refuge, "had avarice for their leader and robbery for their paymaster." Philip had ordered, on the 19th of October, 1569, that the war be carried on "with fire and sword," and was but too well obeyed. Among other deeds of atrocity, a whole city was sacked and burned, its inhabitants put to death, and the ground on which it stood strewed with salt which was ploughed into the soil. Finally, it was determined that men, who through a policy truly diabolical had been driven into rebellion, had no rights whatever; that all their possessions belonged to the Crown; and that the whole Moorish population of the Kingdom of Granada should be transported and scattered in the interior of Spain. They were to be divided into small bands and mixed up with the Spaniards, so as to avoid the danger which might result from their agglomeration on any particular point. No exception was made in favor of a numerous class of them who had remained faithful. They were told with all the gravity of sincerity and in the soft tones of sympathy, which must, however, have sounded to them like cruel mockery, that it was "for their good and security" they were to be removed from the place of their birth, from their paternal roofs and all their broad acres of land. "The Moors," said Philip in the preamble of an ordinance dated on the 24th February, 1571, "who took no part in the insurrection ought not to be punished. We should not desire to injure them." On reading these words we began to breathe more freely and to hope that, at last, a sense of justice had overcome in the breast of the Monarch the malignant influence of fanaticism and the inspirations of a greedy policy. We had, unfortunately, been too hasty, and we confessed to ourself that we did not yet know Philip thoroughly, much as we had studied his character, when, before finishing the sentence, we met with a "but," truly worthy of his genius. "We should not desire to injure them," wrote the Prince, "but they cannot hereafter cultivate their lands; and, besides, it would be an endless task to attempt to separate the innocent from the guilty. We shall indemnify them, certainly. Meanwhile, their estates must be confiscated like those of the rebel Moriscoes." It has been said that Philip, however, pretended to show some consideration for the loyal Moors. Their lands and houses were to be forfeited to the Crown, it is true. *That* he could not make up his mind to relinquish. But their personal effects, their flocks, their herds and their grains would be taken, if they desired it, at a fixed valuation by the Government. What that valuation was we have no means of ascertaining, but we suspect that in that arrangement the unfortunate Moors found themselves unmercifully fleeced by their Royal shepherd. That Royal shepherd, however, if he sheared all the wool from his sheep, ordered that every regard be paid to their personal comfort and security; and it was forbidden to separate, in their removal to distant localities, children from their parents, and husbands from their wives; in short, to divide the members of one family from one another.

"This was an act of clemency," says a Spanish chronicler, "which they little deserved; but his Majesty is willing to give them that satisfaction." If this was an act of clemency which they little deserved, what would the Spaniards have thought if the loyal Moors had been indemnified by Philip for their confiscated lands and houses, as he had promised? Hence that indemnity never came, so far as we can ascertain, and probably the plundered exiles had too much discretion to remind Philip of his pledge. It would have been as unwise as if lambs had bleated to prevent the lion from forgetting their existence.

In the distant localities whither they were transported, the Moors who were not sold into servitude, and who remained free, had but a sorry kind of freedom to enjoy. Not only were they forbidden to seek a momentary oblivion of their miseries by resorting to their national songs and dances; not only were they commanded, under the harshest penalties, not to speak the Arabic, or read any book written in that language, but "no one," says Prescott is his History of Philip, "was allowed to change his abode, or to leave the parish or district assigned to him, without permission from the regular authorities. Whoever did so, and was apprehended beyond these limits, was to be punished with a hundred lashes and four years' imprisonment in the galleys. Should he be found within ten leagues of Granada, he was condemned, if between ten and seventeen years of age, to toil as a galley-slave the rest of his days ; if above seventeen, he was sentenced to death. On the escape of a Morisco from his limits, the hue and cry was to be raised as for the pursuit of a criminal. Even his own family were required to report his absence to the magistrate ; and, in case of their failure to do this, they incurred the penalty of a whipping and a month's imprisonment in the common jail." This is one of the specimens of Philip's internal administration.

In this insurrection of the Moors, and in the war which resulted to subdue them, thousands of Spaniards lost their lives, many of them in the most excruciating tortures inflicted in retaliation by their revengeful foes. The Christian soldiers became demoralized by being permitted to fight like bandits for pillage, and to divide among themselves as slaves the captives of the bow and the spear. Lust, avarice and cruelty in all their refinements became the order of the day. By the massacre of the Moors and the transportation of those who were spared by the sword, the Kingdom of Granada lost its most useful population—a population of most skillful husbandmen, artisans and mechanics ; and, although there was an attempt to replace them by an immigration of Spaniards, who were allured thither by tempting concessions, favors and privileges granted by the Government, that lovely part of Spain, that terrestrial paradise, received a blow from which it has not recovered to this day. Where industry had spread fertility and accumulated wealth, where agriculture had clothed the bosom of the earth with a gorgeous mantle of never-failing harvests, where taste and art had decorated fairy gardens with garlands of fruits and flowers, where the genius of architecture, inspired by poetry and love, had thrown up its aerial palaces, which looked like embroidered lace petrified into stone, indolence and pride, like two fraternal spirits, held communion together amidst decay, ruin and famine. For all these evils Philip had made himself responsible before God and man.

If Philip had proposed to himself to blend together the Spanish and Moorish elements, so as to produce in his Peninsular dominions a unity in religion and nationality, he was signally defeated in his purpose; for the Moors, scattered and oppressed as they were, remained obstinately distinct from their oppressors, notwithstanding some external conformity which they assumed for their own protection, and many of them, who were ostensibly Christians, worshiped in secret the God of Mahomet. If he had intended to diminish their number and destroy them gradually, he was not more successful in his design, for under his successor, Philip III., a census of them having been attempted, they were found to have increased so greatly, that their enumeration had to be given up, from an apprehension of making them acquainted with their strength. Such was the vitality of that extraordinary race! Such was also their industry and economical habits that, notwithstanding the weight of the yoke which bent their necks down to the earth, notwithstanding the disabilities against which they had to contend in the midst of a hostile population who hated them with the pent-up and accumulated hatred of eight centuries, they were, in the course of a few years, accused by many, and among others by such men as Cervantes, of absorbing all the current coin of Spain, which they either concealed in secret places, or found the means of sending out of the Kingdom. They were said to be "sponges which sucked all the juice of the land." They were reproached with being so keen and indefatigable in the pursuit of gain, and so tenacious of it when once clutched by their fingers, that even a Jew would have starved among them. Be it as it may, it is certain that the confiscation of all the lands and houses of the Moors in the Kingdom of Granada, besides other spoils, and besides selling so many of the captives as slaves, did not, as a fiscal resource, prove of much advantage to Philip. For, shortly after the famous battle of Lepanto, in which the naval power of the Turks was destroyed, Don John of Aus tria could not gather from his victory all the fruits which ought to have been expected, "because," as he wrote, "he had not a single real for the necessities of the fleet, but had incurred a debt of many hundred thousands of ducats." What had become of the stream of gold which was to flow from that powerful machinery of confiscations, taxes and contributions so skillfully contrived and artistically put together to pump the Netherlands dry? Certainly the iron hand of the Duke of Alva had squeezed the orange to the last drop. Two or three hundred thousand Moors had been stripped of everything. What had become of their substance? The fact is that, by a just dispensation of Providence, the robber had been robbed, and Philip, if he had been susceptible of being enlightened on the subject, would have come to the conclusion that oppression is doomed to that sterility to which it is said that nature condemns all monsters; that tears are not the vivifying water which blesses the land with productiveness; that iniquity is a bad adviser, and that spoliation is but a poor secretary of the treasury.

CHAPTER V.

Such was the not very flattering condition of Spain, as described in the preceding Chapter, when an event took place, preceded, accompanied and followed by circumstances which admirably portray the character of Philip, together with the manners and morals of the epoch, and which had the most fatal consequences for what remained of the liberties of the Kingdom of Aragon. We have already stated that the Princess of Eboli was suspected on good grounds of having been the mistress of Philip. She had been the wife of Ruy Gomez, who, from being the playmate of the Prince in his boyhood, had risen to become his most trusted and most favored Minister. During her husband's life, the Princess had been supposed to exercise great influence over Philip, by whom she and her family had been loaded with favors. After that husband's death, she did not seem to have lost her long-enjoyed possession of the affection of her Sovereign. She was diminutive in size, remarkable for beauty, haughty in temper, unconquerable in her pride, irresistible in the exercise of the fascination with which she had been gifted by nature, and which she had studiously improved; astute, unscrupulous, loose in her morals, greedy of wealth and power, she excelled in the management of those intrigues which usually secure success in a corrupt court. She had, no doubt, materially aided her husband in reaching and retaining the elevated position which he had occupied until his death; and, after having lost him, she worked in perfect accord with one of Philip's most confidential ministers, Antonio Perez. This man, a native of Aragon, was the natural son of an individual of the same name, who, during many years, had been Secretary of State under Charles V. He had been legitimated, however, by an Imperial decree, and had been employed by Ruy Gomez, in his ministerial Department. He succeeded so well in pleasing his puissant employer, that he soon became an inmate in his house, was recommended by him to Philip, and was granted almost the familiarity and the privileges of a son. Perez had received in Spain a distinguished education, which he had completed abroad. Talent and memory he naturally possessed in a great degree. All the profane and sacred authors were familiar to him, and in his travels he had acquired an extensive knowledge of the world. He was as well versed in the Bible and the writings of the Holy Fathers of the Church, as in those of Tacitus, Machiavel, Horace and Ovid. He wrote and spoke Latin and several other languages with considerable facility. He was so prepossessing in his person, that he always produced a favorable impression at first sight. Refined in his manners, sagacious, artful, flexible, insinuating, a thorough courtier, unsurpassed in dissimulation and self-possession, he had won many of the frail beauties of the Court, and he seemed even to have obtained the first place in the cold heart of his Sovereign. He had unquestionably become the most influential man in Spain with the King. He possessed his most important secrets, dispatched the most delicate affairs of State, and had been constituted a sort of Universal Minister, or depositary of the Royal authority. He had learnt to penetrate the designs of Philip, long before they were made known. He then took care to stand prepared for their gradual unfolding, facilitated their development, or modified their nature, or even frequently checked and thwarted them, according to the promptings of his own interests, without exciting the slightest suspicion in his master's mind. Observing a crafty neutrality, a studied indifference, a shrewd reserve, he never obtruded his advice, but prudently waited until he was consulted by Philip, although he secretly angled for, or gave birth to, the occasion. So far, all had succeeded with him on the slippery and dangerous ground on which he was treading. He had become the favored lover of the Princess of Eboli, and although the demonstrations of her passion were sufficiently imprudent, they seem not to have been known to Philip, which is certainly wonderful, considering his proneness to suspicion, the number of the spies he had in pay, and the wide-spread activity of their minute investigations. Perez had also had the art of gaining the confidence of Don John of Austria, and of his Secretary, Escovedo. He had inspired them with so much faith in the truth of his friendship, that they had nothing concealed from him. The arch-deceiver made use of it to discover all their plans and aspirations, and to communicate them to the King with exaggerations and misrepresentations to suit his purpose. In those conjunctures, Escovedo, who, as well as Perez, had been much indebted to the protection of the Prince of Eboli, and who had remained grateful for it, being indignant at the scandalous intimacy which existed between the Princess and Perez, and which seemed to him to be an affront to the memory of his benefactor, had the imprudence to remonstrate with them on the subject, and threatened them to inform the King of their illicit intercourse, if they did not put an end to it voluntarily. The Princess treated the officious intermeddler with the most lofty contempt; she dared him to the worst, and even scorned to deny her predilection for Perez. This individual, when addressed by Escovedo, was more smooth than the Princess. But the guilty pair instantly resolved the death of Don John's Secretary, and Perez went to work to accomplish it with his usual ability. He persuaded Philip that Escovedo was fanning in Don John the flames of a criminal ambition, and encouraging that

Prince in the pursuit of designs dangerous to the safety of the King and the welfare of the Kingdom. This was enough; the King ordered Perez to put Escovedo secretly out of the way. Twice Perez, showing warmer friendship than ever to Escovedo, and inviting him to his table, attempted in vain to poison him. The daggers of hired assassins were more effectual, and Escovedo ceased to be an object of fear to Perez and the Princess of Eboli. But Philip might die, and, in that case, the resentment of Don John might become fatal to Perez. Be this supposition correct or not, a few months after Escovedo's assassination, Don John had also ceased to exist, and it was thought that on his body were found all the signs of the administration of a deadly poison.

No doubt Perez now thought himself secure against all denunciation, and laid on his pillow a head less disturbed by dreams of royal vengeance. But he was watched by the sleepless enmity of one who, for a long time, had been biding the opportunity to destroy a hated rival. That enemy was Mateo Vasquez, one of the Ministers of Philip, and the blow which he struck at last was well aimed. On the 28th of July, 1579, during the night, by order of the King, his favorite Minister, Antonio Perez, was conveyed to a prison in Madrid, and the Princess of Eboli was surprised to see her palace invaded by an armed force which conducted her to a fortress in which she was incarcerated. What could have induced Philip, who had then attained the mature age of fifty-three, to station himself, mysteriously wrapped up in a cloak, under the porch of the Church of St. Mary, opposite to the residence of the Princess, to look at her as she passed under escort to the place of her destined confinement? If by the light of the torches which flashed round her carriage the eyes of those two personages met, how much may they have told each other in that transient moment! Was it love, was it hatred that had thus drawn Philip to that spot? Or was it a mixture of both? Whatever were the feelings pent up in the King's breast, the arrest of Antonio Perez and of the Princess of Eboli produced almost as much sensation as had resulted from the imprisonment of Don Carlos; and Madrid, particularly in the precincts of the Court, was shaken as if by an earthquake.

Antecedently to this event, Perez and the Princess of Eboli had been denounced to the King by the family of Escovedo as guilty of the murder of that individual, and permission had been asked to proceed to a judicial investigation. This had been done at the instigation of Mateo Vasquez. It was a bold move; for the hired assassins, who were known, had been rewarded, under the sign-manual of the King, with lucrative offices in Milan, Naples and Sicily. The King, however, did not reject the application made for leave to begin a criminal prosecution against his two favorites, but he informed Perez of what was going on and of the manœuvres of his enemies. Perez was much alarmed, and having expressed his fears to Philip, that Prince treated him with affectionate familiarity, tranquillized him as a friend would another, and assured him of his never-failing countenance and support. Thus encouraged, Perez supplicated his kind protector to order that he, Perez, be the only person prosecuted, and that all proceedings be stopped against the Princess in consideration of what was due to the honor of a lady. But the King pursued a different course. He requested the President of the Court of Castile, Don Antonio Pazos, Bishop of Cordova, and the particular friend of Perez, to speak to the son of Escovedo and induce him to withdraw the accusation. "Assure him," said the King, "that it is to my knowledge that the Princess of Eboli and Perez are as guiltless of the death of his father as myself." Escovedo's son, on being thus informed of the Royal pleasure, had of course but one thing to do, which was to desist from his accusation in the name of his family. One would have supposed the affair at an end, but Secretary Mateo Vasquez, notwithstanding Philip's asseveration that the Princess and Perez were innocent, most unaccountably and tenaciously insisted that they were guilty, and became their accuser in his turn. He must have known, or suspected, that in so acting he secretly pleased the King. Thus assailed by one of his colleagues in the Council of his Sovereign, Perez asked leave to resign his post, but Philip did not consent to it. As to the Princess, she haughtily complained to the Monarch of the conduct and enmity of Vasquez. She wrote to him a note, in which she bitterly resented the affront against which she thought that, as a King and a gentleman, he was bound to protect her, and she requested his Majesty to return the note after its perusal, as it contained sentiments which she had ventured freely to express, "under the full conviction that she was addressing a gentleman." The King answered enigmatically, as one who did not seem disposed to give her the satisfaction which she desired, but who, at the same time, was afraid of incurring her displeasure. He appeared anxious that the Princess should become reconciled with Mateo Vasquez, and, with a view to obtain it, he employed the agency of Diego de Chaves, his confessor. But all the efforts of the Priest miscarried against the stately resolution of the Princess, who rejected all his entreaties with imperious harshness. Baffled in that quarter, Chaves turned to Perez, and endeavored to bring a reconciliation between him and Mateo Vasquez; but Perez, being irritated by an affront which he had recently received from his colleague, and, besides, being stimulated by the Princess, showed himself equally inflexible.

It is impossible to imagine that Mateo Vasquez, on that occasion, was acting a part contrary to

Philip's wishes. What the King was aiming at while resorting to all these mysterious plays and by-plays, plots and counterplots, and while confounding everybody with such startling contradictions, it is not easy to conceive. Some believe that his sole object was to gain time and acquire the proof of the relations supposed to exist between the Princess and Perez, and that it was when he became satisfied on this point, that his resentment prompted him to strike the blow which had been so long impending, and to act as we have described, on the night of the 28th of July, 1579. Be it as it may, here are Perez and the Princess of Eboli incarcerated. The cause alleged by Philip for this measure was not their being suspected of murder, but that they had refused to be reconciled with Mateo Vasquez. A singular ground, truly, for a criminal prosecution to rest upon! Another singularity in this case was that, on the next day, the King sent the Cardinal of Toledo to console the wife of Antonio Perez for the misfortune which had happened to her husband, and commissioned his confessor, Chaves, to visit Perez himself in his prison for the same purpose. Among other things pleasant to the prisoner's ears, the Priest told him in a sportive manner to be of good cheer, because "his disease was not mortal." Notwithstanding this assurance, the prisoner had too much sense and sagacity not to understand the perils of his situation, and too much pride not to be mortified by his sudden fall. His health having been altered by his anxieties, he was permitted to be transferred from his prison to his own house. There the Captain of the King's guard, shortly after, presented himself, and, in the name of his Majesty, requested him to swear friendship to Mateo Vasquez, and to promise under the same sanction of a solemn oath that neither he, nor any member of his family, should ever do any harm to that personage. Perez complied with this request, and remained eight months confined to his house, with guards who never lost sight of him. At the expiration of that time, he obtained leave to go to church, to take exercise out of doors, and to receive visits, but not to pay any. Among all the strange features of this strange affair, one which is no less remarkable is, that in this nominal state of arrest, Perez, who had never ceased to be Minister, transacted all the business appertaining to his Department, as if he had been as free as before, and that this most equivocal condition of things continued when Philip, during the summer of 1580, went to Portugal to take possession of that Kingdom. Perez had, as in the past, his official relations with all the Councils of his Majesty in Madrid, and even with the King himself whilst at Lisbon. He corresponded with the Princess of Eboli, and lived with as much luxury and pomp as he had displayed when at the zenith of his favor.

The President of the Council of Castile, Pazos, was very active in his exertions to rehabilitate Perez, and, it was thought, with some probability of success, when the son of Escovedo reappeared on the stage and renewed his accusation. As to the King, he seemed to vacillate between the accused and the accuser, to be sick of the whole affair, and to act like one who was desirous of setting the prisoner at liberty, but was restrained from it by some inexplicable apprehensions. At last, after two years of apparent hesitation, he issued a secret commission directed to the President of the Council of Hacienda, Rodrigo Vasquez de Arce, empowering him to institute secret judicial proceedings against Perez, and instructing him to make the witnesses swear that they would not divulge to anybody what they testified before the tribunal. The trial began on the 30th of May, 1582, and most of the witnesses were of the highest rank. From their declarations it appears that Perez had made enormous profits in the exercise of his Ministerial patronage; that Don John of Austria, that the Genoese Admiral Andrea Doria, that Princes, Viceroys and other exalted personages used, year after year, to make munificent presents to him as bribes for his keeping them in office; that the candidates for office under the Government thought it an economy to give to Perez, in order to obtain the gratification of their desires, what they would have spent whilst dancing attendance in the antechambers of the Court, and that, in thus acting, they accomplished better and prompter results; that having inherited nothing from his father, he nevertheless possessed a colossal fortune, and lived with more splendor than any Grandee of Spain ; that he had a variety of gorgeous equipages ; that his stables were full of horses, and that he kept a multitude of pages and lacqueys ; that the furniture of his house was worth more than two millions of ducats ; that he had ordered for himself a bed like that of the King ; that tables for gambling were always set up in his house, where the Admiral of Castile, the Marquis of Auñon and other magnates had lost thousands of doubloons ; that his intimacy with the Princess of Eboli was scandalous ; that he was in the habit of receiving from her, in the way of presents, mule or horse-loads of silver ; that to him and to the Princess of Eboli was attributed the death of Escovedo. All these testimonies, as it is seen, threw very little light upon the crime of murder of which Perez was accused, and alluded merely to a general rumor on the subject, which could not be received as evidence in any court of justice. The shameful venality of the Minister, the insulting display of magnificence exhibited by the upstart, his dishonestly acquired opulence, his licentious morals and habits, his illicit intercourse with the Princess of Eboli, were sufficiently established, although irrelevant to the prosecution. Notwithstanding all that was thus proved before the Secret Tribunal, there was no change made in the lenient manner in which he was treated, and he remained in the same state of semi-arrest. It is difficult to believe that all these circumstances were not known to Philip long before; for it is a matter of history how marvelously well served he was by his Police of Spies, and what a delight he took in being made acquainted, not only with all the particulars of the life of his Courtiers, but also of some of his humblest subjects. If Philip had not been ignorant of the criminal deportment of his Minister, how came he, for so many years, not only to tolerate it, but even to continue his favor to the perpetrator of such offences? If he had not been aware of their existence, how is it that, as soon as they were revealed to him, he did not punish Perez accordingly, and did not even sentence him to a more rigorous imprisonment? Fearful must have been the secrets which bound together the Monarch and his Secretary of State, and great must have been the precautions which Perez must have taken, and the pledges and securities which he must have had in his hands, to protect himself against such a man as Philip, and keep him at bay in case of necessity.

Nothing further was done for three years, and the prosecution seemed to have gone to sleep, when, in the beginning of 1585, a new turn was given to this affair. The time having come when, according to the usages and laws of Spain, public functionaries had to render to a Commissioner appointed by the Sovereign an account of the manner in which they had discharged their duties, Philip ordered Don Tomas de Salazar, a Member of the Council of the Inquisition, to examine into the administration of his Ministers of State. This was a Special Tribunal, before which the acts of a public functionary were arraigned, without his being given a copy of the proceedings, or a list of the witnesses heard against him. It resulted from the investigations of Salazar, that heavy charges were proved against Perez, and, among others, that he had divulged secrets of State, and that he had made alterations, additions and suppressions in diplomatic dispatches written in cipher ; and, in particular, that he had falsified the correspondence of Don John of Austria. Perez justified himself by saying that, in these matters, he had acted according to the King's instructions. But, notwithstanding this defence, he was condemned, without the observation on his behalf of the accustomed formalities in such cases, and on the simple and mere finding of the Royal Commissioner, Don Tomas de Salazar, to a fine of thirty thousand ducats, to be suspended from office for ten years, to be imprisoned in a fortress for two, and, at the expiration of which, to be exiled from the Court for eight years. According to orders, two Alcaldes went to his house to take possession of his person, and found him quietly conversing with his wife. Whilst one of the Alcaldes was searching for papers, the prisoner very artfully deceived the vigilance of the other, and, entering into a contiguous room, jumped through a window which opened on the Church of San Justo, in which he took refuge. The Alcaldes raised the hue and cry, and with a number of assistants ran to the church. The doors, being closed, were soon battered down on admittance being refused. Nothing intimidated by the sanctity of the place, and after having thus forced their entrance into the temple, the Alcaldes searched it with scrupulous attention, and at last found Perez hidden under the roof of the edifice. They laid hold of him, put him in a carriage, and drove him to the Castle of Turegano, where he was to undergo his sentence. Thus far the Minister appears to have been condemned for peculations and other official abuses, but of the murder of Escovedo not a word was said.

The forcible extraction of Perez from the sanctuary whither he had fled for security, gave rise to a conflict of jurisdiction between the ecclesiastical and civil authorities. The Church demanded the restoration of the prisoner, and censured the Alcaldes for their sacrilegious violation of the sanctity of a sacred place. The Court, in the name of which the Alcaldes had acted, refused to give up the prisoner. This quarrel lasted two years, until Philip made up his mind to order the ecclesiastical censures and other proceedings held in the case by the clergy to be withdrawn and annulled. In the mean time Perez remained in irons in the fortress of Turegano; all his property had been sequestrated, and he had not been permitted to communicate with any of his friends. Such was his condition, when the King went to Aragon to hold the Cortes of that Kingdom, the time for the meeting of that body having arrived. He was accompanied by Rodrigo Vasquez, who was the Judge appointed to take cognizance of the criminal prosecution instituted against Perez in relation to the murder of Escovedo. It looks as if the King was conscious that something would turn up in Aragon concerning Perez, in which the ministry of the Judge would be required. We have felt some curiosity to ascertain whether Judge Rodrigo Vasquez was a relative of Secretary Mateo Vasquez, one of the most ardent prosecutors of Perez, but we have not been able to gratify our desire. Be it as it may, as soon as the King arrived in Aragon, another change took place in this extraordinary trial, which seemed to be constantly assuming different hues like the dying dolphin. It will be remembered that, to this time, very little had been said and still less had been proved about the assassination of Escovedo. But, in Aragon, one Antonio Enriquez came forward, avowed himself one of the assassins at the instigation of Perez, and offered to tell the whole truth about that crime, because, as he stated, his brother's life had lately been endangered by an attempt made by Perez to poison him. His declarations made known, for the first time, all the circumstances of the assassination and the names of those who had participated in it as accomplices. The wife and the major-domo of Perez became implicated in this affair.

Informed of all that had taken place, and afraid of the consequences of the revelations made by Enriquez, Perez sought to fly from his prison. Two mares of extreme fleetness, and shod with shoes reversed, so that his pursuers might be deceived as to the direction he had taken, were kept in readiness by his friends. But his plan was discovered before it could be executed, and he was condemned to an imprisonment still more rigorous. His wife and sons were also incarcerated, and debarred communication with the outer world. Philip's confessor, Diego de Chaves, and the Count de Parejas, President of the Council of Castile, visited her in her cell, and demanded the surrender of the papers of her husband. She stoutly refused for a long time, until Perez, who was afraid, on her behalf, of the consequences of her obstinate refusal, found the means of sending to her a note written with his own blood, in which he requested her to surrender two boxes which he designated to her. She obeyed, and put them, closed and sealed as they were, into the hands of the confessor, who received them with great demonstrations of joy and carried them to Philip. This was in 1587. Eight years had already elapsed since the night when Perez and the Princess of Eboli had been arrested. As soon as the surrender of these boxes was made, the wife and sons of Perez were set at liberty, and he himself was treated with more leniency. He was brought back to Madrid from the fortress where he had been confined, and was permitted to occupy a private house, which was assigned to him as his prison, but in which, to the astonishment of all, he was allowed a considerable degree of freedom of action. He received visits, and was sometimes seen in the streets. The public mind was greatly excited at this novelty. What did it mean? Was a man, whom witnesses had sworn to be guilty of murder and of so many other crimes, travelling back, on the high road of royal favor, to the possession of as much power as he had enjoyed before? Rodrigo Vasquez, the Judge in the case, being interrogated by his friends on the subject, replied: "What shall I tell you? The King himself sometimes stimulates me, and directs the hand with which I grasp the accused, and sometimes pulls it back, and checks all proceedings. I do not understand it, nor do I venture to penetrate into the mystery of the relations existing between the Sovereign and his vassal." Whatever those relations were, it is evident that the King had found his match. Perez knew Philip thoroughly, and had so taken his precautions that the master could not strike at his servant without striking at himself. The two boxes which had been so anxiously coveted did not probably contain all the documents which Philip desired to get back. Perez had been too astute, notwithstanding his apparent compliance, to thrust his head entirely into the lion's mouth, without interposing something to prevent the ferocious beast from bringing together the upper and lower row of his formidable teeth. Hence the trial was kept slowly and innocuously dragging itself along, like a half-torpid snake which might, however, at any time, be sufficiently roused to sting and kill.

But, although moving sluggishly, the trial still went on. The Major-domo, Diego Martinez, and the wife of Perez, denied all participation in or knowledge of the assassination, either as accomplices or otherwise; and, with regard to Perez, six witnesses were, introduced on his behalf to rebut the testimony of Enriquez. The guilt of the accused, therefore, remained a matter of uncertainty, and he wrote to the King several pressing letters, in which he begged his Majesty to bring the trial to a close. But Philip paid no attention to the supplications of his former favorite minister, and contented himself with delivering those letters to his confessor and to Judge Rodrigo Vasquez, with instructions to annex them to the proceedings. On the other hand, the son of Escovedo petitioned the King for further delay, in ord r to look round for other proofs. In these conjunctures, the Royal confessor, Don Diego de Chaves, wrote successively two letters to Perez, exhorting him to confess the truth, which, if known, would clear him from all guilt and open the doors of his prison. "The vassal," said the priest, "who kills another man by the order of his Sovereign, is free from all blame, because the King, being master of the lives of his subjects, can dispose of the same as he pleases, either with or without the formalities of a trial, and in any way he deems it expedient, because he has the right to dispense with all judicial proceedings, and because it is proper to suppose that he takes such a course on just grounds. Thus, the criminal prosecution must stop on your declaring the truth, and Escovedo will have to be satisfied with the action of his Majesty. If not, he will be ordered to keep silent, to leave the Court, and to be grateful that no more is done to him, without declaring to him what it might be, because it is never necessary to make any such revelation on any occasion."

With such confessors to guide his conscience, it is not astonishing that Philip should have acted as he did during his long life, and should have died without remorse, and without fearing that he had forfeited his claims to enter the Kingdom of Heaven. As to Perez, he easily understood that the advice of the confessor was a snare to entrap him. If he admitted that he had murdered Escovedo by the order of the King, he was bound to prove it, or be sent to the scaffold ; and if he proved it by producing some written authority given by his Majesty, he would be guilty of revealing a State secret, of having deceived his master when pretending to have delivered all the papers in his possession, and of having betrayed him at last, notwithstanding the private as well as official confidence so long reposed by the Liege Lord in the fidelity and discretion of his vassal. Perez, therefore, artfully avoided the breakers ahead, to which his bark would have drifted, if he had followed the direction pointed out by the subtle priest, and preferred negotiating with the accuser. In consequence of this determination, Escovedo's son was first intimidated by a threatening anonymous letter, and was next offered a large sum of money to retire from the prosecution and be no longer a party to the suit. He consented to it, and, by a written act formally and solemnly registered in Court, he desisted from all further proceedings against Perez, and declared himself satisfied of his innocence. With this document in hand, Perez prayed that his trial be closed, as the party aggrieved had withdrawn his complaint, unless somebody else appeared against him. Thus this curious affair seemed to be at an end this time, when Judge Rodrigo Vasquez persuaded the King, or the King feigned to be persuaded, that the royal name having been brought into play, and actually committed by a rumor which had spread through the public, and which attributed to him the assassination of Escovedo through the agency of the Secretary of State, the honor of the Crown required, should the rumor be founded on any truth, that Antonio Perez should be compelled to declare and prove judicially the justice of the motive which had led to that summary and sanguinary execution. The accused, who was already congratulating himself on his fortunate escape, was struck with amazement on receiving from the Judge the following communication, addressed to that functionary under the hand and seal of Philip himself: "Mr. President, you may tell

Antonio Perez (and, if necessary, you may show him these lines) that he knows full well the part which I had in the death of Escovedo, and the reasons which he gave me for it. Considering that, for my personal satisfaction and for the rest of my conscience, it suits me to know if those reasons were sufficient or not, I order him to communicate them to you, and to prove clearly that what he had said to me on that occasion was true. I have already imparted to you minutely all that he told me, in order that you should proceed to its verification according to my intentions."

This new complication, in an affair sufficiently dark and perplexing from the beginning, came upon the public like a thunder-clap in a serene day. There were no bounds to the general astonishment. "Sir," said the Archbishop of Toledo to the Royal Confessor, "I am either mad myself, or there is madness in these proceedings. If the King ordered Perez to have Escovedo killed, what account does he ask at the hands of his agent, and to what purpose? Let him reflect and he will see it." But notwithstanding these observations, the accused was subjected to a closer imprisonment, and some of the doors and windows of the house he occupied were nailed or walled up. Perez challenged Judge Vasquez on suggesting probably a want of impartiality, but Philip maintained him in the exercise of his judicial functions. He gave him, however, an adjunct in the person of Juan Gomez, a member of the Royal

Council. The accused, being repeatedly interrogated as to the causes of the death of Escovedo, replied perseveringly that he had nothing to say beyond what was on record against him. Displeased with his refusal to answer the interrogatories, the Judges ordered him to be put in irons, and his wife to be again arrested. But this treatment did not shake the determination which Perez had taken to remain silent, although he was, several times, earnestly pressed to comply with the request contained in the King's letter to the Tribunal. To conquer his obstinacy, the Court determined to submit him to the torture. In vain he invoked in his favor one of the privileges of Spanish nobility —that of being exempt from the application of this barbarous process of obtaining proofs of imputed delinquencies or crimes. The Judges were inexorable, and the grim executioner of the law presented himself to Perez in his dungeon with the terrible apparatus which belonged to his functions. He stripped of his clothes the former Secretary of State and confidential servant of Philip, tied his arms crosswise on his breast, and proceeded to the several operations of the torture in the presence of the Judges, whose silent and ruthless insensibility contrasted strangely with the bodily contortions and the dismal shrieks of the patient. At last, the fortitude of Perez yielded to his physical sufferings, and, to escape from the continuance of his horrible torments, he declared the political causes which had led to the death of Escovedo, and which were such as we have already briefly mentioned in the preceding pages. He also averred that he had been silent thus far, to maintain his fidelity to the King, and to comply with the written order of his Majesty enjoining him never to reveal that secret. The infliction of the torture produced a very serious illness, which endangered the life of Perez. A physician declared that Perez had been thrown into a violent fever, and that death would certainly ensue, if he was not properly attended to, as his situation required. Due attention was paid to the medical recommendation, and Perez was permitted to be assisted by a servant. Shortly after, his disconsolate wife, who had been released from her imprisonment, and his afflicted children, were so incessantly active in their solicitations, that they obtained, by dint of imploring tears and touching lamentations, leave to have access to the sufferer and to offer him their consolations and ministering cares. It was then that Perez, convinced that his implacable enemies had resolved on his utter ruin, meditated and prepared to fly as soon as his health should permit. When that time came, every arrangement having been made, Perez, assuming the dress of his wife, and concealed under the long veil which she usually wore, passed through his guards without being discovered at nine o'clock in the evening of the 19th of April, 1590, and, without encountering any other danger than that which he ran on meeting a patrol, succeeded in joining some friends who were awaiting him outside of the walls of the city. Although very feeble, and still with aching limbs, he took to horse, and did not stop until he reached Aragon in safety. It will be recollected that he was a native of that Kingdom, under the shield of whose privileges and immunities he had always intended to seek shelter, and where he hoped to find assistance and protection.

On the next day, the flight of Perez being known, his wife and sons were incarcerated, and an order was sent to Aragon to seize him and bring him back dead or alive. The order overtook him in Calatayud, the second town of that Kingdom in importance, but he had already taken refuge in a convent of Dominicans, and when the King's Emissary presented himself to arrest the fugitive, he was opposed by a Deputy of the Kingdom, Don Juan de Luna, at the head of forty Arquebusiers. From Calatayud Antonio Perez wrote a very humble letter to the King, in which he explained the reasons of his flight, apologized for it, and begged that his wife and children be sent to him. He forwarded copies of his letter to Cardinal Quiroga and to the Confessor of Philip, Don Diego de Chaves. In the mean time, Gil de la Mesa, a relative of Perez, had gone to Saragoza to claim for that individual the benefit of the privilege of the *Manifestacion*, which constituted one of the most remarkable franchises possessed by Aragon. What was called

Manifestacion was the act by which the accused, the prosecuted, or the aggrieved, presented himself in person, or through some duly authorized agent, before the Chief-Justice, or any of his delegates, to solicit the protection of the Court. From that moment, the King lost all judicial authority over his subject, was reduced to the part of an informer, or accuser, and was bound by the decision of the Chief-Justice, from which there was no appeal. The place where the persons seeking the protection of this privilege were detained was called the prison of the *Manifestacion*, or of the Fueros. Perez, being transferred to Saragoza, was put in the prison of the *Manifestacion* under the tutelary ægis of the Supreme Magistracy of the Kingdom. He had taken care, beforehand, to gain the sympathies of his compatriots. But when he showed them the marks of the torture on his limbs ; when he told them that such was the arbitrary and cruel treatment inflicted on a nobleman and one of their fellow-citizens, in defiance of the privileges to which he was entitled as his birthright ; when he told them that he appealed with confidence to those glorious laws of his free native country which had, for centuries, been found sufficiently powerful to protect the weakest against the strongest, the Aragonese, among whose national traits of character that of being disposed to side with the oppressed and to bridle the royal authority had been conspicuous in all ages, exhibited the most intense interest in his favor.

The King, in conformity with the customs, laws and usages of Aragon, appeared by proxy before the Chief-Justice, and accused Perez of the death of Escovedo, of having falsified ciphered dispatches, of having revealed State secrets, and of having criminally fled from the prison where he was legally detained by virtue of the Royal authority. The Marquis of Almenara, who had been sent by Philip to Saragoza on a special mission, to obtain from the Aragonese that they should renounce the privilege which they possessed of having for their Viceroy no other than a native of that Kingdom, was instructed, besides, to press the trial of Perez with the most earnest diligence. In the meanwhile, the lingering criminal prosecution so long pending in Madrid was now pushed on with vigor, as if Perez had been present, and embraced additional charges, among which was that of his having poisoned Pedro de la Hera and Rodrigo Margado. His scandalous amours with the Princess of Eboli, which do not seem, however, to have constituted any offence punishable by law, became also the subject of the most searching examination, and copies of all the proceedings and testimonies were sent duly sealed and certified to the Marquis of Almenara in Saragoza. At last, on the 10th of June, 1590, the Court sitting in Madrid found Perez guilty, sentenced him to death, and to be paraded, before his execution, through the streets, according to the established usage. His head was to be cut off, and hung up conspicuously in some public place. His whole property was confiscated for the benefit of the Crown, after deducting from it what might be found necessary to pay the costs of the trial. But this judgment could not be executed against the person of Perez in Aragon, and was to remain a mere *brutum fulmen*, unless sanctioned and enforced by the authorities of that Kingdom.

But whilst Perez had been doomed to the scaffold in Madrid, he had been writing from his prison in Saragoza several letters to the King. At first, his tone was humble and bland, but it soon became resolute and threatening. He begged Philip not to compel him to make certain disclosures which might damage the reputation of persons of much consequence, and might even affect the honor of his Majesty, because, although it was believed that he had parted with all his papers, he still had retained some which might be sufficient for his discharge. Not satisfied with this, he sent to Court Father Gotor, to whom he had confidentially shown certain original notes from Philip, commanding him to put Escovedo to death. The priest was instructed to give the King to understand verbally, that it would be decorous for the Crown to stop all prosecution against Perez and to restore him at once to liberty. Seeing, however, that the King answered not his letters as he had hoped, but, on the contrary, was doing the very reverse of what he prayed for; that the Judges in Madrid had condemned him to capital punishment; that in Aragon his trial was continued, and that his imprisonment had been made more rigorous at the request of the agents of the King, he resolved to justify himself before the Judges of that Kingdom, by presenting to them a memorial which contained copies of the original notes from the King in relation to Escovedo's death and other matters, and also copies of the letters of the Confessor Don Diego de Chaves, to which we have already referred. By these documents Perez proved that, if he had altered the sense of dispatches in ciphers, it was by the authority of the King and of those very personages from whom they came, and also that he had caused Escovedo to be killed in conformity with the Royal pleasure.

The boldness with which Perez made these revelations, and his avowed determination to divulge other mysteries, alarmed Philip to such a degree that he solemnly desisted from the criminal prosecution which he had begun in his name before the Supreme Court of Aragon. The reasons which he gave for taking such a step are consigned in a document under his Royal seal, which purported to be issued "in the name of God," and which he ordered to be filed in Court, "to make those reasons known to all;" and it is not the least extraordinary feature in this extraordinary affair, that he should have made the confessions which are thus on record. "It would not have been difficult for us," said the King, "to have convicted Perez of all the accusations brought against him, and to have obtained his being punished for his crimes. It is because it was our intention to have proved his guilt to the satisfaction of all, that he was prosecuted in the usual way, in conformity with all the dilatory formalities of the law. But Antonio Perez, taking advantage of this our Royal disposition, and fearing the result of the proceedings against him, defends himself in such a manner that, in order to meet him on the ground where he has placed himself, it would be necessary to treat of affairs more grave than usually come within the province of judicial investigations, to divulge secrets which it would not be proper to make public, and to bring forward persons whose reputation and dignity it is more important to preserve than to secure the condemnation of said Perez. For these considerations, I have deemed it less inconvenient to cease to prosecute the accused before the High Court of Aragon." The King, however, took that occasion to asseverate "that the delinquencies of Perez were so heinous, not only in their nature, but also on account of the time and manner of their perpetration and of other circumstances, that no vassal had ever been guilty of the like toward his King and Liege Lord. Wherefore he had desired it to be recorded, in order that it should never be forgotten, and, in so doing, he only complied with his obligations as King." Philip declared moreover in that document, "that he wished it to be distinctly understood that he made a special reservation of all the rights which he possessed as King of Aragon, and as King of Castile, jointly and severally, to prosecute Antonio Perez, when he chose, either criminally or civilly, by way of accusation, or in any other form as he might please, for any of the delinquencies which that individual had committed, as a servant against his master, as a Minister against his Sovereign, and as a vassal against his Liege Lord." Thus we see Philip, notwithstanding his implacable temper, sacrificing what must have been his intense desire to punish one "who had done him such wrongs as no subject had ever been guilty of against his Prince," to the fear of the revelation of certain secrets. How terrible and infamous must they have been! It is inexplicable that a man so cautious as Philip should have driven the possessor of such secrets to such an extremity of despair, as to compel him to make known to the world that there existed such a partnership of dark criminality between the Monarch and the fallen Minister. It is probable that he would have long before dealt with Perez in a more summary way, and secured his silence by those occult means which he never scrupled to use, if he had not apprehended, or been informed that, in such a case, there would be found an avenger, in whose hands the proofs of those secrets had been safely placed.

But the King, notwithstanding the relinquishment of his complaints before the Supreme Tribunal of Aragon, had not given up his intention of destroying his hated subject. He had found the path in which he had ventured to be perilous, and he resolved to take some other one which might lead him more safely to the gratification of his vengeance. One of the expedients to which he resorted was to charge Perez, after having dropped all other accusations against him, with having poisoned Pedro de la Hera and Rodriguez Margado. The other was to call in Aragon for a court of inquest (*enquesta*), which was equivalent to that of *Visita* or *Residencia* in Castile, whose special jurisdiction was to examine the manner in which public officers had performed their functions. Perez argued with great force that, having never filled any office in Aragon, he could not be subject to any Court of Inquest in that Kingdom. He also defended himself with much ability against the accusation of his having administered poison to La Hera and to Margado. And well did he need all his consummate skill and the assistance of all his friends to cope with the tremendous influence which the King brought to bear against him; for the agents of Philip were innumerable; they were indefatigable, and some of them were of the highest rank. Threats, promises, blandishments were used unsparingly; even the seductions of gold were not left untried. The main object was not to have Perez condemned to death, because it was doubtful whether such a sentence could be obtained and executed in Aragon, but to get him out of that Kingdom and bring him back to Castile. Therefore his enemies were content with soliciting a mere decree of banishment from Aragon, well knowing that he would then fall infallibly into the hands of the King.

The Junta or Council of Madrid, in a deliberation of the 20th of September, 1590, resolved on advising the King to have Perez dispatched in any manner that should be effective; "because," as they said to their royal master, "there is no reason to scruple about the choice of the means to execute the sentence pronounced against him, if it cannot be done in the ordinary way. If it is lawful for any individual to kill any bandit who has been doomed to capital punishment by a Court of Justice and who cannot be seized by its officers, it follows that your Majesty has a much more evident right to order the execution, in any form which may be deemed expedient, of him whom you have found guilty, and who has fled from the application of your sentence. Princes, for the good government of their dominions, are in the habit of using strong and extraordinary remedies, when mild and ordinary ones are not sufficient to check crimes, or cure evil practices. To carry into effect the intended execution of Perez, there is no lack of means . . . . and, in case it should be necessary, those means will have to be considered." The logic of the Junta was not unacceptable to the King, for he put the following note on the margin of the document which contained the reasonings and conclusions of his advisers: "It will be proper to examine all that which may be done in conformity to what is here expressed. But in relation to what is said about the means of execution in case they should be required, it seems to me that it would be better to treat of them at once, and to resolve upon them beforehand, so as to meet all the exigencies which may happen, and have everything prepared, should there be any understanding on the subject, because otherwise the emergencies might come when too late to execute what might be determined." Nature had not given Philip a generous heart to counteract the baleful effects of a bigoted mind, and when it is seen in whose custody he had placed his religious, moral and political conscience, it may not be so difficult to understand how he may have deluded himself into the belief that he was acting uprightly, as is maintained by those who have endeavored to defend his memory, when he was committing acts of atrocious villainy.

Judgment was on the eve of being pronounced in Aragon by the Court of Inquest in relation to the manner in which Perez had discharged his functions as Minister of State, and also by the other tribunal to which the accusation against him for poisoning La Hera and Margado had been referred, when the accused was, by a new expedient, withdrawn from their jurisdiction. This was due to a sudden inspiration of the Marquis of Almenara, which seemed excellent to Philip, and which consisted in a device to surrender Perez to the Inquisition. That active agent of the King suggested to him that Perez, being claimed by that terrible tribunal, could not invoke against it the protection of the laws of Aragon, and that he would be taken out of the prison of the *Manifestacion* to be carried to the dungeons of the Holy Office, where the royal resentment would reach him with ease, secrecy and security. But what could be the charges on which to proceed against him before the Inquisition? They were difficult to be found, and yet it will be seen what slight pretext was sufficient to make a man amenable to the dreaded jurisdiction of that tribunal. Perez had fled from Castile with his Secretary, who was a Genoese named Juan Francisco Mayorini, and who became the companion of his captivity in Aragon. Although surrounded with so many friends in that Kingdom, and shielded by its *fueros*, or privileges and immunities, both, being alarmed for their safety, determined again to take refuge elsewhere, and resolved to repair to the small Principality of Bearne, between the Kingdom of Navarre and that of France. That was enough. On their plan being discovered, they were accused of heresy, merely because they had intended to go to a country full of heretics. Besides, there were witnesses who swore that they had heard Perez and Mayorini utter certain phrases, or exclamations, which it is not unusual for men to use in fits of anger, impatience, or despair, and which really mean nothing, but which might sound like blasphemies, if taken literally. These were certainly slim and narrow grounds, but they afforded space enough for the goat-like foot of the Inquisition to stand upon, and to reach its intended victims. Among other inconsiderate things, Perez had said, on his being accused by the King of having deciphered dispatches falsely and revealed secrets of State, that "he had proceeded to justify himself without being deterred by considerations for the honor of anybody, and that he would slit the nose of God the Father Himself, if He should attempt to prevent him (Perez) from showing in what a perverse and ungentlemanly manner he had been treated by the King." Such expressions, with others, more or less irreverential, were submitted to Philip's confessor, Don Diego de Chaves, who was also a commissary of the Holy Office, and he pronounced them to be scandalous, offensive to pious ears, and smelling of heresy. In consequenee of this declaration of one of its officers, the Supreme Tribunal of the Inquisition ordered its subordinate one in Saragoza to immure Antonio Perez and Mayorini in one of its secret prisons. On receiving this mandate, the Inquisitors of Saragoza issued a decree by which they revoked and annulled all the privileges of the *Manifestacion*, so far as they impeded the free exercise of their authority. They demanded of the *Justicia* or Chief-Justice, and of his delegates, the surrender of the bodies of Perez and Mayorini, under the penalty, in case of a refusal, of excommunication in the first degree, and they threatened to subject to their judicial proceedings whomsoever should dare to oppose the execution of their requisition. The *Justicia Mayor* or Chief-Justice, Don Juan de Lanuza, had been spoken to and gained by the Marquis of Almenara, and he was in the Council-Room with the five subordinate dignitaries who constituted his Court, when the Secretary of the Inquisition presented himself. The order was immediately given to deliver to him Perez and Mayorini, and he had them transported at night, in a close carriage, to the prison of the Holy Office.

But notwithstanding the secrecy with which the transfer of the prisoners had taken place, the news of it spread instantaneously among the people, who rushed tumultuously into the streets, shouting: "Breach of privilege! Breach of privilege! Long live our liberties!" And the same excitement diffused itself like an electric fluid through the whole of Aragon. Perez, who had for many years foreseen that it would be the best shelter he might have against the storm with which he saw himself threatened, had neglected no means to secure powerful friends among the magnates of that Kingdom and to gain the favor of the middle classes and of the populace, and had met with complete success. But the interest which he excited was not merely personal, although they considered that, if not innocent, yet he was hunted down rather with the fierceness of blind hatred, than fairly put on his trial with that impartiality which justice requires. Granting even the commission of all the crimes with which he was charged, some of them at least were attended with attenuating circumstances in the opinion of the multitude. Besides, he was the victim of royal persecution, his body bore the marks of the rack, and he had been eleven years in prison! They forgot the delinquencies of the once omnipotent Minister, and, with characteristic generosity, remembered only the sufferings of the wretched fugitive, who was stripped of all his wealth and honors, and who begged but for life. The popular feeling, therefore, ran high in favor of Perez, for he had had the address to connect his cause with that of the maintenance of those privileges and liberties of which the Aragonese were so proud, and from that moment the personal interest which he had inspired had merged into a national one. To save Perez, or to save the *Fueros*, or franchises of the Kingdom, became a synonymous idea in the mind of the people. Hence the sudden rising of an infuriated mob and the deafening cries of "Our liberties, or death!" A column of the rioters marched in the direction of the palace of the Marquis of Almenara, one of the most active agents of Philip, and to whom they attributed chiefly the violation of their privileges. The Marquis, on his arrival in Saragoza, had displayed an ostentatious mode of living to which the inhabitants of that city were not accustomed. It certainly was not in harmony with the simplicity of their tastes, the frugality of their habits, and the austerity of their disposition. They had been highly disgusted with the object of his mission, and their pride had been shocked by what they thought an arrogant manifestation of superiority of rank and wealth. The aversion which the Marquis had inspired was such, that it was impossible to be his friend, or even to associate with him, without being looked upon as a public enemy. Such being the sentiments entertained for him, it was evident that his danger had become imminent. Therefore, on receiving notice of the commotion in the city, he had barricaded himself in his palace, which, with the aid of his numerous household, he prepared bravely to defend, for he was a man of resolution. The *Justicia*, or Chief-Justice, with his subordinates, and his two sons, Don Juan and Don Pedro de Lanuza, had hastened to his assistance, and were endeavoring to save his life by assuring the people that they had come to arrest him. They told the most furious of the rioters that it was their duty to retire and to leave the object of their hatred in the hands of the regularly constituted authorities, in whom they were bound to have confidence. This, however, did not satisfy them, and they battered down the doors of the palace with a beam which they used like a ram. They found Almenara in the midst of a group composed of the Chief-Justice and other public officers, who had made a rampart of their bodies to protect him. This sight checked the populace, who permitted the Marquis and his escort to come out, and to proceed in the direction of the place where he was to be incarcerated. But in the streets the crowd thronged around them, and seemed to labor under increasing excitement. The shouts were deafening, and the imprecations and gesticulations became more alarming, as the Marquis and his guards advanced toward a public square near which they were to pass and which was full of people. It became almost impossible to push them back, and they pressed so hard and so close on the small band that was conveying Almenara to a place of safety, that the Chief-Justice, who was old and infirm, fell down and was so much bruised that he had to retire. The enemies of the Marquis availed themselves of this circumstance, and, no longer satisfied with applying to him the most opprobrious epithets, they inflicted serious blows on his person, and several times struck him in the face with their daggers. Faint, dizzy, and covered with blood, he reached at last his destined prison, but died fifteen days afterward from a fever caused, it is said, more by his mortification at the insults which he had received than by the gravity of his wounds.

Whilst some of the rioters had been invading the palace of Almenara, others had gone to the Tribunal and prison of the Inquisition, and had boldly demanded that the two prisoners be remanded to the prison of the *Manifestacion*, from which they had been removed. As the Inquisitors did not seem disposed to yield, the vociferations of the rioters showed that their fury was thoroughly aroused, and voices were heard crying: "If you do not surrender the prisoners, we will burn you as you burn others." The Inquisitors were still deliberating on what they had to do, when they received a note from the Archbishop, advising them to grant what was desired, as it was the only way to put an end to the popular tumult. The Bishop of Teruel, who was Viceroy of Aragon, many magistrates, many members of the Clergy, and several magnates, such as the Counts of Aranda and Morata, presented themselves successively before the Inquisitors, and urged them to comply with the request of the multitude, if they did not want to give occasion to worse excesses than what had already happened at the palace of the Marquis of Almenara. After much hesitation, the majority of the Inquisitors became inclined to follow this prudent advice ; but one of them, Father Molina de Medrano, vehemently protested against it, on the ground that it was better for them to be buried under the ruins of the building which they occupied, than to gratify the rebellious rabble. This, however, did not seem to be to the taste of his colleagues. At last, after having received a second and a third note from the Archbishop, pressing them not to persist in their refusal, they consented to give up their prisoners, reserving to themselves the right of considering Perez and Mayorini, when in the prison of the *Manifestacion*, as being there in the name and by the authority of the Holy Office. The rioters either did not hear of this reservation, or probably cared very little for it, as it was, after all, but a senseless fiction, with which it was unnecessary to quarrel. The important point was to gain possession of the prisoners, and when they were delivered to the Viceroy and some of the judicial magistrates of the Kingdom, the people were satisfied with their triumph. They surrounded and escorted the coach which contained Perez and Mayorini, shouting with joyous enthusiasm: "Liberty! liberty! Long live our liberties!" They even recommended to Perez to show himself three times every day at the grated window of his prison, in order that they might be sure that their *Fueros*, or privileges, had not been again secretly violated. As soon as the doors of the prison of the *Manifestacion* closed on Perez and his companion, the mob quietly dispersed, and their leaders, who, most of them, were men of distinction, went to their respective homes. But, fearful of another attempt on the part of the Inquisition to seize again their intended victims, they summoned to Saragoza numerous bands of the stout and hardy inhabitants of the neighboring mountains. They accused two of the subordinate officers of the Chief-Justice of being partial to Almenara, and the Tribunal *de los Judicantes*, which was composed of seventeen men specially commissioned to take cognizance of similar denunciations, condemned the accused to deprivation of office and exile. In the mean time, the people patrolled the streets at night in imposing force, and would occasionally fire shots at such of the employees of the Holy Office as they met accidentally. Whilst the populace was thus testifying its hatred for the Inquisition, learned men were rummaging the archives of the city and studying documents to show that the Inquisition had ceased to exist legally, on account of the infringement of those conditions on which it had been introduced in the Kingdom.

Philip was then engaged in a war against France. He probably thought that his hands were full. Partly for this reason, no doubt, and partly because of his natural sluggishness and of his love for temporizing, he acted with but little energy against those who had thus set him at defiance in Saragoza, and seemed even to shrink in some sort from the necessity of inflicting punishment. He wrote to the principal cities of Aragon that it had never been his intention to violate their franchises, and that his sole object had been to deliver to the proper tribunal those who had sinned against the true faith. He contented himself with instructing the Inquisitors to publish the Bull of Pius V. against all those who should oppose the free exercise of the authority of the Holy Office, and to take the necessary means to have Perez and Mayorini replaced in their possession. Philip did not indicate those means, and to find them was no easy task for those to whom he had signified his desire. The Bull, however, was published as he wished, but it was received with very little respect by the Aragonese. They assailed it with pasquinades and insulting writings which they posted up in all the public places, and with satirical songs which were attributed to Perez. Every day gave birth to similar productions, in which the wit of the natives was taxed to express their detestation. The Inquisitors were intimidated, and did not dare to act as they were recommended. The same Molina de Medrano who, on the day of the riot, had been disposed to bury himself under the ruins of the house of the Holy Office, rather than yield to the populace, and who was the most harsh and inexorable of all the members of that implacable tribunal, allowed his courage to ooze away and asked permission to leave Aragon, because "his life was in constant peril." His apprehensions were not groundless, because, according to the description given by the Inquisitors themselves of the spirit which animated the whole population, it appears that the Clergy and even the Nuns were so excited that they talked of nothing else but resistance, and vowed that there was no danger which they would not brave in support of the liberties of the Kingdom. The people were unanimous in swearing that they would sooner lose their lives than permit Perez to be taken away. Therefore the Inquisitors informed the Government that there would be another riot, should they attempt to exercise their authority, as the public mind was so prejudiced that "it seemed to be bewitched."

In the mean time, investigations were going on in Madrid in relation to the recent occurrences in Saragoza, testimonies were taken down, written statements recorded, and a new Junta, or Council, created to take cognizance of the affair of Antonio Perez. The King consulted this Junta on what he had to do, and, not satisfied with this step, for never was a man more addicted to fortifying himself with advice, took the opinion of thirteen learned men in Saragoza, who met in a body to deliberate on the subject submitted to their consideration, and whose Jesuitical conclusions were well suited to the atmosphere of the Court of Philip, if repugnant to morality and to the logic of common sense. They declared that the privilege of the *Manifestacion* could not be annulled, but that it could be suspended ; and having discovered this curious way of solving the difficulty by maintaining theoretically the franchises which were so dear to the Aragonese, whilst destroying them practically by justifying the King in acting as if they did not exist, in consequence of their temporary suspension, these sage and conscientious advisers of royalty concluded that the Inquisitors could claim Perez and transport him to their prison, on condition of remanding again their prisoner to the place of confinement from which he had been taken, if they did not think proper to release him. Ridiculous as this may appear, it was probably thought to be a middle term, ingeniously contrived, on which the contending parties might meet and be reconciled, but it had the fate of all such contemptible devices, and failed entirely in obtaining its object. Unfortunately, the singular interpretation given by these learned men to the charter which secured the franchises of Aragon, this manifestation of weakness and subserviency on their part, greatly encouraged Philip, who knew well how to avail himself of these favorable circumstances. From the Escorial where he was ensconced, he, with that indefatigable pen which he was so fond of wielding, wrote to the Viceroy of Aragon, to its Magistrates, Magnates, and other distinguished personages, making a personal appeal to their fidelity, ordering them to dismiss from Saragoza the turbulent mountaineers who had been called to that city, and giving them other directions for the re-establishment of the Royal authority. Most of the Nobles gave their adhesion to the King; the *Justicia* and other Magistrates began to waver; the Count of Aranda and the Duke of Villahermosa, who had been the most conspicuous among those of their Order to side with the people, hesitated, and showed signs which indicated that they were disposed to go no farther. The Inquisitors, whose zeal and courage were revived by the support which they felt to be at hand, and by the symptoms of irresolution which they observed in their opponents, ventured to issue, on the 17th of August, a new mandate for the transfer of the prisoners to the dungeons of the Holy Office.

As soon as the determination of the Inquisition to retake possession of Perez and Mayorini was made known, the people began to move like an angry sea under the first blast of the tempest. There could already be discerned that long and heavy swell which announces the strength of the perturbing power. There were heard in the distance the deep-toned mutterings of the coming storm. It was evident that the people were preparing for another outbreak. The most energetic and influential of the Nobles were either openly or secretly at their head, and those by whom they had been abandoned had never possessed much of their confidence. Antonio Perez, on the other hand, was not inactive in his prison, and, despite his jailers, or perhaps with their connivance, found the means of scattering abroad spirited writings, which contributed to inflame the public mind. At night, numerous bands of armed men, in a state of great excitement, perambulated the streets, and occasionally fired at the patrols, which the magistrates of the city headed in person. In these skirmishes several individuals were killed and wounded, and the advantage remained with the populace. The danger was so apparent that neither the Viceroy nor any other authority would venture to execute the mandate of the Inquisition, although a certain number of troops had been collected for that purpose. Nevertheless, Perez became apprehensive of falling into the hands of that Tribunal, and resolved on a speedy flight. Already had he sawed asunder the iron bars of the window of his prison with a pair of scissors which he had converted into files, when he was denounced by a Jesuit to whom he had opened himself. In consequence of this discovery he was removed to a safer room, and precluded from having any intercourse with anybody.

At last the Inquisitors, with that tenacity of purpose which characterized their institution, after having come to a satisfactory understanding with the *Justicia* and his Lieutenants, resolved, cost what it might, to obtain, a second time, the delivery of the prisoners into their sacred hands. The 24th of September was chosen for it—a fatal day for Saragoza—a day which is forever to be gloomily remembered in the annals of Aragon, and which had deplorable consequences for the whole of Spain. On that day the officials of the Inquisition, accompanied by the Viceroy and some of the high dignitaries of the city and of the Kingdom, by a crowd of noblemen followed by some of their vassals, and by six hundred arquebusiers, marched in great pomp and in military array to the prison of the *Manifestacion*, to execute the mandate of the Inquisition. But the popular wrath, at such a spectacle, exploded like a mass of ignited gunpowder. The Viceroy and other authorities had to take refuge in houses, which were attacked, set on fire, and from which they escaped through the roofs. The officials of the Inquisition were indebted for their safety to the same agility, and the doors of the prison being battered down, Antonio Perez and Mayorini were rescued by their friends, and, taking to horse, fled rapidly out of the city through the gate of Santa Engracia. The Secretary of the Inquisition, who was an eye-witness, and who relates all the details of this riot, says: "I certify that the soldiers and the nobles made so little resistance that it cannot be doubted that they did not intend any, and even some of them went over to the other side." At five of the afternoon the people, having overcome all obstacles, being in complete possession of the city, and tired of shouting "Long live our liberties! Long live our privileges!" retired to rest like a lion, who, exhausted by the fury into which he had lashed himself, and no longer seeing anything on which to vent it, utters a last growl, folds his paws under his shaggy breast, and composes himself to sleep, with the satisfaction of a monarch whose sway remains undisputed. The authorities, when night came, being made aware that the many-headed monster had abandoned the battle-field and withdrawn to its den, dispatched couriers in every direction to arrest the fugitive Perez, for whose capture they offered a reward of two thousand ducats. But their alarms at what every moment might bring forth were intense. The Viceroy wrote to the King to ask permission to remove with the Royal Audience to some other place, on account of the little security which they could rely on in Saragoza. The several districts in which the city was divided had demanded, through their Representatives, that its defence be intrusted to them, and that the troops be sent out of its precincts. Already were the authorities preparing to accede to their wishes, and to make a distribution of the arms which were in the arsenal, when there came an order from the King, prescribing to take special care that the people should not have access to them. He was obeyed.

The political Constitution of the Kingdom of Aragon, with its numerous franchises, privileges and immunities, which imposed such restraints on the Executive as almost to annul it in some cases, was not compatible with the character of such a Sovereign as Philip, who was so greedy of power as to regret to delegate the least particle of it, and who thought it impious on the part of subjects to attempt to throw the lightest ligament round the neck of royal authority. Therefore the liberties of Aragon and all the ideas of Philip in relation to his divine rights of sovereignty were as antagonistical as day and night. It is even to be wondered at that they had not, long before, come to a collision. But Philip's attention and Philip's armies, since his accession to the throne, had chiefly been engaged abroad—in Africa, in America, in Turkey, in Italy, in the Low Countries, in England, in France, and in Portugal. His eyes, being mostly fixed on distant and more important objects, had not been afforded the leisure to dwell on this offensive one which lay nearer to his person. Besides, it was not in accordance with his habitual policy to attack openly and in front institutions which had been for so many centuries deeply rooted in the hearts of the Aragonese. He knew that their bravery was equal to their proverbial stubbornness, and he felt that it would be dangerous to provoke wantonly a people so warlike and so free, dwelling in a rugged country where war could be prolonged indefinitely among mountain fastnesses, and which was situated on the frontiers of France. Foreign assistance might be too readily obtained. He was also wanting in pretexts to show his latent hostility to the Aragonese. They had always exhibited a great deal of loyalty, had served him faithfully in peace and war ; and with a docility to which they had not accustomed their Sovereigns, they had, notwithstanding their independent spirit and their economical habits, granted to Philip all the ordinary and extraordinary subsidies which he had required of them, besides allowing him, on several occasions, with spontaneous generosity, very large sums in the liberal shape of donations.

Philip had, therefore, contented himself with undermining secretly the edifice which he had more than one reason not to assail with unconcealed weapons. But if he spared the thunderbolt which, in a serene sky, would have been observed of all, and which, amidst the crash of shattered columns and tottering walls, might have produced a conflagration more extensive than he was prepared for, he noiselessly crept to their foundations and laid under them the seeds of destruction. He had, since the beginning of his reign, from time to time, when the occasion favored his designs, warred in detail against the liberties of Aragon. Some of them he had indirectly abridged by a sly extension of the royal authority; others he had wounded, crippled, or weakened by stealthy side-blows, as if with the midnight dagger of an assassin. There were in Aragon franchises common to the whole Kingdom, and franchises which appertained only to particular localities. These latter he first operated against, in order gradually to arrive at the former, which were of far more importance. His plan was to accustom the people by degrees to these infractions of their rights, and to break one by one those shafts which, if united in a bundle, might have resisted his efforts. He knew that the successive destruction of the immunities of localities, between which there were frequently intense jealousies, and about which there could be felt no general interest, was far more easy to accomplish than the overthrow of any of the franchises which were common to the whole Kingdom. He went to work accordingly in this matter with diabolical skill, whenever he could divert his mind from those machinations with which, far and wide, he kept the world in a state of perturbation. He would, on such occasions, turn his cold gray eyes toward Aragon, and if he saw in any particular spot any cause of discontent, he took care to make it worse. Were a magnate and his vassals quarreling, he widened the breach, until he found the opportunity to step in, and it was always to the detriment of both parties. Was any community disposed to turbulence, his agents fanned it into an actual outbreak, which afforded the chance to strangle some of its beloved immunities. Were a city and its constituted authorities on terms of disagreement, he so manœuvred that anarchy soon ensued, and he then intervened to restore order at the cost of some of their prerogatives. Thus he had been slowly and cautiously breaking down the spirit of the people and familiarizing them with strokes of royal authority, without their thinking that these encroachments were of sufficient importance to call for a well-organized and general resistance. In this way some of their most valuable privileges had fallen into desuetude, or been emasculated, and others had been suspended, if not absolutely abolished ; when it was discovered by some of the most patriotic and enlightened minds of Aragon that it would be fortunate if something occurred to wake up the zeal of the people for their antique liberties ; and the Sovereign, on the other hand, came to the conclusion that the favorable time had arrived to strike a final blow. These were the respective relations existing between Philip and Aragon, when the desired opportunity for a struggle was given by the affair of Perez.

CHAPTER VI.

On the 15th of October, thinking that the time for action was ripe, and having sufficiently pondered on the measures to be taken in connection with the events which have been related, Philip wrote to the authorities of Saragoza that he had determined to send to that city the army which had been assembled under the command of Alonzo de Vargas, to carry on the war existing between Spain and France. He also announced to them that the object which he had in view was, "to re-establish the respect due to the Holy Office of the Inquisition, and secure the free use and exercise of their *fueros.*" In another letter he assured them with more explicit precision, that "he had no other intention than that of protecting their *fueros*, and that he would not permit them to be violated by anybody." Notwithstanding these royal declarations, the approach of the army filled the Aragonese with consternation. They suspected that Philip meant the very reverse of what he professed in relation to their privileges and franchises ; for the mere sending of an army into Aragon without the consent of the Cortes was thought to be an infraction of their *Fueros.* Therefore the inhabitants of Saragoza resolved on resistance. The manifestations of the public spirit were such, that the Viceroy sent two emissaries to Vargas, to request in his name, and in that of the Kingdom and the city in particular, that the march of the troops be stopped until further orders from the King; and, at the same time, he dispatched two other emissaries to His Majesty, to supplicate him to defer for awhile the entering of the army into Aragon; if that could not be done, he begged to receive timely notice of it, so that he might retire for safety, with the members of his Council, into the fortress which commanded the city. He suggested, moreover, that, in his opinion, it would be expedient to convene the Cortes in Calatayud, and to delay their proceedings by proroguing them from time to time until some means be found to settle satisfactorily the questions which had disturbed the tranquillity of the Kingdom. In these conjunctures, its most learned jurisconsults, having been consulted, decided unanimously that the entering of Philip's army into Aragon would be a breach of privilege, and that, in such a case, it would be the duty of the proper authorities to use all the resources of the Kingdom "to resist and expel those intruding strangers." (*Gentes estrangeras.*)

Philip, on his part, acted with his usual slowness of deliberation. He did not hasten the march of his army to anticipate the movements of his opponents, but he sent the Marquis of Lombay to Aragon with minute instructions as to the steps which he should take to restore peace to the Kingdom. It was prescribed to him at full length how he was to deal with the magnates, the universities and other corporations, in order to separate them from the cause of the people. He was commissioned to repeat that the sole object of the King was to re-establish the authority of the Inquisition, and " to secure the uncontrolled exercise of the franchises of the Kingdom," although the Aragonese could not understand how the antagonism of these two hostile elements could be reconciled ; for it seemed that the existence of the one excluded the other as effectually as water extinguishes fire. In the mean time, Vargas, who was slowly progressing with his army, gave also assurance to an Aragonese Committee, who had come to remonstrate against his further advance, that he was specially instructed by the King "to preserve the Fueros."

Informed of the approach of the army, which was chiefly composed of troops from Castile, the inhabitants of Saragoza compelled the Justicia to march a short distance from the city to meet the coming foe. The Justicia was no longer the old man, Don Juan de Lanuza, who had figured in the first disturbances. He had died since, and had been succeeded in his office by his eldest son, who bore the same name. This new dignitary, although young and robust in body, had a timid and vacillating mind. He had with him an undisciplined force of scarcely two thousand men, with whom he certainly could not hope to offer a successful resistance to the veteran troops which were approaching. Catalonia and the Kingdom of Valencia had not responded to the appeal which had been made to them; the other cities of Aragon, with the exception of barely half a score of them, had remained indifferent, and even these had sent but a scanty aid. The Count of Aranda and the Duke of Villahermosa, who were suspected of being traitors, took refuge in the Monastery of Santa Engracia, which was attacked by the populace with great fury, and it was with considerable risk that these nobles escaped by scaling the walls of the garden of the Monastery, at a spot which was not sufficiently guarded by the assailants. They fled to the neighboring town of Epila, whither also retired in dismay the Justicia and several other chiefs and magnates, after having reluctantly come out of Saragoza with the rabble, who had rather dragged them onward than followed them. The insurgents, who acted like a confused mob, and not like a body of armed men organized for battle, on finding themselves deserted by those to whose personal rank and official dignity they looked up as a protection and encouragement in their hazardous enterprise, returned to Saragoza in much disorder. From Epila the Justicia and his companions published an address to the Kingdom, in which they justified their conduct on the plea of necessity, as their forces were totally inadequate to the object which they had in view, and were even so mutinous as to threaten the lives of their chiefs "at every step." On the other hand, the Count of Morata, who was one of Philip's most zealous adherents, wrote to him to boast of having defeated the plans of the insurgents and to recommend the severest chastisement without any regard to the Fueros.

It was certainly an ill-concerted affair, and a most lame and abortive attempt at resistance. It was evident that there was no general disposition on the part of the people of Aragon to engage in a struggle against the royal authority. There had been a spasmodic convulsion in one of the limbs, but the body had remained quiescent. Even Saragoza opened its gates to Vargas, who entered without the slightest opposition on the 12th of November. Under such circumstances, the prudent commander very properly abstained from any act of rigor. Moreover, he wrote to Philip that it seemed to him opportune to grant a general pardon to all, with the exception of a few persons among the most guilty, and he invited the Justicia, the Deputies of Saragoza, the Duke of Villahermosa, the Count of Aranda, and others, to return without apprehension, and with assurances on his part that the Fueros would be preserved intact. A few days afterward, Vargas, in a communication to the King, advised again a general pardon. "It is much required," he said, "that the pardon be as full as possible, and that your Majesty, in granting it, should use words calculated to tranquillize them on the preservation of their *Fueros*, about which they have run mad. Let there be only a few persons excepted from it and brought to trial, and things will work well." He added that it would be proper to appoint as Viceroy a native of the Kingdom, and he assured His Majesty that this measure and others of the like nature would bring the whole people back to their senses and to their duty. Wise and humane as these suggestions were, they failed to be adopted. They neither suited the temper and usual policy of Philip, nor his designs on that occasion. There was no feeling more repugnant to his cold and relentless heart than that of clemency. Most of the leaders of the insurrection had fled, some to Catalonia, others to the mountains, and emissaries had been sent in pursuit. But the Justicia, with other magistrates and magnates of the land, relying on the conciliatory language and professed indulgence of Vargas, had presented themselves to him in testimony of their unbroken allegiance. The Marquis of Lombay, who had come as the special representative of Philip, renewed to them the promise that their *Fueros* would be respected ; and the most rigorous measure which he proposed to the King was the temporary disfranchisement of the Kingdom and city. He also recommended that the Justicia and other competent authorities be called upon to acknowledge that the entering of the army into Aragon was no violation of their privileges, and that their antecedent declarations to the contrary had been extorted from them by the mutineers. This he thought would be a sufficient reparation. But the Inquisitors were of a much more inexorable disposition. Molina de Medrano, who had come to Madrid to claim the reward due to his services, to his zeal, and to the dangers he had run, gave his opinion to the Inquisitor-General on the course which he deemed advisable to pursue. It smelt of brimstone, it breathed vengeance, it was hot with the fire of the stakes which it proposed to kindle, and called for the shower of blood in which the imagination of this fanatic Priest was already luxuriating. Harsh, indeed, were the measures advocated by him for the present correction and future amelioration of the Aragonese. In connection with this document, he presented to the head of the Inquisition a minute list containing the names of those whom he thought the most guilty. That list embraced laymen and ecclesiastics from the highest to the lowest, and even condescended not to ignore most obscure and humble individuals among the peasantry and among the dregs of the populace of cities.

Tranquillity, however, had been restored in Saragoza, and it seemed as if all these disturbances were destined to have everywhere a pacific termination. The Marquis of Lombay, who was known to possess the instructions of Philip, and whose deportment, therefore, was supposed to be indicative of the intentions of the Sovereign, had alighted at the house of his uncle, the Duke of Villahermosa, and become his guest. There also Vargas and the other officers of the army were duly entertained. It was augured from these circumstances that the Duke and others who had been connected with the recent popular commotions had very little to apprehend. The Justicia had resumed his functions and opened his Court. The people were quiet and submissive; everything looked fair and promising, and wore a smiling aspect. All were rejoicing at the policy of conciliation and leniency which appeared to have been adopted, when suddenly the serene horizon was overcast, and the storm of royal resentment which, unperceived, had been secretly gathering in the distance, swept over the devoted city. The theatrical effect which had been produced in Brussels on the 9th of September, 1567, by the treacherous arrest of Egmont and Horn, who had been decoyed by the blandishments of the Duke of Alva, seemed to have been fondly remembered by Philip, who determined to have something like a repetition of the scene in Saragoza, although with different actors. On the 19th of December, 1591, at noon, the Justicia, with his lieutenants, was leaving the palace where they had been assembled in the regular discharge of their duties, and was proceeding to the neighboring church of St. John to hear mass, when, in obedience to secret orders forwarded to Vargas, he was arrested, to his utter amazement, in the name of the King, by Captain Velasco, at the head of a company of Arquebusiers, and conducted to the headquarters of Vargas, who committed him to the custody of Colonel Francisco de Bobadilla. On the very same day, with no less deceitful management, the Duke of Villahermosa and the Count of Aranda were made prisoners, and transported, the one to the castle of Burgos, and the other to the fortress of the Mota de Medina. Terror hung like a funereal pall over Saragoza, and Philip may well be supposed to have rejoiced, a second time, at the grand stage effect of his dramatic combinations.

On this occasion he acted with more promptitude than was his wont, and this departure from his habits was the more striking from the fact that there was no necessity for it. Poor Lanuza, notwithstanding his illustrious name and his exalted station, was not a dangerous man, and it was evident that he had been but an unwilling tool in the hands of the insurgents. As soon as the opportunity had presented itself, he had abandoned them, carrying away with him the national standard of St. George and the banner emblazoned with the coat-of-arms of Aragon, round which their disorderly band had tumultuously rallied. If he had deserved any punishment at all, it would probably have been limited, under any other Sovereign, to a severe reprimand, or an incarceration of a few months. He was the head of one of the greatest families of Aragon, and, almost by hereditary right, filled the office of Justicia, which was the highest under the Crown, and which for near two centuries had been in his family as an heir-loom. But these circumstances were no protection to him, and were, perhaps, the very cause of the harsh doom to which he was subjected. On the night following the day of his arrest, he was notified to prepare to die on the next morning. "What!" exclaimed the unfortunate man, "who condemns me?" "The King himself," was the answer. "But," replied the prisoner, "I cannot be tried and judged by any other authority than the King and Cortes assembled together for that purpose." All his remonstrances were useless. No accusation was brought against him; he was not even interrogated; and there was not the shadow of a trial. The King had merely written to Vargas: "You will arrest Don Juan de Lanuza, and you will have his head immediately cut off." This laconic sentence was sufficient to put to death the Supreme Magistrate of Aragon, among whose attributes was that of checking the royal power and compelling it to act in conformity with the Constitution and laws of the Kingdom. In preceding ages, the Aragonese would have risen to one man, nobles and peasants, to resist such an attempt against the sacred person of the Justicia. But the times had changed; the people had gradually been tamed to servitude, and not a hand was raised to strike for the expiring liberties of Aragon. No effort was made to save Lanuza thus summarily disposed of, as if he had been the slave of some Turkish Bashaw, and not the free subject of a Christian Prince. He was given the Jesuit Ibañez for his confessor, and a certain number of priests were designated to accompany him to the scaffold, which was erected during the night in the market-place; for Philip always pretended to take great interest in the salvation of the souls of his victims. At one in the morning, the whole army being under arms and batteries of cannon enfilading the principal streets, Don Juan de Lanuza, chained like a common malefactor, and attired in the same black costume which he habitually wore on account of the recent death of his father, was taken in his own coach to the place of execution, where trumpets sounded and proclamation was made that the King had ordered his head to be struck off, his houses and castles to be razed to the ground, and all his earthly possessions to be confiscated, as a punishment for his having, "with banners displayed," opposed the royal army. The axe of the executioner was soon crimsoned with the best blood of Aragon. Unfortunately, it was not one man only who had perished under that blow, but all the liberties of the Kingdom; and it was what Philip had meant by that symbolical death. "The record of that sad day," says an Aragonese historian, "should be chiseled on a black stone, as a testimonial of mourning for what we then lost forever."

The royal vengeance was not satisfied with the death of the Justicia, which was merely the signal for throwing aside the mask of dissimulation and inaugurating a reign of terror and cruelty. The King vented his rage even on inanimate objects. The palace of Lanuza, from which his aged and disconsolate mother was expelled, and which ought to have been defended by the glory of the historical deeds of its former possessors, was destroyed to its foundations. All the houses of the nobles who had participated in the late disturbances had the same fate. It is impossible to imagine anything more senseless than this wanton destruction of property, which, if taken away from traitors, granting them to be such, would in other hands have still constituted a portion of the public wealth. But the wrath of Philip seems to have been tinctured with a degree of insanity. The best streets of Saragoza were choked with heaps of ruins, as if an Attila had passed through with his Barbarian hordes. The destruction of so many noble edifices announced but too clearly what Philip would have done to their proprietors, if he had got hold of them. The blow of the executioner's axe would have sounded still more gratefully in his ear than that of the mason's pick engaged in the work of demolition. Some of his intended victims, not trusting to his hypocritical mansuetude, had fled in time, but too many, however, had remained in his power. The Duke of Villahermosa and the Count of Aranda had died in their prison before sentence had been pronounced against them. Their destiny had been a singular one. Distrusted by the people, who had threatened their lives and compelled them to fly for safety on account of their supposed attachment to the King's interests, they were imprisoned and perhaps put to death by him on account of their fancied zeal in the cause of the insurgents. Don Diego de Heredia, Baron of Barboles, and Don Juan De Luna, Lord of Purroy, had their heads struck off, after having been subjected to torments which it would be sickening to relate. Others soon followed, and the planks of the scaffold had no time to dry. They were kept reeking with plebeian and noble blood—the blood of the patrician, the commoner and artisan—the blood of the aged and the young, without discrimination and mercy. Some were beheaded, others strangled, many quartered and disemboweled ; and all these sacrifices to Moloch were marked with a variety in the mode of execution which showed a striking fertility of imagination in the contriver. Each dish offered at this banquet of death was cooked up in a different style to stimulate, as it were, the appetite of the grisly Monarch. Heads were stuck up plentifully in the most conspicuous places of public resort, with what was thought to be appropriate inscriptions. The baptism of blood and tears was not confined to Saragoza, but extended to Teruel, a considerable town, and to various other points. Something new and entirely original closed this scenic representation of which Philip was the author, and for which he certainly deserved the plaudits of the inmates of Pandemonium. Before the curtain fell, the hangman was hung by his own aid. It was, we presume, intended as one of those laughable farces which are generally given to the public after the performance of tragedies. The mood of the populace must have been suddenly moved by it from grief to joy, and it is not to be doubted that they enthusiastically clapped their hands at the perpetration of this grim joke.

At last Philip, having glutted his ire, imitated his father, who had granted an amnesty after having destroyed the chief participators in the insurrection of Castile. Charles had been most sanguinary, and his son willingly trod in his footsteps on an occasion of a similar nature. The pardon granted by Philip was after the fashion of the one vouchsafed by Charles more than half a century before. It purported to be general, but there were so many exceptions that the number of the excepted exceeded that of the pardoned. What made this document still more striking, was the complacency with which the King complimented himself on his paternal indulgence and wonderful benignity of heart. In Castile, after having crushed those among the inhabitants of that Kingdom who had attempted to defend their time-honored liberties, Charles had, on the 28th of October, 1522, granted a *general amnesty*, which pardoned only those who had no need of his mercy, because they could not be reached by the law, even in its most far-fetched interpretation and application. In Aragon, on the 24th of September, 1591, Philip repeated the same fraudulent act of clemency.

There was the same family resemblance in these two acts—a uniformity of bad faith, hypocrisy and cruelty, which showed that both proceeded from kindred sources.

There is hardly on record an instance of more exquisite mockery than this general pardon. It was not enough that the number of the excepted exceeded that of the pardoned ; but the Inquisition, encouraged by the Royal protection, having gone to work with great zeal and on its own account, independently of the action of the civil authorities, the wretches who had escaped from Charybdis fell into Scylla. The Holy Office swept into its dungeons about one hundred and thirty persons who had eluded the grasp of the Courts of secular jurisdiction. As they were tried before an Ecclesiastical Tribunal, the natural inference would be that it was for offences against religion or the Church. But such was not the fact, except in a few cases. Most of the prisoners were only found guilty of having assisted the flight of Antonio Perez, or of having done or said something or other to resist the Royal army. One could hardly have supposed that such offences were cognizable by the Inquisition, but it was held by that Tribunal that Antonio Perez having fled from its prison, into which he had been cast on a charge of heresy, all those who had given him aid and comfort under any pretence whatever, and who had attempted, directly or indirectly, to oppose the army which had been sent to support the Holy Office, were necessarily heretics, wherefore it pronounced sentence upon the accused, and for its execution handed them over to the civil authority. Some were put to death, some banished; on others lighter penalties were inflicted. As to Perez, he was decreed to be guilty of heresy in the last degree; and in consequence of his having taken refuge in France, his effigy, with a high conical hat on its head, and dressed in a long yellow robe on which were represented the flames of hell, was burned in an *auto de fé* which took place on the 20th of October, 1592, and lasted from eight o'clock in the morning until nine at night. From its duration, it is easy to imagine the number of its victims. When the last had been reduced to ashes by those worse than cannibal monsters, the effigy of Perez, which had been reserved to close this demoniacal exhibition, was pitched into the blazing pile. His sons, his daughters, and all their male descendants, were declared incapable forever of possessing any ecclesiastical or secular dignities, benefices, or offices whatever, and were prohibited from having on their persons any ornament of gold or silver, or pearls, precious stones, or corals—from using silk, camlet and fine cloths as articles of dress—from riding on horseback — and from doing many other things which were usually interdicted to persons who had incurred the excommunication of the Holy Office.

Thus, hand in hand, went to work in harmonious

accord the Grand Inquisitor and the King; the jackal hunted for the lion. Philip had attained his object: he had struck such terror into the Aragonese, that it was evident he could henceforth do anything he pleased without expecting the slightest resistance. They had been taught that their boasted privileges, franchises and immunities had become but the fantasies of an idle dream, and that, in reality, they were at the mercy of an inflexible despot. Their conscience must have told them, besides, that they were suffering the consequences of that retributive justice which is sometimes awarded to nations as well as to individuals. About seventy years before, when they had been called upon by the Castilians, their neighbors, to help them in maintaining their liberties against Charles the Fifth, they had remained indifferent and egotistically inactive. Those liberties were extinguished on the battle-field of Villalar. Now the turn of Aragon had come; and when she also cried for assistance, an army of those enslaved Castilians, who remembered perhaps but too keenly how their ancestors had been abandoned to their fate on a similar occasion, drowned in blood her long-enjoyed and hereditary liberties. It must also be admitted that the protection which the Aragonese granted to Perez was injudicious. He was a very wicked man, and it is not in support of one so little worthy of the sympathies of a high-minded and generous people, that they ought to have gone into a contest about their *Fueros*. That individual was accused of having committed crimes in Castile, and had fled to Aragon as to a sanctuary. We cannot but think that he ought to have been surrendered. It looks like an unwarrantable pretension on the part of the Aragonese to have insisted on his being tried in Aragon, because he was a native of that Kingdom, for acts which he had done in Castile. If this was one of their privileges, it would have been wise to have relinquished it, because improper, and to have saved the rest by this prudent and just concession. It would at least have left Philip without a pretext for aggression.

Notwithstanding his easy triumph, Philip thought it expedient to give an aspect of legality to the new relations which brute force had established between the Crown and the Kingdom of Aragon. With that view, he convened the Cortes at Tarazona, to revise and reform the Aragonese *Fueros*. It was customary for the King in person to open their session; but alleging that it would be inconvenient for him to meet them at that time, he had himself represented by the Archbishop of Saragoza, who read the royal speech. Shortly after, the Archbishop having died, the King appointed as his representatives the Magistrate Don Juan Campi and Doctor Don Juan Bautista de Lanuza, who were then performing *ad interim* the functions of Justicia of Aragon. He associated with them a learned jurisconsult, named Geronimo Perez de Nueros. There appears to have been a fatality attached to those who, at that session of the Cortes, were personating the King; for Campi and Nueros also died shortly after the Archbishop, leaving their colleague Lanuza to act by himself. Probably after having ascertained that the temper of the Cortes was sufficiently pliant to suit his purposes and to invite his presence, at last came the King with his son, Don Philip, the Hereditary Prince, who was sworn before that assembly as his successor. The Cortes seem to have crouched servilely under the heavy iron rod which Philip had extended over the Kingdom, for instead of resenting the tyrannical and bloody course which he had lately pursued, they voted a larger sum of money as subsidy than had ever been granted to that Monarch by any of their predecessors. Fully aware that they shared in the general consternation, convinced that they were broken down in spirit and ready for the yoke which he had prepared for their necks, Philip availed himself of these favorable circumstances to obtain the modification or repeal of all the *Fueros* which he considered incompatible with the absolute power of the Crown. To pass certain laws and to tax the people, a unanimity of votes had been indispensable in the Cortes of Aragon. It was reduced to a bare majority, as in Castile. The nomination to some important offices in the magistracy was conceded to the King. Even the appointment of the Justicia was left to him, and he could remove at will that exalted functionary, who therefore ceased to be independent. It had been the main column which had supported the whole edifice of the liberties of Aragon ; for that magistrate had been for ages the embodiment of the power and majesty of the people and a counterpoise to the royal authority, in the same way in which the Tribunes of Rome had checked the Consuls and Senate of that Commonwealth. It was an immemorial institution, which was venerated and cherished by the Aragonese as the guarantee of their franchises. It was now reduced to a mere shadow. The name was retained, but the substance was gone. The Justicia had become a mere royal functionary instead of being the representative of the people. He had not even the privilege of appointing his own lieutenants. Philip took that into his hands, still with the acquiescence of the Cortes. They no longer had anything to refuse. Clearly the wild unicorn had been tamed, and bore the saddle gently. Ready to vault into it at will, despotism, booted and spurred, stood by with looks of self-complacency and with whip in hand.

Pleased with the results of the castigation which he had inflicted, Philip thought that the moment had come for showing some degree of clemency. He therefore relieved the city of Saragoza from the presence of the army which he had quartered on its inhabitants, but he left in its citadel a garrison sufficiently strong to maintain his authority, should there happen to be again any disposition to oppose it. Such was the end of the famous trial of Perez, which had lasted for so many years, and which made so much noise at the time. He had succeeded at last in flying from the Kingdom where he had so long wielded so much power, to pass the remainder of his life in exile ; and Aragon, his native land, had to submit to radical changes in its constitutional and fundamental laws. Perez, however, was less the cause of it, than the occasion. Whilst Aragon had remained a distinct Kingdom, the Barons and the Commons had been able to bridle successfully the royal authority, although the frequent struggles between the sovereigns and their subjects had been attended with much bloodshed, and with alternate success on either side. But the people, on the whole, had stood their ground and retained their liberties, only allowing to their kings a limited power. However, when Ferdinand, the future conqueror of Granada, married Isabella of Castile, when the Iberian Peninsula, with the exception of Portugal, after the subjugation of the Moors, was united under one sceptre resplendent with glory, in the hands of the great Emperor Charles V., when by successive events the Sovereign of Spain became so powerful as to threaten the independence of Europe, the continuation of the existence of the franchises of the Kingdom of Aragon must have appeared to many more than problematical. Sagacious minds must have foreseen that their destruction was inevitable ; that it was a mere question of time, of opportunity and expediency. The nobles had been seduced by the splendors of a Court which had been refined into the most polished and brilliant in the world. The immense patronage of the Crown had attractions which could not be resisted. There were, not only in Spain, but in the four quarters of the globe, a multitude of viceroyalties and other magnificent offices to be distributed with a profuse hand. Thus the Barons had been gradually tempted to exchange the rude independence and petty royalty which they enjoyed in their castellated domains among their native mountains, for the distinctions and honors, the titles and wealth which disguised from the world, and perhaps from their own eyes, the state of gorgeous servitude into which they had passed. Besides, in the march of ages, and in the changes which it brings, the days had gone by, when the poor but proud and warlike population of Aragon, who thought themselves compensated by the blessings of freedom for the barrenness of their soil and the harshness of their climate, and who had long enjoyed republican institutions under the ostensible form of monarchy, could say to their Sovereign, on his taking his coronation oath : " We, who, individually, are as good as you are, and who, collectively, are more powerful, make you King, on condition that you shall observe our laws and respect our liberties. If not, no." This was very well when that Sovereign, in his circumscribed territory, was but little above the great magnates of his realm, and when he admitted himself that he was but the "comrade of his vassals." But such language had ceased to be true, and could therefore no longer be addressed with effect to kings in whose dominions the sun never set, and whose power had grown to be an object of terror to nations in comparison to which the Aragonese sank into insignificance. Hence, dazzled by the achievements of the glorious Emperor Charles V., remembering how easily the Castilians had been crushed by him when attempting to resist his encroachments on their liberties, raised in the belief that the power which he had bequeathed to his stern son was irresistible, the new generation of Aragonese, when called upon to rise in arms like one man, or lose those franchises which had become hoary with age like the weather-beaten towers of their old castles, proved unequal to the noble and arduous task. The hope of success did not dawn upon their hearts, and therefore their efforts were but feeble, and almost confined to the city of Saragoza and to its populace, instigated by a few noblemen, friends of Perez, whose chief object probably was rather to liberate him by the outbreak of a sudden riot, than to engage in a serious and protracted struggle for the *Fueros* of Aragon against the overwhelming forces which Philip had at his command. In this way may be reasonably explained the want of energy and unanimity which has been observed, and the easy surrender by the Aragonese of all those rights and immunities which had been so dear to them. The sap of the tree had ceased to be healthy;

the canker-worm was under its bark, making its way to the heart; its roots had become loose; so that, at the first blow of Philip's axe, the pride of the forest fell to the ground without the honor of a sturdy resistance.

As to Perez, whom we have left flying out of Saragoza, he reached the Pyrenees, where he remained concealed in a mountain cave three days, with no other aliment than some bread and wine. At night he went out in search of water. Being informed that he was surrounded by his pursuers, and that all the passes to France were guarded, he had the hardihood to return to Saragoza, where he thought he would be in greater safety. In that city he remained hidden in the house of Don Martin de Lanuza, a kinsman of the Justicia, who was soon to perish on the scaffold, until the approach of Vargas with his troops; when, two days before they entered the city, he again escaped, after having eluded the vigilance of the Inquisition. At last he succeeded in crossing the Pyrenees, and arrived at Pau, in the principality of Bearne, on the 21st of November, 1591. There he presented himself to the sister of Henry IV., Catherine of Bourbon, to whom he had previously written to secure her protection. The agents of Philip followed him and invited him to return to Spain, on guaranteeing a speedy adjustment of his difficulties with the King. But Perez, who was informed of the atrocities perpetrated against his partisans in Saragoza, was proof against deception. Being frustrated in their design to inveigle Perez, those agents attempted his life several times and in several ways, but without success. In February, 1592, he and some of his friends, having obtained from the Princess Catherine the assistance of some companies of men-at-arms, penetrated into Aragon in the hope of producing an insurrection, and pushed as far as the town of Biescas; but, being attacked by the inhabitants of Huesca and Jaca, and by Vargas with a portion of his army, he was routed with great slaughter and compelled again to take refuge in France, where he offered his services to Henry IV., who accepted them. Henry probably thought that Perez, with his thorough knowledge of the character, plans and secrets of Philip, might be a useful instrument, and, in the Spring of 1593, admitted him into his presence at Tours, where the King and the exiled minister had long and frequent conferences, from which it resulted that Perez was sent to Queen Elizabeth with letters from Henry. Whilst in England, Perez gained the good-will of the Earl of Essex, through whose patronage he obtained a pension of one hundred and thirty pounds. During his residence in that country he published a political pamphlet under the name of Raphael Peregrino, in which he made certain revelations concerning Philip, and increased the irritation of that Monarch. Shortly after, two Irishmen, who had been sent by the Count of Fuentes, Governor of the Low Countries, to kill Perez, were arrested and executed. In 1595, war being formally declared between Philip and Henry, Antonio Perez was recalled from England by the latter Prince, who had availed himself of the Spaniard's influence with the Earl of Essex to prevail upon Queen Elizabeth, of whom that nobleman was the favorite, to assist France in carrying on hostilities against Spain. Whilst in Paris, Perez was very near being assassinated by two emissaries from Spain, who had come for that special purpose. One of them was seized, put to the torture and executed. These repeated attempts caused great alarm to Perez, who, although he had been allowed a pension of four thousand ducats and seemed to enjoy all the confidence of Henry, was so restless and so apprehensive of the consequences of Philip's resentment, that he would have sought shelter somewhere else, if Henry had not persuaded him that he could be nowhere more safe than at his side.

In the Spring of 1596, Antonio Perez was sent a second time to England to assist in the negotiation of an offensive and defensive alliance between that country and France against Spain. But, this time, he found that a change had come over the disposition of his former friend, the Earl of Essex. This nobleman avoided seeing him, and Perez had to return, wounded in his pride by the conduct of Essex, and with the mortification of not having contributed to the treaty which was made between France and England. But he still continued to be in high favor with the King, to whom he must have been conscious that he had rendered greater services than are on record, since he prayed for rewards, which were promised him, and which, from their magnitude, show the extent of the appreciation in which he was held by the King: 1st. A Cardinal's hat for himself, if it turned out to be true, as reported, that his wife had died, and if not, for his son Gonzalo. 2d. A pension of twelve thousand crowns, secured on ecclesiastical benefices, and transmissible to his sons. 3d. The continuation of the pension of four thousand ducats which he already enjoyed. 4th. A liberal allowance of money to allow him to establish himself in the possession of the office of Royal Counselor, recently granted to him by the King. 5th. A guard for the security of his person. 6th. In case of a treaty of peace between France and Spain, the liberation of his family and the restoration of his confiscated property to be expressly stipulated in one of its articles. But, in 1598, when the treaty of Vervins restored peace between the two countries, the promise made to Perez was forgotten, or could not be carried into execution. No stipulation was made in his favor; and if Philip had not died shortly after, the fugitive minister would probably have fallen a victim, in the end, to the implacable hatred of that Prince.

It is reported that Philip, a few days before his death, drew from under his pillow and handed to one of his ministers in waiting a paper which, among other things, contained the following expression of his desires: "Provided that the wife of Antonio Perez shall retire into a monastery, whatever property she has a right to may be restored to her, and her children permitted to inherit it." Be it in consequence of this recommendation, or of the friendship which had always existed between Perez and the family of the Duke of Lerma, the omnipotent favorite and minister of the new King, Philip III., this Prince, when he went to Valencia to celebrate his nuptials, in 1599, ordered the wife of Perez out of the prison in which she was detained. She immediately came to Madrid, and obtained from the Count of Miranda, who had succeeded, as President of the Council of Castile, Don Rodrigo Vasquez de Arce, the old enemy of Perez, that her seven sons be set free from their incarceration. It had lasted nine years! When, after his marriage, Philip III. went to Saragoza, he would not enter the city before the heads of the wretches who had been put to death, in 1591, were removed from the conspicuous places which they had so long occupied. It is a sad illustration of the spirit of that age that these ghastly objects should have been exposed for so many years to the public gaze in one of the large cities of Christendom. Philip intended them, probably, as long as they did not crumble to dust, to serve as a memento and warning to all whom it might concern. His son and successor, in conformity with the advice of the same Duke of Lerma, granted also, on that occasion, a general pardon to all the Aragonese exiles, with the exception of Perez, who had hoped for more clemency from his new Sovereign, and who desired ardently to return to Spain, particularly since he had been made aware that he had fallen into discredit at the French Court, and found it to be a laborious task to obtain the payment of his pension. On the death of Philip II., in whose side he was a thorn, he had necessarily ceased to be of importance to Henry, and he was discarded accordingly.

At last, in the hope of ingratiating himself with Philip III., the exile left Paris, renounced his pension of four thousand ducats, and went to London to expedite the peace negotiations which, in 1604, were pending between Spain and England. But the French Secretary of State, taking in ill part this conduct of Perez, influenced the English Court against him, so that this unfortunate and restless man, finding that he was not welcome there, and also that his offered assistance was not favorably received by the Spanish negotiators, had the mortification to be compelled to return to France, and to make again an appeal to the generosity of Henry IV., whose pension he had had the imprudence, in an evil hour, to renounce. But he supplicated in vain, and he became so reduced in his circumstances that he had to humble himself so low as to apply to the French Ministry for a mere pittance to save himself from perishing from want. His extreme destitution increased his desire to return to his native country, and he importuned two Spanish ambassadors who succeeded each other in Paris to use their influence in his favor and procure for him the permission to close his days in Spain. But he learned the dire lesson that, when a man has grown old and poor, when he is withering in exile in a foreign land, and when nothing is to be hoped or feared from him, few, if any, are the ears that will listen to his prayers; and, in 1608, the once powerful minister of Philip II., who had enjoyed so long a share of that absolute and immense power which had made itself felt in the four continents of the world, now infirm, neglected, forgotten, sad in heart and broken in spirit, was dragging a miserable existence in one of the suburbs of Paris—a fit retribution for his vices and crimes, and a striking instance of the vicissitudes of life!

In this state of isolation and wretchedness, Antonio Perez passed the last years of his long and eventful life. His sole consolation was to have obtained of the Pope absolution from the ecclesiastical censures which had been decreed against him, and permission to have an oratory in his own house, because he was too feeble to walk to church. In 1611, he applied to the Supreme Court of the Inquisition for leave to present himself before the Tribunal of the Holy Office sitting in Saragoza, or before any other which might be designated, to establish his innocence of the charges of heresy of which he had been found guilty in his absence. But his petition was received with no favor. A few months afterward he became very ill, and was attended by some Aragonese exiles who were united together by the bond of common misfortune. As the dying man could no longer write, he dictated to Gil de la Mesa, a faithful friend, who had never left his side since his career of adversity had begun, the following declaration: "In the situation in which I am, and conscious that I am soon to render my accounts to God, I aver and swear that I have always lived and that I die like a true Catholic Christian, and I call upon God to be my witness." If Perez believed what he thus solemnly asseverated, it was another melancholy instance of the aberrations to which the human mind is liable. If not, it was a piece of profane hypocrisy which can hardly be accounted for, because it could be of no service to him in the world which he was leaving. It might, however, be supposed that he imagined it might benefit his wife and children, about whose welfare he had always exhibited much solicitude. We see the proof of that solicitude in the following declaration which he also dictated: "I say that, if I die in the Kingdom of France and under its protection, it is because I could not do otherwise, and because I have been driven to it by the violence of my persecutors. I assure the world that this is the truth, and I supplicate my King and natural Liege Lord that, in his great clemency and magnanimity, he be pleased to remember the services rendered by my father to the father and grandfather of His Majesty, hoping that they may incline him to be merciful and gracious to my wife and to my sons, who are orphans and in destitution, and that those afflicted and miserable objects of my affection will not lose, on account of their father's residence and death in a foreign land, the favors which they deserve as faithful and loyal vassals, which I recommend them to be, to the end of their career." A few hours after he had made these declarations, he expired on the 3d of November, 1611, at the age of seventy-two. His widow and sons immediately presented a petition to the Holy Office, to obtain permission to vindicate the memory of the husband and of the father. It was granted, and, in 1615, the Tribunal of the Inquisition sitting at Saragoza pronounced a sentence which rehabilitated "the good name and memory of Antonio Perez," and declared his sons and other descendants to be apt to fulfill all offices of honor and profit. As to the papers concerning this famous trial of Antonio Perez, which had remained in the hands of Judge Vasquez de Arce, they were burned, in consequence of an order left by Philip to that effect. It had lasted thirty-one years, during which had happened all the events which we have related.

Perez had died in the arms of Gil de la Mesa, a kinsman and a friend, whose disinterested and unwavering attachment to the fallen minister and wandering beggar, who was pursued by the sleepless wrath of such a man as Philip, deserves to be recorded forever in justice to his memory and for the honor of the human race. The meeting of such a character as De la Mesa is as refreshing to the heart of the historian, in his dreary journey through an interminable avenue of selfish passions and interests, as is a bubbling fountain to the parched lips of the traveller in the deserts of Arabia. From the night of the 28th of July, 1579, when Perez had been arrested, to his death in 1611, a period of thirty-one years of adversity, Gil de la Mesa had forgotten himself to think only of the friend he loved with such intense fidelity as to challenge belief. The icy atmosphere which always environs misfortune had no chilling effect on him. There was too much sunshine in his noble soul; and the colder blew the wind round his persecuted and forlorn friend the more tightly he hugged him to his own warm bosom. It is beautiful to see such a striking example of self-abnegation. With the fearless energy of a man and the tendernesss of a woman, he watched incessantly over the waning fortune of Perez, through all the various phases of its downward course. He had constituted himself the guardian angel of the destitute, and, reversing the order of things to which we are accustomed, he had made himself the satellite and worshiper of the orb of day, not when it ascends with gorgeous splendor to its meridian, but when faint and weak, and with its diadem of light struck off its brow, it sinks, on the brink of the western horizon, into an ocean of angry and tempestuous clouds. As long as there had been a chance of saving Perez by court intrigues, by solicitations, and prayers addressed to the King, and by influences brought to bear upon his enemies, his judges, his accusers, and the witnesses to be heard on his trial, Gil de la Mesa, by day and by night, had worked with a skill which had only been equaled by his indefatigable zeal. After Perez had been put to the torture and his ruin appeared to be irrevocably determined upon, it was Gil de la Mesa who had contrived his flight from his prison and had carried him to Aragon. There again he was the shield which interposed between Philip and Perez. There he plotted, cajoled, bribed, and became the spirit which infused itself into the Aragonese, rousing them to armed resistance to the King. It was he who led the rioters who delivered Perez; it was he who accompanied the fugitive in all his wanderings in the Pyrenees, and at last conducted him safely to France. With Perez he re-entered Spain sword in hand; with him he fought at Biescas; and when defeated, again fled with him through a thousand perils. In France, in England, wherever Perez went, there was Gil de la Mesa, watching over a life so precious to him, warding off the assassin's blow, or detecting the more subtle attempt of the hired poisoner. In sickness, in destitution, in exile, in perils by land and by water, in those depths of humiliation which are only known to the mighty when fallen from their high estate, whenever the soul of Perez was ready to droop in despair, there was Gil de la Mesa whispering consolations and ministering assistance. His was the only fanaticism permitted to man and which will find favor with God—the fanaticism of friendship. Poverty, sorrows of all sorts, dangers of all descriptions, seemed to have attractions for Gil de la Mesa, if they only gave him the opportunity to prove his devotion to his friend. Truly, Perez, with all his load of guilt on his shoulders, must have been gifted with endowments of a very winning nature, and must have possessed something wonderfully lovable to have inspired the egotistical heart of man with such a passionate attachment as was displayed by Gil de la Mesa during more than thirty long years. It seems to have grown stronger with age, and finally it stood at the grave of Perez, unchanged, unspotted, as vigorous as ever, and dropping tears so pure that a seraph's wing might have carried them to Heaven. In the history of our race, those men who have made themselves famous for their genius are innumerable; but how few are they who have made a disinterested sacrifice of themselves to their country, and much less to one of their fellow-beings! Hence the amazement which such a friendship as Gil de la Mesa's must excite in the human breast, and surely a sort of tender and reverential admiration is due to him who carried the noblest sentiment of the heart to its very highest degree of sublimity.

The end of Philip's reign was marked by another criminal trial, which is one of the historical curiosities of the epoch, and which has since been a fruitful theme for writers of novels and dramas. The last King of Portugal, Don Sebastian, with the inexperience of youth, the romantic extravagance of chivalry, and the fiery zeal of religious fanaticism, had, against the unanimous remonstrances of his wisest counsellors and of his uncle, Philip II. of Spain, undertaken a Quixotic expedition against the infidels of the Kingdom of Morocco—an expedition which terminated in his death on the battle-field of Alcazarquivir, and in the extermination of the flower of the nobility of Portugal. The body of the King had never been found, and the Portuguese, having been subjugated by Philip, who had claimed the vacant throne on the ground of his possessing the strongest hereditary right to it, entertained the fond hope that Don Sebastian was still alive and would one day make his appearance to resume his sceptre. Years had elapsed, and the report was still current among the ignorant multitude that their beloved and heroic Sovereign, after doing penance in some cave or monastery for his sins and for the blood imprudently shed in his ill-starred enterprise in Africa, might be expected to return at any time. Such popular delusions have not been of unfrequent occurrence in other nations and at different epochs, and have given rise to serious disturbances, and even civil wars. It is not astonishing, therefore, that several impostors should have presented themselves to make the best of a persuasion so deeply rooted in the hearts of the Portuguese people. The most remarkable of them all, and the only one who gave some uneasiness to Philip, was an individual called Gabriel de Espinosa, commonly known in history and in fanciful compositions under the name of the pastry-cook of Madrigal, which is a small town of Old Castile. The education and talents of this man were not, it is said, above his condition, although there was something noble in his air, and his manners were not destitute of a certain elegance. He undoubtedly must have been very bold, and must have possessed a considerable degree of natural shrewdness, to have adapted himself so well to the part which he assumed, and which, owing to a concourse of circumstances, instead of remaining an obscure village farce, rose to the importance of an historical event of sufficient magnitude to be recorded.

The author of this imposture was a Portuguese and Austin friar, named Miguel de Los Santos, who had attained high preferments in the Order to which he belonged. He was a man of much ambition, of restless habits, but of no real capacity. Having been one of the most violent partisans of the Prior of Crato, the royal bastard who had been the competitor for the crown of Portugal against Philip, he had been transported from that Kingdom to Castile, where he had been appointed Vicar to the

Austin nuns of Madrigal. This turbulent friar, having observed that there was in Espinosa a striking likeness to Don Sebastian, and that their age would have corresponded if that Prince had been alive, persuaded the pastry-cook to personate the King, assuring him that it was easy to pass himself for that personage upon the credulous Portuguese, and that their enthusiastic attachment would open to him the way to the throne. The pastry-cook accepted with thoughtless presumption the dangerous part which was presented to him, and prepared himself for it under the tuition of the friar, who had known much of Don Sebastian. Among the nuns of the Austin monastery, of which he was vicar, was a natural daughter of Don John of Austria, and, as such, a niece of Philip, whose name was Dona Anna, of much simplicity of mind, and of very little vocation for a cloistral life. In her extreme disgust at the condition into which she had been forced, she used to request her confessor, whenever he said mass, to pray God to have mercy on her, and put her in a situation less repugnant to her disposition, and in which she might better fulfill her duties to Him. It struck Don Miguel de Los Santos that this nun might be made a useful instrument in the execution of his plans, and he gradually filled her too easily deceived mind with the pretended revelations which, whilst officiating at the altar, he had received from God and His Holy Apostles. According to those revelations the highest destinies were reserved to her. She was to become the spouse of Don Sebastian, who was still alive, and ascend with him the throne of Portugal. When he saw Dona Anna fully convinced of the truth of these miraculous communications, he presented to her the pastry-cook, Espinosa, as the King of Portugal. The ingenuous nun, whose weak head was completely turned, surrendered her heart to the good-looking impostor, and there commenced an amorous correspondence between her and him whom she considered as her future husband. As a token of her love, she gave him all the money she could command and her richest jewels, to facilitate the recovery of his Kingdom. In her letters she called him "your Majesty," and the friar used to address him in the same manner. This intrigue lasted for some time, during which this friar caused many persons to come from Portugal who recognized Don Sebastian in the pastry-cook, until this affair began to produce some considerable excitement in Portugal and Castile. Gabriel de Espinosa was soon arrested, and the letters of Dona Anna brought to light. As members of the Church were implicated, there was, as usual, a fierce conflict of jurisdiction between the civil and ecclesiastical Courts, which was finally set at rest by the appointment of an Apostolic Judge for this particular case. Many persons were thrown into prison, some were put to the torture, and there was much scandal. Philip, on this occasion, did not show his well-known impassiveness. For some reasons which it is hard to guess at, he took an extraordinary interest in this affair—much greater than its circumstances seemed to call for. There must have been at the bottom of it something more serious or painful than our penetration can seize. He exacted a most minute account of all the proceedings and incidents of the judicial investigations, as they progressed; and some of the facts which they developed elicited, to the astonishment of all those who knew Philip, the manifestation of considerable emotion in that cold breast which had always been thought so little susceptible of any. It is a circumstance of his life involved in mystery, like several others which remain unexplained. At last sentence was pronounced on the leading personages in this intrigue. Gabriel de Espinosa was decreed to be put in a sack and dragged to the place of execution in Madrigal, where he was hung and quartered. His head was exposed in an iron cage, and the other parts of his body were suspended from two gibbets, with inscriptions, at different points on the public roads. The friar, Miguel de Los Santos, after having been degraded by the judgment of an ecclesiastical Court, was delivered to the civil authority and hung in Madrid, on the 19th of October, 1595. Dona Anna of Austria, who, one would suppose, was sufficiently punished by the mortification of having been a dupe, by the painful sense of the ridicule which she had incurred, by the shame of having been the cause of so much scandal, and by the loss of her trinkets and other valuables, was condemned to be transported to the Monastery of Avila, and to a rigorous confinement of four years in her cell, during which she was to be put on bread and water, every Friday, as a penitential fast. She was also declared forever incapable of any ecclesiastical dignity, and deprived of the title of "Excellency," which she had hitherto enjoyed. The silly young nun, the poor deluded daughter of Don John of Austria, was certainly entitled to be treated with more compassion by her royal uncle. Among the other participators in this plot, some were sentenced to be exiled, some to work on the King's galleys, and several to be whipped publicly. Such was the tragical end of this political and amorous conspiracy between a nun, a friar, and a pastry-cook. It was a rich theme for a comedy, ready found for the prolific pen of a Lope de Vega; but Philip, who was not prone to laughter steeped it in blood. His great and magnanimous contemporary, Henry IV. of France, if anything of the kind had happened in his Kingdom, would no doubt have treated it with good-natured contempt. He would probably have obtained for the inflammable damsel a dispensation in relation to her vows; he would have provided her with a suitable husband, immured the intriguing and would-be king-making priest in a convent, and assigned in his royal kitchens a place to the ambitious pastry-cook.

CHAPTER VII.

We have already mentioned that the Spanish Cortes, that great bulwark of Spanish liberties, had been gradually and systematically robbed of their pristine importance, first by Charles V., and next by Philip II. It was a wheel, however, in the political machine, which was still kept turning, but turning to very little purpose. The circular motion was seen, the usual noise was heard as it revolved on its axle, but no useful result was produced. Thus under the Roman Emperors, the deliberations of the Senate and the appointment of Consuls were still kept up as under the expired Republic, but the substance of power had departed from these shadows. It was Cæsar who decided everything, and if it be true that the Senate was once called upon to determine by its patrician vote which was the most appropriate sauce for an extraordinary turbot offered to the master of the world, and that a favorite horse was derisively appointed Consul by an imperial jester, nothing could more forcibly represent the changes which had taken place since that body had ruled all the nations of the earth, and the Consuls had rested their feet on the necks of kings. The Cortes, it is true, had not come yet to such a degree of degradation, but their virility had been emasculated. They no longer possessed any procreative faculties ; they could no longer initiate measures, inaugurate a system of external and internal policy, and have the destinies of the nation in their own keeping. They and the King were no longer the Government ; the King was the State. They could only appear before him as suitors do before a court of justice, besides their being a very convenient sort of assessors to tax their constituents to the very marrow of their bones—reluctantly, it is true, and not without remonstrances, but still to the ultimate satisfaction of the King. They might address respectful petitions which might, or might not, be granted, and that was all. They expressed the desires of the people without being able to enforce them ; they were a voice crying in the wilderness, but nothing else. Well aware that the Cortes would not even make a feeble effort to check his unlimited authority, Philip seems to have liked to convene them and to have them at hand. He knew that they were the brain and the heart of his subjects, and he was fond of ascertaining from them what there was in that brain and that heart. Such knowledge, as long as he was sure that both these noble organs could not emancipate themselves from the pressure of his iron grasp, might be useful to him, without there being any danger to be apprehended from the source from which it was derived. Thus the sessions of these assemblies became more frequent under Philip than they had been under any of his predecessors. We think that a succinct analysis of their proceedings will complete the picture which we have attempted to draw of the reign of that Prince, as they are the reflection of the social life of the epoch, and will give some accurate idea, not only of the administration of the Kingdom in all its branches, but also of the wants and grievances, the aspirations and prejudices, the customs and habits, the moral and intellectual physiognomy of the Spanish people in the Sixteenth Century.

We have already referred in preceding pages to some of the doings of the Cortes from 1558 to 1567. After a short interruption of three years, they met again in Cordova, for it was the custom of the Sovereign to convene them from time to time in different places. One of the first acts of the Cortes, when they assembled at that city, was to claim that no further taxes, general or particular, be levied without being granted by them. They reminded Philip that this had been one of the fundamental laws of the Kingdom, "established by the Cortes, and by the Kings, his predecessors, of glorious memory, such as Alonzo and others." They said that they knew very well that the excuse for it had been the alleged necessity to provide for the expenses incurred by his father and by himself in those long wars which had been undertaken for the defence of Christendom, but that this justification did not satisfy the people in their pretension that the observance of this ancient right, sanctioned by a law of extreme antiquity, be faithfully complied with. They therefore supplicated His Majesty that, for the future, no tribute whatever be exacted from the people, without the previous assent of the Cortes, according to immemorial usage ; that the collecting of such as were illegally demanded be stopped, and that the people be exempt, as heretofore, from the payment of them, "because other means might be sought and found to assist His Majesty without doing so much damage to the Kingdom." This petition of the Cortes was as respectful as it was well grounded. Philip replied that the necessities which had compelled him to act in this manner had not only not ceased, but were even increasing every day, and therefore that he could not but continue to do as he had done. Formerly no king of Castile, or of Aragon, or of any other Kingdom in Spain, save those parts where Moslem despotism was enthroned, would have dared to send this arrogant answer to his Cortes, or if he had, he would soon have repented of his presumption. But times had changed, and this change had begun with the Austrian dynasty. The Cortes were no longer Sovereigns, they were beggars at the foot of the throne ; beggars not for favors, but for what was legitimately due to them, and had been their possession by the prescriptive sanction of centuries.

The duties on all sales and the two-ninths levied

on ecclesiastical tithes had been fixed for twenty years, and as this term was nearly at an end, it was asked that it should be renewed. Constantly anticipating fresh applications for money on the part of the Government, and, consequently, the laying of heavier burdens on the shoulders of the people, the Cortes had always been anxious that the taxes be determined in "an unchangeable manner as long as possible, and, if practicable, forever," as experience, they contended, had demonstrated that it was the system the least vexatious and oppressive. The King answered that the term of years referred to had not expired, and that, when such should be the case, it would be time enough to take their request into consideration.

The administration of justice, the attributes of the Courts and the rules by which they were governed, had been the source of frequent complaints from preceding Cortes, who had unsuccessfully presented numerous plans of reforms. The Cortes of Cordova returned to the same subject with the same pertinacity. They proposed that there should be an appeal from the Council of the Treasury (Hacienda) to the Royal Council, which inspired more general confidence than any other tribunal. The ever-increasing number of attorneys at law and of other individuals who lived by fomenting litigation having become a serious evil, they proposed that it be restricted. They also proposed the abolition of many offices which seemed to have been created for no other purpose than to make the ordinary transactions of life, particularly among the laboring and mercantile classes, more difficult, more expensive and more liable to confusion. The Judges and Alcaldes were frequently absent from the districts where they should have resided permanently. The Cortes begged that this evil be remedied. Some of the Judges were in the habit of holding court during the harvest season, much to the inconvenience of the peasantry. The Cortes desired that it should be otherwise. They denounced the long and interminable writings and formalities by which notaries and other public officers who lived by the exercise of the quill contrived to vex and plunder the people, and they pointed out multifarious reforms which might be beneficially introduced in the trial of civil and criminal cases. The abuses complained of were so gross, that one would have supposed that the dullest eye would have seen them and taken offence at these sores of the social body. But to most of these petitions Philip returned the answer, that it was "not expedient to make any changes," or that he would "look into the subject," or that he would "reflect and do what was right."

In conformity with the notions of political economy prevailing at the time, the Cortes insisted on the necessity of enforcing strictly the prohibition of exporting corn and those animals whose flesh is used as food—what they designated as "bread and meat." The impropriety of fixing the market price of corn was generally felt, and yet the only remedy which they found for it was to change the rate of the tariff, thus modifying the effect of an error instead of attacking it in its source. The Cortes of Cordova reiterated the complaints of former ones, that the sale of so many titles of nobility, which exempted their purchasers from tax-paying, was extremely unjust and injurious to the poor and to all those who remained in the Plebeian class, because their contribution to the Treasury of the State had to be raised in proportion to the increase of the number of those who were exempt from such a charge. Nothing could be better founded than this appeal to the sense of justice which ought to have existed in the Royal breast. But Philip replied: "That he had used this expedient, among others, to relieve his necessities; that he could not do otherwise; and that, in so doing, he had only exercised legitimately one of his prerogatives." When they remonstrated against the alienation of villages and rural estates belonging to the Crown, together with the exemption from taxation and other privileges appertaining to that sort of alienated property, he answered: "That he had made those sales for just and valid reasons; but that, in the future, he would see that nothing be done in matters of this kind which should not be required by the circumstances of the case." Such was the constant evasiveness of his replies. It is astonishing that it did not tire out the patience of the Cortes, and did not induce them to put an end at once to deliberations and petitions which had become, with a face of apparent solemnity, an absolute and positive farce in reality. They were probably afraid of offending the Monarch if they ceased to keep up this semblance of popular representation.

We have stated in the course of this review of Philip's reign, that he was in the habit of appropriating to himself the gold and silver which came from America for the account of individuals. At different epochs in the past, the Cortes had clamored against these royal outrages. A discontinuance of this practice had been promised by the King, but it seems that the present Cortes had a strong suspicion, if not actual proof, that this abuse was still in existence, for they returned to the subject about which their predecessors had expressed their disapprobation, and dilated on the injury which such a high-handed stretch of authority inflicted on the commerce and prosperity of the Kingdom. On this question the King condescended to be more explicit than usual. He assured the Cortes that he had ceased to take the gold or silver referred to, and would continue to abstain from applying it to the wants of the State.

It had been found that, wherever the King repaired with the numerous and magnificent court by which he was always followed, the price of lodgings rose to a fabulous price. This was ruinous for those who were compelled to be in attendance upon the

Sovereign or his Ministers, for the transaction of public or private business. The Cortes begged his Majesty to form a commission composed of two or three of those who let out lodgings, and of as many other persons to be appointed by the Municipal Council of the city, town or place in which his Majesty should happen to reside, with instructions to establish a tariff for rooms and habitations, setting forth the precise price for each one, and prescribing a penalty for the violation of such regulations. This seemed equitable enough, and one would have supposed that it was, after all, a point on which there would have been no objection to gratify the national will; but the King did not think proper to depart, on this occasion, from the habit of giving vague and dilatory answers. He contented himself with informing the Cortes that "the subject would be discussed in his Council."

The cities and towns of Spain, whenever they were called upon by the Sovereign to assist him in his wars, had enjoyed the prescriptive right of appointing the commanders of the troops which they furnished ready equipped. In the last war against the Moors of Granada Philip had usurped that ancient right, of the violation of which the Cortes respectfully complained. They begged that the King be pleased to leave it as it stood before. He admitted for once the justice of their petition, and promised that "he would act accordingly in the future." He added that, if he had acted differently in the war against the Moors, it was on account of the peculiarity of the service which the cities and towns had been invited to render on that occasion. What that peculiarity was does not appear, nor is it possible to ascertain why there was a greater necessity for the King to appoint in this war than in any other the captains of companies or other commanders.

Some of the petitions of the Cortes of Cordova give a sad idea of the morals, customs and habits of the epoch. They dwelt, like their predecessors, on the necessity of not permitting any male visitants, either of the clergy or laity, to penetrate into the interior of the convents or monasteries of female recluses, and recommended that the visits paid to these institutions be confined to the common reception parlor, or some other place where iron grates intervened between the visitant and the visited. It must have been exceedingly difficult to eradicate the practice which is thus denounced, because it had been, for years past, the constant theme of the complaints of the Cortes, and the disorders which prevailed in many of those monastic establishments must have been very great, since we find that Philip was obliged to send instructions to his Corregidores* to investigate, "with secrecy, adroitness and dissimulation," the excesses which were pointed out to him, and which scandalized the people in conse-

* A Magistrate in Spain. It is derived from the word correct, or castigate.

quence of the bad example presented by so many persons consecrated to the worship of God. "You shall report to me on this subject," he said, "in order that these delinquencies be punished according to law." It seems that the policemen and municipal guards who patrolled the cities and towns of Spain to maintain order were themselves the cause of frightful disorders; for, under various pretexts, they entered the houses of honest citizens, carried away their wives and daughters, and made them the victims of their lust. The Cortes denounced to the King and deplored the habitual perpetration of these nefarious deeds, and begged that the policemen and municipal guards be prohibited from entering at night any other houses than such as were occupied by women of the town and concubines. The regulations applicable to prostitutes which Philip published in 1571, are a striking exemplification of the depraved laxity of public morals at the time. This Royal ordinance is composed of fourteen articles.* They contain details which, curiously characteristic as they are, it is impossible to relate without doing violence to decency. We shall only mention the twelfth, which ordered prostitutes to adopt a certain costume by which they were distinguished from honest women. They were prohibited from using cloaks, bonnets, gloves and light shoes, and had to wear a short yellow mantilla or mantle, under the

* Archives of Simancas.

penalty of three hundred maravedis,* and of losing by confiscation any article of their dress which should happen to be different from the one prescribed.

Some petitions, in relation to the study of medicine and surgery, are an evidence of the little progress which these two sciences had made in Spain. The Cortes expressed the wish that no student of medicine should graduate before having previously obtained the degree of bachelorship in astrology, "because," they said, "practitioners, from the want of a proper knowledge of the critical days and of the movements of the planets, fail to cure many patients." The Cortes remonstrated against the naturalization of foreigners; they solicited that the Kingdom be supplied with arms, and insisted on the policy of renewing the breed of horses, as the race of those noble animals, for which Spain had been so famous, was rapidly deteriorating. Many other points of internal administration did not escape their attention. The number of petitions which they presented amounted in all to ninety-one, of which but very few were granted, and even three years elapsed before these few began to be acted upon.

In the year 1573, the Cortes met in Madrid. They reproduced the complaints of their predecessors in those matters which had been so frequently

* A small copper coin, equal to three-tenths of a cent, American money, or a little less than a farthing sterling.

submitted to the consideration of Philip, and pressed upon him the urgent necessity of such reforms. To a few of these petitions the King vouchsafed a favorable answer, but to the great majority of them he replied as usual, that "he would see what was proper to be done," or that he would "examine into it," or that he would "confer about it in his Council." These Cortes of Madrid represented to the King that many members of that assembly were public officers, and therefore in his pay as such; that this circumstance prevented such deputies from possessing that degree of liberty which was necessary to propose such measures and give such votes as the interests and welfare of the Kingdom required; and besides, that there was "a grave inconvenience" resulting from this state of things, which was, that such members were suspected by the rest of their colleagues, and that it destroyed the general harmony and confidence which ought to exist among them. They, in conclusion, supplicated his Majesty that persons holding office under the Crown, or being in the enjoyment of any pensions or favors from it, be not eligible to their body. Questions of this kind have been repeatedly agitated in modern times in various countries where representative Governments have been established. This petition, addressed to such a man as Philip, shows the spirit of independence which was still lurking in the Cortes, notwithstanding the curtailment of their powers, the diminution of their importance, and, in fact, the state of servitude to which they had been reduced. They were even so bold as to make observations on the rewards which the King granted to those who served his personal interests in that assembly, and designated several recent instances of these improper remunerations and of this corrupting influence. The nature of this petition must have been disagreeably new to Philip. It had an air of possible resistance to his authority and of condemnation of his acts. There was a ring of the true metal in it which must have grated harshly on the despot's ears. He resolved that the odious sound should not be repeated, that the voice of something like that of freedom should not be heard again, and therefore his answer, on this occasion, ceased to be evasive. It was abrupt, short and categorical. We can almost fancy that we hear the peremptory tone of stern reprobation with which it was uttered.* "I answer you," said the King, "that it is not proper to make any change in this matter."

The prevailing opinion in Spain had been, for a long time, that the diminution of the revenues of the Kingdom and that its general impoverishment were due to the immense quantity of lands held in mortmain by the Clergy, and to the vast accumulation of unproductive and uncirculating wealth which was locked up in their monasteries and other religious

* A esto vos respondemos que no conviene hacer en ello novedad.

establishments. Those corporations never parted with anything, and their acquisitions were incessant. The enormous leech always sucked, but never disgorged. In conformity with the express instructions of their constituents, the Cortes had clamored against this evil. It had been a fruitful theme for the complaints of the Cortes of Valladolid, in 1517 and 1523, of the Cortes of Segovia in 1532, of the Cortes of Madrid in 1534 and 1563. Those remonstrances were repeated in 1573. It certainly was the undoubted and settled expression of the national will, as evidenced by the frequency, the unanimity and pertinacity with which it was conveyed to the throne. But Philip returned the invariable answer which he had often given on that subject: "It is not expedient that there be any change." The same prayer ascended from year to year from the heart of the nation, and it met, every time, the same frigid and unrelenting denial.

Notwithstanding the proverbial reputation of the Castilians for sobriety of habits, extravagance in dress and in the furniture of houses had become so great, that the Cortes had frequently thought themselves under the obligation to propose to the King measures for its repression, although the experience of ages had demonstrated the futility of sumptuary laws. It appears that women, when they married, used to spend for their bridal clothes and jewels as much as their dowry was worth. The Cortes petitioned the King to prohibit parents from giving to their daughters in trinkets and dress more than one-twentieth part of the value of their dowry, and notaries from framing any marriage contract without inserting that stipulation under the sanctity of an oath. They also petitioned that no article of wood or of copper, or of any other metal, be gilded or plated, except such as were destined to divine worship, to the embellishment of arms or accoutrements for horses, and that the violation of this ordinance be visited with appropriate penalties. The reason which they gave for it was, that, in consequence of such follies, the Kingdom was, for the present, considerably drained of all the gold and silver "with which it had been so abundantly supplied by God."

There had been already, in former times, several royal ordinances intended for the repression of the excessive luxury which women displayed in their apparel, but they had remained dead letters, or rather had been like those withered leaves which no one cares for, and which are left to be the sport of the wind. The Cortes attributed the non-observance of those regulations to the ingenuity of the tailors and other dressmakers, who daily invented fashions and ornaments, and threw so many irresistible temptations in the way of the foolish and frivolous. They said to the King that a large number of men were engaged in a kind of occupation which was fit only for females, instead of serving his Majesty in his wars, or of tilling the ground, or raising cattle, or sheep, or other useful animals, in those places where they were born ; and that they preferred repairing to the large cities or towns, where they lived by plying the needle, and led a life of much greater ease and comfort than they could otherwise have done, had they remained at their respective rural homes, and performed the hard but beneficial and praiseworthy labor to which they had been originally destined. This petition, although it met with favor from the King, who subsequently issued a pragmatic in conformity with its spirit, had no more effect in curing the evil complained of, than if it had been aimed at the ebb and flow of the sea. The intentions of the Cortes were undoubtedly very good, but they were not practical. The morals of a nation never were suddenly established or purified by a mere legislative decree enforced by executive authority. Whether good or bad, whether in their primitive formation, or in their progressive decay, or under the reaction of reform, they are slowly generated by causes and circumstances in which the folly or wisdom of man may have a considerable share, but which work, nevertheless, in conformity with the final and inflexible laws of nature. In such matters, a pure religion, and a sound domestic education, strengthened by conspicuous example at the apex of the social pyramid, are the most powerful legislators to be relied on, when they have once succeeded in getting the mastery.

Coaches had been lately introduced into Spain,

and had become so much in vogue, that all families must set up one, under the penalty of being nobodies. The consequence was, that those who had but a small fortune, or even hardly any at all, made ruinous sacrifices to keep up what they considered an evidence of social position and a recommendation to respectful consideration. The Cortes came to the conclusion that this kind of luxury was not only detrimental to individuals, but injurious also to the State, because it withdrew from agricultural labor the mules who were taken for so many coaches, and raised considerably the price of these animals, who were now bred in preference to horses, in consequence of which the acquisition of good horsemanship would be neglected. They therefore supplicated the King that, considering "these inconveniences and others not mentioned," and considering that, "for so many years, Spain had done very well without coaches," His Majesty be pleased to prohibit the use of this new invention. The Monarch replied that "the subject had been already under advisement, and that he would provide for it in the way most fit and proper."

These Cortes, like the preceding ones, lamented the progressive deterioration of the breed of horses, as well as the notable diminution of those animals in the Kingdom; and, among the measures which they proposed to remedy this evil, was the exempting of those who were bound when called upon in case of danger to do military service with horse and arms, from the performance of that feudal duty, on condition that they should keep as many as six mares. It was thought of the utmost importance, not only to encourage the raising of horses, but also the study of equitation, and particularly the knowledge and use of a certain kind of horsemanship called *La gineta*; and the Cortes of Madrid, thinking that the suppression of bull-fights ordered some years before according to the wish of their predecessors, had been injurious to the attainment of these objects, petitioned for the re-establishment of that old and favorite amusement "as soon as it could be done." Never was a petition so graciously received by the King. He replied that "he would instruct his Council to take the subject of their request into speedy consideration, and not to lose sight of it until justice had been done to its merits." The wish of the Cortes was soon gratified, but it is not a little singular that, before complying with it, Philip should have deemed it expedient to consult the Holy See. It was hardly to be expected that the Pope should have been asked permission for the restoration of the national entertainment of bull-fights in Spain.

Many salutary reforms were pointed out as proper to be made in the Department of Justice, particularly with a view to avoid the long delays, heavy costs and other vexations so well known to litigants; for most of the tribunals of Spain had the unenviable reputation of the English Chancery, in which it is not uncommon for suits to outlive many generations.

The Cortes begged that new courts be established in certain localities for the convenience of the population, and that no one be sued out of the district in which he resided. They turned also their attention to public education, and, among other things, prayed that a faculty of law be established in the University of Alcala, with the same privileges and advantages possessed by similar institutions in Salamanca, Valladolid, and Bologna in Italy. The answer of the King on this matter was, "that he would look into it and do what would be proper." The Cortes recommended that each town and village be required to put up at the end, or head, as it might happen, of every road terminating or originating within their precincts, or at every cross-road, or at every point where a road forked, in the district within which they were situated, some indication by which travelers would be guided as to the direction they might wish to take, be it in the shape of wooden crosses, stone posts, or sheets of lead. It was a measure which would have cost little, and the utility of which could not be questioned. One would hardly have anticipated that such a suggestion could fail to be readily adopted. Not so with Philip, who replied that "he would think on it," and as usual with him in most cases when any sort of internal improvement was recommended by the Cortes, he dismissed it forever from his mind.

The Cortes met again at Madrid in 1576, and remained in session until 1578, a period sufficiently long, one would suppose, to do a world of business. They elaborated seventy-three petitions. In the first which they presented to the King they remonstrated, as the Cortes of Cordova had done in 1570, against the illegal practice of levying taxes on the people which had not been previously granted by their Representatives, and they begged that all the royal ordinances on that subject which had been issued in violation of the fundamental laws of the Kingdom be revoked. In the second, they complained like their predecessors, six years before, of the wasteful alienation of the domains of the Crown which was still going on to meet the wants of the King. But spendthrifts have always paid very little attention to the monitions of their friends or well-wishers, and Philip was not an exception. In the third petition, the Cortes desired the Monarch, if his multifarious and laborious occupations prevented him from paying occasional and personal visits to the different parts of his Kingdom, from seeing with his own eyes its condition, and from ascertaining the wants of his subjects, to be pleased to have himself represented by delegates of his authority, whose ministry should be to investigate the manner in which public officers performed their functions in the provinces, and punish those who should happen to fail in the discharge of their duties. Among other abuses was the appointment for life to certain municipal officers, and sometimes with a right of transmission to the heirs of the incumbents, in return for a sum of money paid to the Crown. The Cortes complained of the injury to the public which resulted from such a practice, and prayed that those officers be elected annually as formerly. They also clamored, as in a preceding session, against the use of coaches, and solicited their prohibition, on the ground "that they were an occasion for display, and not for exercise." The King viewed the subject in the same light, and, in order to diminish the number of these objects of luxury, decreed that no one should sport a coach or carriage in cities, or within a radius of five leagues around them, "without driving it with four horses owned by himself, and not hired, or borrowed," under the penalty of forfeiting the carriages and horses, with their harness and other appendages.

The Cortes felt the importance of providing the youths who destined themselves to the priesthood, with the means of acquiring a moral and religious education, and petitioned for the establishment of seminaries and schools of divinity in connection with metropolitan churches and cathedrals, as decreed by the Council of Trent. They recommended that young men, however brilliant the success in their studies might have been at the universities, and however great their legal attainments, should not be appointed to the highest offices of the magistracy, without their having previously given proofs of their discretion and morality, and without their having shown that they knew how to make a good use of their science and a practical application of it in the inferior tribunals. They were still more scrupulously exacting as to the qualifications of the ecclesiastical judges. One single fact will give an idea of the extent of the encroachments which the clerical authorities had been gradually permitted to make over the jurisdiction of the secular. For instance, they had fallen into the monstrous habit of fulminating excommunication against individuals, even for petty debts when not paid. It was at that epoch a terrible weapon, of which it is not easy in our age to realize the power. In vain those wretches pleaded their extreme poverty, in vain they sued for delay and offered sufficient security for ultimate payment; they were inexorably excluded from the Church, and deprived of all its rights and privileges—a penalty which, at that time in Spain, was as serious a one as could be inflicted, short of death. It is probable that the Clergy, as a plea for their interfering in such matters, assumed that it was sinful to get in debt. But the Cortes remonstrated strongly against this enormous abuse. They begged that excommunication be no longer permitted in such cases, and that debtors be cited to appear only before the civil courts. They proposed that certain magistrates and other officials connected with the administration of justice be better paid, and be given salaries which would enable them to live with the decorum required by their station; that the municipal officers of those cities and towns which sent representatives to the Cortes be not permitted to exercise any of the mechanical arts, or engage in any trade or gainful pursuit, on account of which their persons would be discredited ; that the salaries of the members of the Cortes who represented cities be not paid by those cities only which elected them, but by the whole province, whose interests they also represented ; and that no one be privileged to engross two incompatible offices or employments. The political wisdom of these propositions was apparent, but Philip received them with his usual indifference. There was in that man an unconquerable force of inertia.

The Cortes had seen with much displeasure that the nobles were gradually less addicted to those military exercises and that wholesome art of horsemanship which had made them agile, robust and adroit, and which had so eminently qualified them for the hardships and perils of war. In order to put a stop to this growing effeminacy, the Cortes thought that it was expedient to revive the ancient spirit of the nobles by re-establishing, with a suitable degree of splendor, those exciting entertainments in which the patrician order used to take the lead and make itself conspicuous by its achievements. Thus it had been customary for Grandees and men of gentle blood to be members of the associations for bull-fights, or to be their patrons and sponsors. They also entered the arena as combatants, and performed the parts which are now left to professional and salaried artists. It was not then uncommon for the proudest Grandee to excite the frantic applause of the multitude by appearing sword in hand in front of the enraged bull, and killing him with as much skill as bravery. For the reasons which we have alleged, the Cortes of 1570 and 1573 had petitioned for the restoration of that national amusement, and those of 1576 had proposed that the municipalities of all those towns which were of sufficient importance to pretend to having bull-fights, should at their expense have a place prepared for such exhibitions; that they should supply with lances such gentlemen as might desire to go through a preliminary course of practice; and that they should furnish the music, whenever those entertainments were given to the public. It was almost the only petition to which the King granted his approbation with promptitude and in explicit terms. He answered the Cortes that, in this matter, "it should be done forthwith as they desired." As to the other propositions, he met them in his accustomed style of: "We shall see," or, "we shall reflect," or, "we shall deliberate in council."

Hardly had the Cortes closed their session on the 31st of December, 1578, when their successors met in the beginning of the year 1579, and continued their labors until 1582. They complained that so many petitions presented by their predecessors had remained unattended to, and they prayed that the King should henceforth answer their prayers before their adjournment, and that no law and no ordinance be published by the Crown before consulting them, when they were assembled. They reproduced almost all the former petitions of the Cortes which had not been granted, and expressed the desire that certain custom-houses, recently established by a Royal decree, be abolished ; that a number of offices which had been created by the same authority in several branches of the administration be also abolished, and that there be no further creation of the kind ; that the royal revenues be farmed out, and not collected by administrators ; and that new laws and ordinances be made in relation to the discovery and working of mines. They insisted on the importance of preventing the amortizement of lands and tenements in favor of the clergy, and supplicated the King to remember that the Cortes had never ceased to remonstrate against this abuse since the beginning of the reign of the Emperor Charles V. They added : ' Until now no remedy has been applied to it, but experience has demonstrated how just and necessary is this reform, because the churches, monasteries and other pious institutions have possessed themselves of the greater portion of the real estates of the Kingdom. We supplicate your Majesty to stop this ever-increasing evil, when it is yet time to provide for it." On this occasion, at last, the King did not answer as before, that "it was not proper to make any change," but that, "by his command, this matter was under advisement in his Royal Council, and that such application as the case required would be made to the Holy See."

The Cortes presented a remarkable petition against that favorite tool of Philip—the omnipotent Inquisition. "The officials and ministers of the Holy Office," they said, "are so highly favored in consequence of their station, that they meddle with many things which concern them not, and whenever any one of them is involved in a quarrel or dispute, or takes a part in any transaction, or is connected with any affair, it affords a pretext to the Inquisitors of the district to assume jurisdiction over the case, and to incarcerate many persons, to whom much harm results. The public hears of the imprisonment, but is not informed of the cause of it. The supposition is that it is in consequence of delinquencies against the Church and the true faith. It throws a stain on those unfortunate beings and their descendants which they are scarcely ever able to wipe out, and they are much injured in their character, in their social position, and in their pursuits or avocations." The Cortes, therefore, supplicated his Majesty to instruct the Inquisitors not to correct anybody except in cases of heresy, or offence against the Catholic faith. That assembly drew as many as ninety-five petitions on matters of administration and political economy. Some were founded on those erroneous maxims prevailing at the time concerning the management of public affairs, and proposed, for certain abuses, reforms and remedies which were more prejudicial than salutary, but most of those petitions recommended measures which would have been highly beneficial if adopted by the Government. The same may be said of the preceding Cortes. It is impossible not to come to the conclusion that, if Philip had listened to the representations of those faithful exponents of the wants and aspirations of his subjects, the decline of Spain would have been arrested, and that with renovated vigor she would have entered into a new career of prosperity and grandeur.

CHAPTER VIII.

The financial condition of Spain, when Philip II. ascended the throne, was such as to have justly created the most serious alarms. It required only common sense to be convinced that this disorder must be stopped, or that the country could not fail to fall into the most poverty-stricken helplessness. It was in vain that the New World continued, with ceaseless abundance, to yield its countless treasures to the avaricious grasp of its conquerors ; it was in vain that the subjects of the Spanish Monarchy were groaning under ever-increasing taxes, the Royal treasury remained empty. This was due to Philip's unwise foreign policy, which involved him in wars and intrigues by which immense sums were absorbed, and to an internal administration in which corruption, imbecility and oppression combined their efforts to dry up all the resources of the Kingdom. Loans after loans were procured by paying the most usurious interests, and mountains of debts rose on each other in endless succession, whilst laws were made which repressed, instead of developing, commerce and industry in all its branches, and whilst exemptions from tax-paying were sold to an extent which is hardly credible. The exigencies of the hour were satisfied by destroying the sources of revenue; the most ruinous means to raise money which penury run mad could devise were resorted to, and made the national bankruptcy a proximate certainty. A proper system of retrenchment and economy, order, vigilance, honesty and responsibility introduced in the various departments of the administration, an inflexible determination to bring the expenses to a level with the income of the State, and the appropriation of a sinking fund for the gradual extinguishment of its obligations, would have been the policy pursued by a wise and patriotic Monarch, but Philip went on plunging heedlessly into the financial chaos which he found gaping before him, giving new energy to its wild uproar and confusion, making darkness darker, and gathering round his random and starless course more inextricable difficulties, which he himself had produced. With the rashness of the prodigal, who seems to be intoxicated by the very sight of the ruin to which he rushes, and willing to drown in the riotous enjoyment of the present all care of providing for the necessities of the future, he wasted with a sort of headlong extravagance, which looks incompatible with his phlegmatic temperament, as much of his inheritance as he could dispose of, and he mortgaged the rest. He himself, in a note to his treasurer, Francisco Garneca, expresses very pithily the extremity of destitution to which he had been reduced by his own folly. "Having already reached," he said, "my forty-eighth year, and the hereditary Prince, my son, being only three years old, I cannot but see with the keenest anxiety the disorderly condition of the treasury. What a prospect for my old age, if I am permitted to have a longer career, when I am now living from day to day, without knowing how I shall live on the next, and how I shall procure that of which I am so much in need!" It is hardly to be conceived how this Prince came, in his lifetime, to be surnamed the "Prudent." He certainly performs the part and holds the language of a young spendthrift, whom the dissipations of Paris or London have stripped of his patrimonial acres and doomed to tardy repentance.

In order to remedy this deplorable state of things, the King formed a Junta or Commission, composed of individuals chosen out of the several Royal Councils, and instructed them to report with the utmost diligence on this urgent and vital subject. They went to work without loss of time as desired, but their united wisdom could not devise any other measure than such as despoiled the creditors of the State and violated the sanctity of contracts. To this act of iniquity, which was to be as fatal to its perpetrators as to those against whom it was directed, Philip gave his approbation. The payments to which those creditors were entitled were suspended, the stipulated interests reduced, and new obligations or promises, under a different form, and framed in accordance with the views and necessities of the

Government, were given to those who had claims against it. This immoral and impolitic breach of faith elicited loud and indignant complaints from its Spanish and from its foreign creditors. It divulged to Europe the whole extent of the financial distress under which Philip labored, it gave the final blow to his already tottering credit, it proclaimed to his enemies the secret of his growing debility, and instead of relieving, it increased the embarrassments of the treasury.

There is, however, a work of public utility, for which it gratifies us to give credit to Philip, for we have had little occasion to praise him, and it is much to be regretted that it was not completed. It was designed to be a vast repository, not only of statistical, but also of geographical and historical information, and it would have been of great use for establishing a just and accurate basis for the assessment of property and the apportionment of taxes. The instructions given for its execution were ample and minute, and might serve as a model worthy of imitation, even in this our age of advanced civilization. The work progressed so far as to produce several valuable folios, and yet withered before maturity, in consequence of the paralysis which was slowly spreading over the whole country. Philip had desired also a general map of Spain to be made, and had intrusted the surveys which it required to Don Pedro Esquivel, a celebrated mathematician and professor at the University of Alcala, but they were abandoned on account of his death and that of his successor during their operations. This has been but too often in Spain the fate of useful projects—a beginning, and no termination—a spasmodic effort, and a collapse.

The financial distress which pervaded the Kingdom was not without its anomaly, and the national atrophy without its exception and contrast. If the creditors of the State were defrauded, if public officers clamored in vain for their meagre salary, if armies mutinied or melted away from the withholding of their pay, if contractors abandoned their works because their wages were not forthcoming, if fleets could not sail because they were unprovided with everything they needed, if Philip pretended that there was not one day when he knew how he should live on the next, if the artisan's shop had to be closed from the want of employment, if fertile fields remained uncultivated by the husbandman, who calculated that his labor would not produce enough to meet the demands of the tax-gatherer, if squalid beggary swarmed where industry had once smiled with contentment, if a fatal drowsiness seemed gradually to benumb the faculties of a noble race, there was at least one spot where flowed a continual stream of gold, where work had its merited guerdon, and where repose was pillowed in the lap of abundance. That spot was formerly an obscure, deserted and miserable village in the vicinity of Madrid. Now it was alive with the presence of thousands of mechanics and laborers of all sorts, and had become the residence of many artists of genius, who strove, in emulation of each other, to produce architectural prodigies and masterpieces of sculpture and painting. There, was royalty itself giving assiduously to the whole work a superintendence of love, acting with unwonted familiarity and good-nature, smiling approbation, encouraging with look, word and gesture, pouring gold into horny palms which heaved up ponderous stones, and into those delicate hands which gave a visible form to the glorious conceptions of taste and imagination. There, was Philip stirring up himself and others, and there, grew the Escorial from its Cyclopean foundations. There, a city of canvas structures, of tented workshops, of thatched huts, of sheds, pavilions and wooden buildings of all sorts had suddenly arisen to accommodate the multitude which the King had summoned to erect a monument for the wonder of all ages. There, all was action and noise and bustle from the early dawn until night darkened the scene ; there, the music of the hammer and the music of the human voice ; there, the varied songs of all the provinces of Spain, for they were all represented, and the agglomerated volume of sounds proceeding from an infinite variety of machines, vehicles and tools. It was the tumult of Babel, without its confusion.

The pieces of stone used for the construction of that gigantic edifice were so enormous, that it was not uncommon to see forty or fifty pairs of oxen engaged in transporting a single one of those detached fragments of neighboring rocks. Whole mines seemed to have been exhausted to furnish the iron, lead, copper and tin which were used ; the quantity of bronze was in proportion. Jaspers of various hues and Lapis Lazuli, the most beautiful marbles of Spain and Italy, the most precious woods of Europe and America, with other materials for inside and outside decoration, which are too numerous to be described, were collected with a profusion which struck with amazement those who saw the gorgeous exhibition This far-famed edifice is a rectangular parallelogram of some 744 feet from North to South, and 580 from East to West.* It stands about 2,700 feet above the level of the sea, and looks like a natural part of the mountain of granite out of which it has been constructed.† The square of the building covers 3,002 feet ; there are 63 fountains, 12 cloisters, 80 staircases, 16 courtyards, 3,000 feet of painted fresco, and 11,000 windows, which are said to have been intended as a compliment to the memory of the virgin martyrs of Cologne. An eye-witness wrote, that the number of the men who built the Escorial can no more be ascertained than that of those who erected the Temple of Solomon. "So many‡ works were carried on at the same time," he said, "that, although I lived many years in their midst, I am still at a loss to comprehend how it

* Madoz, vii., 527. † Murray's Spain.

‡ Cabrera's History of Philip, c. 17.

could be done; and, vanquished in the attempt to relate it, I leave the task to other historians, as I feel like St. John the Evangelist, who despaired of describing what he saw of the Transfiguration."

The Spanish historian, Modesto Lafuente, to whom we are so largely indebted in this composition, says of the Escorial: "Various and even conflicting judgments have been passed, from the beginning to this time, on this gigantic, austere and marvellous edifice. Some have considered its author as the prototype of piety, and others, of religious fanaticism. As to ourself, we think that he was a compound of both. It seems to us, also, that it is impossible to deny with justice the splendor of the conception. It is certainly wonderful that, when Europe was convulsed with wars, when nations saw their fields uncultivated and their treasures exhausted, when in other Kingdoms the hands of the Protestants were occupied in demolishing the Catholic churches, there should be found a Monarch who, in a corner of Castile and at the foot of a barren and rocky mountain, raised and consecrated to religion a monument of such colossal dimensions — a peaceful and silent abode for Kings and monks to live together, as if he had flung defiance at the world, and said: 'I will build up an inexpugnable fortress against the new doctrines, and an adamantine shelter where religion and royalty will feel assured that not a single one of those ideas which agitate and perturb the world can penetrate.' If it was true piety, the grandeur of the inspiration was worthy of its origin; if it was religious fanaticism, its effect was the same, although proceeding from a source less pure.

"In an economical point of view, it is difficult not to consider the Escorial as an ostentatious and magnificent error. When the nations over which extended the sceptre of Spain were daily complaining of the insupportable weight of the tributes imposed upon them, when so many ordinary and extraordinary taxes were not sufficient to cover the expenses of the Kingdom, when the Spanish troops, who were shedding their blood to subject to the arms of Castile distant regions, were every day mutinying from the want of pay; when the King himself was lamenting his own personal state of destitution, to invest immense sums in the construction of an edifice which, however admirable in its religious and artistic aspect, was at least not necessary, seems to have been an unjustifiable deviation from common sense and judgment. It is impossible to approve of impoverishing a nation to build a sumptuous dwelling for one hundred and forty monks." The chronicler, Father Siguenza, who is the most fervent apologist of that superb monument, could not but confess that "the Spaniards had deeply rooted in their hearts the sad conviction that it was the cause of all their poverty, sufferings, taxes and tributes." We have already stated, in the course of this work, that the whole cost of the Escorial had been at least six millions of ducats ; a sum equal to the total amount of the revenues of the Kingdom, and equivalent to about twenty-five or perhaps thirty millions of dollars in the gold and silver currency of the United States, if we make a proper allowance for the comparative difference in the value of money in those days and in ours ; and it must also not be forgotten, in order to have an accurate idea of the magnitude of that cost, that salaries and wages of all sorts were then so low, and materials for building, with articles of food for the workmen, so very cheap, that the like of it would be considered in our age as fabulous.

The Cortes of 1583 soon resumed, as it were, the continuation of the labors of those who had adjourned in 1582, for they petitioned on many of the same subjects. They insisted particularly on reforms in the administration of justice, and on the necessity of remedying the evils resulting from the delays of judicial proceedings, in consequence of which suitors were so long kept out of their rights, and prisoners were indefinitely detained in prison before judgment was given. Among the administrative measures which they recommended was the humane one of having stores of corn in the chief town of every district, to assist the poor among the peasantry in the years of short crops, or in case of famine. It is to be remarked of the Cortes of 1583, that, being convinced at last of the inutility, if not the impropriety, of the existing law which repressed as much as possible the use of coaches, they proposed that it be made much less restrictive, because it was impossible to subdue, as they alleged, "the torrent of fashion and the rage of imitation." One of their petitions gives but a sorry idea of the state of discipline which prevailed in the army at that epoch. "The men of war and soldiers of this Kingdom," they said, "move together and in companies from one place to another, and on their way they commit such outrages, particularly in small towns and villages, that the inhabitants fly from them to the mountains and to desert places, and prefer to abandon to their depredations their houses, with the furniture, goods and supplies which they contain, rather than to expose their persons to insolence and indescribable atrocities." Whenever any of the delinquents were seized by the civil authorities, the military power interfered and set them free. The Cortes denounced these abominations, and proposed measures to put an end to their perpetration.* Notwithstanding the former protestations of that body, the Inquisition had not ceased to arrest and judge persons for causes unconnected with religion and the Catholic faith. The Cortes of 1583 addressed the King on this subject; they begged that this usurpation be checked, and that the civil authorities be protected against it.† But they had to put up with the same answer which he had given to their predecessors. It was: that his Maj-

* Petition No. 39. † Petition No. 77,

esty "had ordered the contents of their petition to be examined, so that what was proper might be done." This assembly also remonstrated against the levying of illegal taxes—that eternal theme of complaint from the representatives of the people. The Royal reply was as usual: "We have been compelled by our necessities, as our Cortes have been more than once informed, to have recourse to such ways and means, but we shall see what may be done in the matter for the future." He received as unfavorably another address concerning his continual sales of towns, villages, regiments and offices of all sorts, and concerning his practice of enlarging, on the payment of a sum of money, the jurisdiction of certain magistracies. Out of eighty-four petitions which the Cortes presented to Philip only twelve were granted. They related to subjects of no very great importance, and yet he seems to have assented to them churlishly; for one, two and three years elapsed before all the ordinances which he framed accordingly were promulgated. It was as if Philip had said: "I cannot decently refuse you all that you ask for; hence I reluctantly throw before you these few bones; make the most of my condescension." The Cortes appear to have felt it: for they prayed the Sovereign to shorten their sessions, because their remaining so long assembled was a cause of expense which their constituents, who had to pay for their services, could hardly bear.* They would

† Acts of the Cortes of 1583 to 1585; printed in Madrid in 1587.

probably have added, if they had dared, that they were heartily tired of this semblance of freedom, of their purposeless deliberations, of their contemned remonstrances, of their shadowy projects of law, of their stillborn plans of reform, of the vain parade of their effete existence, and of this solemn farce of popular representation.

In 1586, Philip again convened the Cortes in Madrid for no other purpose, one would suppose from his past treatment of that body, than to have the pleasure to discard their petitions. That assembly, however, made an attempt to rescue themselves from the nothingness to which they had been reduced. They presented to the King an energetic address, in which they said in substance: "We, the Representatives sent to the Cortes, who have met according to your royal summons, have come as usual with the desire to do all that your Majesty's service may require, to perform with equal zeal the work which the inhabitants of this realm and its subjects expect of us, and to give satisfaction to their wants in all matters of a general and particular nature. In our conferences and deliberations we are determined to pray, with all the suitable propriety of form and manner, for nothing which shall not be just and necessary." After this preamble, they complained that, in violation of an organic law to which they specially called the attention of the King, no answer was given to their petitions before they adjourned, or if any was returned, that it was evasive, and that, if favorable and explicit, long delays intervened before any action followed in conformity with its tenor, in consequence of which the welfare of the Commonwealth suffered not a little, and the people no longer enjoyed the fruits which were formerly obtained from the institution of the Cortes. "We therefore supplicate your Majesty," they said, "that all the provisions of the law which we have cited be observed." The King replied, in his habitual half-shuffling and half-contemptuous way, that henceforth he would respond to their petitions "with as much promptness as there would be occasion for." * As to the ordinances which he caused to be drawn according to such of their views as he adopted, he did not have them promulgated before two years had elapsed since their adjournment.† This was the manner in which he treated their remonstrances about the dilatoriness of previous publications.

With the same firmness of tone and precision of language they informed the King, that his subjects felt at last "fatigued" under the increasing burden of so many and so heavy taxes for the ordinary and extraordinary service of the State, and that it was impossible for them to pay such enormous contributions. They desired him to keep in mind that according to the Constitution of the Kingdom, no tax could be laid and collected which had not been

* Que en adelante mandaria responder á las peticiones con la brevedad que hubiere lugar.

† Lafuente. History of Spain, p. 435, vol. XIV.

previously voted by the Cortes. They told him that this was emphatically the law, the most ancient usage of the Kingdom, the practice observed by his predecessors, and sanctioned by the "natural logic of reason," and they begged that the people be relieved from such impositions on persons and property as had been thus illegally decreed. To this request, which, for years, had been repeatedly made, the King had but one stereotyped answer: * "That the great necessities under which he had labored to provide for the protection of the Holy Catholic faith and for the preservation and defence of the realm, had been the cause of his having used some ways and means to which it was impossible not to have had recourse, but that he would take care to order that this thing be looked into, and that the desired remedy be procured, whenever the aforesaid difficulties should permit its application." Those "necessities," and consequent violations of the law, lasted the whole of Philip's reign. The King's impassive perseverance in disregarding the protests of the Cortes was equal to the pertinacity with which they were sent. It was a long struggle of patience between

* Lafuente, History of Spain, p. 436, vol. XIV. La respuesta del rey fué la de costumbre: "A esto vos respondemos que las *grandes necesitades* á que nos habemos puesto por acudir a la defension de la Santa Fe Catolica, y conservacion y defensa de estos reinos, han sido causa de que se haya usado de algunos medios y arbitrios sin haberse podido escusar, y tendremos cuidado de mandar se vaya mirando y procurando el remedio *en cuanto las dichas necesitades dieren lugar.*

him and that body—the patience of prayer on one side, and the patience of denial on the other.

These Cortes fell again into the old inveterate error of praying for the passage of sumptuary laws. It was one of those few subjects on which Philip was pleased with their interference, and, on such occasions, he never failed in his answer to depart from his usual laconism ; for if it be true, as Motley maintains in his "History of the Rise of the Dutch Republic," that he was "the most tautological of writers," it must be confessed that, when it suited his mood and purpose, he knew how to be brief and precise. Be it as it may, he readily listened to the application made by the Cortes for the repression of extravagant habits of living, and, in compliance with their expressed desire, he promulgated an ordinance specifying how men and women should be dressed in his dominions. It will be recollected that he had already prescribed what they should eat.* This pragmatic about the cut, make and materials of habiliments is certainly a most curious and quaint document, which is more worthy of a tailor than of a powerful Monarch. But these minutiæ were precisely what Philip most affected. He liked to be felt by his subjects in the humblest details of life. He wanted them to be automatons, and he the regulator of all their movements. In many instances this meddling may have been well

* See p. 126 of this work.

meant, but it must have been far more insupportable than his worst acts of oppression ; for Macaulay says with truth in his essay on Frederic the Great : "We could make shift to live under a debauchee, or a tyrant ; but to be ruled by a busy-body is more than human nature can bear." Spanish nature bore it, however, not from servility, but from that chivalrous loyalty which generally made the Spaniards of those days loth to question the King's authority. Any tailor or dressmaker, violating any of the provisions of the ordinance we have mentioned, was to be punished with exile for four years from the place of his residence, and with a fine of twenty thousand maravedis, to be divided in equal parts between the King, the Judge and the denunciator. Minute instructions were given to men, whatever was their age, condition, quality, and the class they belonged to, as to their garments in general, down to the sort of shirt they had to wear ; and the ordinance even forbade its being starched, according to circumstances, under the penalty, in case of disobedience, of forfeiting the shirt, with its ornaments, and of paying a fine of thirty ducats.* A better ordinance was the one which prohibited women from wearing

* Y asimismo mandamos que ningun hombre, de cualquier clase, condicion, calidad y edad que sea, pueda traer ni traiga en *los cuellos, ni en puños, ni en lechuguillas, sueltos or asentados en la camisa,* ni en otra parte, guarnicion redes, ni deshilados, ni almidon, ni arroz, ni gomas, verguillas, ni filetes de alumbre, oro, ni plata, ni alquimia, ni de otra cosa, *sino sola la* lechuguilla de holanda or lienzo, con una ó dos vainillas chicas, so pena de perdicion de la camisa, cuello y puños y de treinta ducados, aplicado segun dicho es.

masks when they went abroad. It was a general and mischievous usage. Men* borrowed the female apparel, and, in that disguise, committed, said the Cortes, who remonstrated against this abuse, "all manner of iniquities and sacrileges." According to the same authority, "Fathers met their daughters, husbands their wives, and brothers their sisters without recognizing them, whereby there resulted much offence to God and injury to the public." The existence of such a custom certainly implied a very singular state of society. If it was romantic, it cannot be denied that it tempted to immoralities, and it was, therefore, the fit subject of a prosaic police regulation, for each infraction of which there was to be paid a penalty of 3,000 maravedis. This sum, equal to nine dollars in the currency of the United States, or in reality to about thirty or thirty-five dollars, considering the relative value of money between that time and ours, was evidently not sufficient to restrain women of rank, fashion and wealth from continuing this evil practice on such occasions as

* Ha venido á tal estremo (said the Cortes) el uso de andar tapadas las mugeres, que dello han resultado grandes ofensas de Dios y notable daño de la repùblica, á causa de que en aquella forma no conoce el padre á la hija, ni el marido á la muger, ni el hermano á la hermana, y tiene la libertad y tiempo y lugar á su voluntad, y dan occasion á que los hombres se atrevan á la hija ó muger del mas principal como á la del mas vil y bajo, lo que no seria si diesen lugar, yendo descubiertas á que la luz dicirniere las unas de las otras, porque entonces cada una presumiera ser y seria de todos diferentemente tratada y que se viesen diferentes obras en las unas que en las otras, demas de lo cual se escusarian grandes maldades y sacrilegios que los hombres vestidos como mugeres, y tapados sin poder ser conocidos, han hecho y hacen.

they might deem convenient. For this reason, and from the difficulty of enforcing such an ordinance against persons of influence, it would be presumed, if not known, that the custom of wearing masks was not entirely discontinued by a certain class, until it was put down by the more powerful edict of public opinion. The Cortes proposed also many reforms in all the branches of the administration of the Kingdom. If we are to judge, by the contents of their petitions on the subject, of the morality of the officers of the Government, we must come to the conclusion that it was at the lowest ebb.*

Philip, be it on account of the energetic and independent spirit with which he had been addressed by these Cortes, or for some other cause, was more liberal to them than he had been to the preceding assemblies; for he granted them thirty-one out of the seventy-one petitions which they presented to him.† It is a singular feature of this singular reign, that Philip kept the Cortes always in attendance on his person, with but short interruptions; that each session lasted between two and three years, and that, during this prodigious length of time, about eighty petitions, on an average, were elaborated, of which more than three-fourths were invariably rejected, or met with the usual answers which we have recorded. It is evident that the Cortes were not overworked,

* Acts of the Cortes of Madrid from 1586 to 1588, published in that city in 1590.

† Lafuente's History of Spain, p. 438, vol. 14.

and could not be much gratified at the results which they obtained from their labors, such as they were. Indeed, it is a puzzle to imagine how they could still preserve the appearance of being at work, whilst months followed after months in endless succession, without their being prorogued. What could they be writing, talking, or deliberating about? It is not astonishing, therefore, that they did earnestly pray the King to shorten their sessions, which had become so expensive for their constituents. To be assembled a couple of years with no other object to be attained than to have a score or two of petitions attended to, and the few petitions that were thus favored being generally such as were the least important, must have discouraged the most zealous reformer who ever sat in that body. When the Cortes could easily have done in two or three months what it took them as many years to accomplish, when they themselves and the cities, towns and districts which sent them and paid for their services united in the wish that they be dismissed to their respective homes, when Philip had predetermined hardly ever to acquiesce in anything they proposed, it is difficult to understand why he thus prolonged their sessions. No ostensible reason can be seen for it. Was it to disgust his subjects with popular representation by giving them a surfeit of it, or making it so costly a luxury? It remains one of the inexplicable features of that mysterious policy which Philip loved to pursue.

The passion of the King for scribbling, his policy or his natural inclination to go himself into all those details of business which he ought to have left to his ministers; his mania to read and correct, not only the papers which issued from the several Departments of State, but also those which were received, and to fill them with interlines and underlines, with comments and marginal notes, were the cause of great delays and embarrassments. The Cortes of 1588 applauded the excess of his zeal, but represented to him that, if he did not assume to do himself what should be left to others to perform, and if he attended less to minutiæ, he would have more time to devote to those general and large interests which were worthy of his attention, and that the Kingdom would, in consequence of it, derive more advantage from the wisdom and many other endowments of the royal mind. Philip received graciously this complimentary remonstrance, but returned no other* answer than that "he would order it to be looked into, and would have that done in the premises which the good service of the Kingdom might require." The Cortes further represented that his Majesty had instituted a certain number of Councils, such as the Council of State, the Council of War, the Council of the Treasury, the Council of Grace and Justice, and others, which they thought to be sufficient for the wants of the Government,

* Que mandaria mirar y proveer en ello lo que conviniera al buen servicio del reino

without the creation of so many special Juntas or Councils and special Tribunals, whose powers were sure to conflict with the jurisdiction of the regular and ordinary authorities, and that it produced confusion and many difficulties which greatly retarded and perplexed the transaction of public business. Their complaint was certainly well founded. The curriculum of the State was already but too notoriously known as a slow coach. It was intolerable to have poles thrust athwart its wheels further to impede their sluggish rotation. The Cortes prayed, therefore, with much reason, that this evil be remedied. Their master, however, turned as usual a deaf ear to their supplications.

As their predecessors had done many a time, they remonstrated against the inordinate duration of their sessions. They begged to be kept no longer assembled than they used to be in the reigns of their former Monarchs ; they said that their procrastinated absence from home prevented their attending to their own private affairs, which, from such neglect, went to wreck, and that their constituents were also ruined by being compelled to pay for the expenses of such interminable assemblies. The King replied that "he would dismiss them as soon as possible." So much for his word. But what did he do ? He unmercifully detained them four years, hanging on his skirts ! Was it on pressing business ? No. For, what they did and was accepted by the King was promulgated only a year after they had been permitted to adjourn. If this was not intended as a mockery, what else could it mean? It is no wonder that Spanish patience has become proverbial. We see that it was proof against all the trials which Philip inflicted upon it, and it must be admitted that he had ways of his own which would have exhausted the endurance of a population of Jobs.

Philip, notwithstanding the remonstrances of his subjects, had not ceased to tax them according to his will and pleasure, without the concurrence of their Representatives. This evil became more difficult of eradication in proportion as it struck deeper roots into the soil. The Cortes of 1588 were aware of this, and therefore addressed the Sovereign with increased energy on the necessity of returning to the scrupulous observance of one of the most important of the organic laws of the State. Their language was explicit and vigorous. They prayed him to remember all the complaints of their predecessors on the same subject. Making allowance for the "necessities" which he always alleged for his justification, they no less bitterly deplored that he had no other answers to give* than that "he would look into it and would find a remedy," when that remedy never came, and the abuse remained as full of life as before. They depicted in vivid colors the extreme distress of the nation, and supplicated his Majesty that the continuation of this illegal mode of taxation be effectually and thoroughly stopped.† The reply

* Que se fuese mirando y procurando el remedio. † Que el abuso cesará de todo punto. Peticion, No. 9.

of the King was more bland than was his wont, but it had lost none of its characteristic evasiveness. It neither promised nor granted anything. The conciliatory mildness of his language was an opiate he was willing to apply to a sore which he knew to be really painful. It was an emollient with which he intended to soothe, but not to cure. Nothing ever was further from Philip's mind than to permit the Cortes to hold the strings of the public purse.

When a State is diseased, and those to whose care its health is committed are at a loss what to do for the recovery of their patient, empirics present themselves with all sorts of panaceas and nostrums, and their number, solicitations and obtrusiveness increase in proportion to the pressure of the necessities which they pretend to be able to relieve. Such was the case when Spain was discovered to be in the deplorable financial condition of which we have given but a feeble sketch. Visionary projectors and crafty schemers pullulated at Court. The Cortes complained of those charlatans, who, they said, were molesting by their importunities the King and his ministers; who succeeded in obtaining from them long and repeated audiences; and who, if their propositions were listened to, would finish devouring what remained of the substance of the Kingdom.* They cautioned the King against lending too favorable an ear to the trumperies of those quacks who

* Peticion, No. 10.

pretended to have made such wonderful discoveries in the field of political economy. Among the numerous propositions offered to the Government, there was one, however, which was favored by some members of the Cortes. The author of it was a man of some distinction for his erudition and literary attainments. His name was Simon Abril. In an address to the King he made this remark: "Having observed, in the course of my investigations, prompted as they were by my zeal for the service of your Majesty, that the pecuniary embarrassments of the State have been produced by the wars of Germany and the Low Countries, which have been undertaken against heretics and rebels in defence of the Church and the Holy Catholic faith, I have come to the conclusion that it is just to look to the Church for the remedy." He then suggested a mode of taxing the Clergy during twenty years, by which a sufficient sum would be obtained, during that lapse of time, to extricate the national treasury out of its difficulties, without any real detriment to any particular individual. It appears that this project had been first presented by Simon Abril to the Council of Finance, who treated it lightly, like many other plans of notorious extravagance. Repulsed in that quarter, Abril applied to the King, and in a communication to his Majesty said, with much pathos, "I know* that there will be no lack

* Archivo de Simancas, Est. Leg. 163. Yo sé que no han de faltar gentes que este mi trabajo y estudio que yo e puesto en servicio de V. M.

of people who will find fault with the conceptions which I have placed at the service of your Majesty, and who will endeavor to discredit them. Therefore, I supplicate your Majesty, by the entrails of Jesus Christ crucified, to hear all, but to decide for yourself, and to notice that, in the whole commonwealth, there is not a body of men on whom hands may be laid, in such pressing circumstances, with so much justice and less prejudice. Your Majesty will also take into consideration how tired the people are of paying so much annually to the Clergy, etc." This Simon Abril must have been a bold man, indeed, and it is to be wondered at that the Inquisition did not devise some means to get hold of him. His suggestions were not, of course, of such a nature as to be acceptable to Philip. Near two centuries and a half were to elapse before the overgrown and unnatural prerogatives of the Clergy could be successfully attacked, and before their colossal acquisitions in lands, churches, seminaries, convents, monasteries and other sorts of property were to be thoroughly subverted.

Although the Clergy were exempt from taxation, yet they had voluntarily granted, for many years past, an annual subsidy, of 420,000 ducats, for the object of building, arming and keeping up sixty galleys in the Mediterranean to check the depredations

lo disacrediten, ó á lo menos traten de disacreditable ; y asi suplico á V. M. por los entrañas de Jesu Christo crucificado que oyga á todos, y mas á si mismo, y considere que en toda la masa de la república no hay parte de que tan sin perjuicio y con tanta justicia sé pueda echar mano para un negocio tan urgente ; y mire quand fatigado está, &.

of the Moslem Corsairs, but this sum had since been gradually diverted to other purposes. The galleys had rotted away, or were remaining idle and neglected in several ports from the want of crews and many other things, which, of course, could not be had without pay. The consequence had been that the turbaned rovers had been emboldened to land frequently on the coasts of Spain, and to spread far and wide the desolation which we have before mentioned.* The Cortes begged that this annual subsidy of 420,000 ducats be applied to its original destination.† The manufacturing of powder had become an exclusive privilege. The natural result ensued — the powder was execrable. The Cortes very judiciously remonstrated against the continuation of such a policy. They also reproduced a petition which had been already presented to the Crown in 1548. In its style and sentiments it shows in a striking light what may be called the *local color*. No wine ever tasted more strongly of the soil by which it is produced. It is characteristic of Spain and of the epoch. "Our predecessors," they said, "supplicated your Majesty not to permit the introduction into these Kingdoms of baubles, glassware, dolls, fancy knives and other knick-knacks which came from abroad. These articles are unnecessary to the support of human life, and yet we exchange gold for them just as if we were Indians. If, because they were obtained for little money, this evil

* See p. 126, chap. IV. of this volume. † Petition, No 11.

was, at that time, of a limited nature, now a great amount of pure gold and silver is extracted from these Kingdoms for manufactured articles of these metals, containing however much alloy, which come from France, and consist in chains, tinsel ornaments, brass and gold wires, rosaries, false stones, colored glassware and other trinkets, which are sold at first for large sums on account of their novelty, and which, in the end, the vendors themselves show to be of no value by parting with them at very low prices. Next comes another invention and novelty which they sell again very high. Thus there is nothing but buying, and wasting an infinite quantity of money, as long as life is in the body. Nothing ot any value is got for it in return. All these things turn out to be worthless at last, whilst in the meantime the gold and silver which had been acquired with so much labor, and which had been procured from the Indies and the remotest parts of the world, are carried away from these Kingdoms." They therefore supplicated His Majesty to prohibit the introduction of those articles and the selling of them by any French or other foreign pedlers, in any manner whatever, "because among such traders who traveled over the whole country under the pretext of trafficking in pins, combs and rosaries, there were many spies, and because those foreigners took all the gains and profits out of the hands of the natives." This petition, founded on false and contracted notions of political economy, was of the nature of those which Philip always received favorably. Hence he did not fail to gratify the Cortes on this occasion with ready and ample compliance. The importation and sale of the described articles was forbidden, under the penalty of confiscation and of paying besides as much as they were estimated to be worth.*

The last session of the Cortes in the reign of Philip began in 1593, one year after the adjournment of those who assembled in 1588. One of their first acts was to complain that many laws of the realm, although useful and necessary, had fallen into desuetude, or were set aside, or not executed, "much to the discredit of the law and lawgivers." They remarked with too much truth that this was a chronic infirmity in Spain.† They prayed that the majesty of existing laws be vindicated, and that stability and vigor be secured to the enactments of future legislation. To this the King assented. They prayed that the tax called "Cruzada,"‡ and the tax known as the "Subsidio y escusado," which was one levied on the Clergy by virtue of a bull of the Holy See, be invariably employed in keeping up the armies and fleets which were destined for the defence of the realm and the Catholic faith, and that they be not diverted to other purposes; that the comp-

* General proceedings of the Cortes of Madrid, who met in 1588. Printed in 1593.

† Lafuente's History of Spain, p. 444, vol. XIV.

‡ It was a tax which, by a special grant of the Pope, was paid to the King of Spain by his subjects for permission to eat eggs and cheese in Lent.

trollers of the exchequer be instructed not to violate the privileges and franchises of the people ; that the faculty granted by former Cortes to equip privateers for the guard and defence of the coasts be permitted to have its full effects ; that the Clergy be prevented from acquiring lands and tenements in mortmain, in accordance with the wish expressed "an infinite number of times," by the Cortes. As to this last request, so often reproduced, * Philip went on answering, until the grave closed over him, "that he would look into it, and do what would be expedient in the matter." Another object of complaint on their part was, that the peasantry were not paid for the sacrifices they had made to furnish provisions and supplies of all sorts to the armies of His Majesty. They represented that, in order to fulfill this patriotic duty, estates had been sold, or debts incurred, and that many persons were ruined in consequence of it. They insisted on the necessity of indemnifying promptly those who had thus suffered for the service of the Commonwealth. They also desired some reforms concerning the Alcabalas,† with a view to having them more justly established and less oppressive for certain classes. These Cortes further suggested many ameliorations in relation to the judiciary and to the system of political economy then prevailing in Spain. All their petitions, even those which were short-sighted and erroneous in

* Lafuente's History of Spain, p. 444, vol. XIV.

† Alcabalas are duties levied on all sales.

principle, show that they were animated with an earnest and sincere desire to improve the condition of their country. But Philip was impervious to their suggestions.

We have said before, we believe, that, with the accession of the Austrian dynasty, there had begun a struggle between the liberties and franchises which were the natural growth of Spain, on one side, and the absolutism which had been imported from Germany, on the other. One of the adversaries had finally triumphed in the fields of Villalar and in the streets of Saragoza. The Cortes were the embodiment of the popular element, and Philip, during his long reign, pursued with indefatigable pertinacity the ancestral policy of rooting out what was to his race a traditional subject of terror and hatred. He had but too well succeeded, as we have demonstrated. The Cortes had been stripped of the robust power which they had formerly possessed. They could no longer make laws, or refuse their assent to anything the Crown desired. All that which they were permitted to do was to present plans and projects, accompanied by humble prayers for their adoption, and we have seen the way in which those prayers were received. They had, however, continued for a long time to claim as their prescriptive privilege, that the Crown should not legislate without their concurrence. But, gradually debased and humiliated, they had lost so much of their antique spirit as tacitly to concede to the King the right to frame laws, decrees, or ordinances, without consulting them. They now contented themselves with begging that his Majesty be graciously pleased not to promulgate any law, or publish any edict, whilst they were in session, before ascertaining if they had any observation to address to him on the subject, any modification to propose, or objection to point out, "because," they said, "the Representatives of the people were bound to know better than the King and his ministers the condition of the country at large, and the peculiar necessities of each province." They finally concluded with this phrase, which was tantamount to signing with their own hands the death warrant of their political existence: "His Majesty's Council * will, nevertheless, retain the same faculty which they had before, to do what they please, notwithstanding what they may hear from the Cortes." This declaration, of course, consigned that formerly august and energetic body to the tomb of the Capulets. Then Philip probably felt that his work was accomplished, and turned his mind, with the gloomy satisfaction peculiar to his temperament and to his family, to the contemplation of his own sepulchre in the Escorial, convinced, as he was, that he would leave his feeble successor in the undisturbed possession of the most despotic power in Christendom, and that he had, with the pneumatic engines he had so skillfully contrived, pumped out

* Que al consejo le quedaba la misma facultad, habiendo oido al reino, para hacer, sin embargo, lo que tuviera por mas conveniente

of his subjects their hereditary love of liberty, and that fierce spirit of independence which had so long checkmated the encroachments of their Monarchs. He in fact died shortly after. But comprehensive, humble and abdicative as had been the concession of the Cortes, it failed to conciliate the haughty despot, whose pride seems to have been intensified by his triumph. His reply to what we shall call the piteous groan of his prostrate Cortes was: "It is not proper* to make any innovation in this matter, because when our Council deems anything expedient, it is done. On such suitable occasions as may offer, what the Cortes desire will be considered." It is consolatory to think that, neither in the Spain of the present day, nor in any other country where a representative government is established, such imperial insolence would be tolerated.

Philip, Count of Flanders, who married that unfortunate daughter of Ferdinand and Isabella, the mad Queen Juana, was the representative of the rights and pretensions of the House of Burgundy. Until the death of Charles the Bold, with whom had expired the male line of that princely race, the Court of Burgundy had been one of the most magnificent in Europe. The household of those wealthy Sovereigns was established on the most extensive and gorgeous scale of feudal pomp and pride. The

* Que no es bien que se haga en ello novedad, porque cuando el consejo ve que conviene, se hace, y en las occasiones que se offrecieren se mirará lo que convenga.

menial offices, or at least offices with menial appellations, were filled by the highest nobles, and the etiquette which surrounded the Prince was a barrier between him and even his magnates. It seemed intended to make the distance between them still greater and more impressive. Under the auspices of the Count of Flanders and afterwards of his son, the Emperor Charles V., the Royal household of Spain had been transformed and organized after the fashion which had prevailed in Burgundy, much to the mortification of the Spaniards. The Cortes had more than once remonstrated against this innovation. In Spain the King had been but the first gentleman of the Kingdom. He was the head of the nobility, but not a master to be approached with servility. The Grandees were his peers, although he was armed with greater power and his person more sacred, and they kept their hats on their heads in his presence. Some degree of familiarity was not excluded. The haughtiness and ceremonial of the Court of Burgundy had been, therefore, a distasteful importation. Philip was again addressed on that subject by the Cortes who had assembled in 1593, and who availed themselves of the opportunity offered by the marriage of his daughter Isabel Clara Eugenia with the Archduke Albert, to whom he had ceded Flanders in consideration of that union. "The Court of Castile," they said, "should no longer be kept in the style of Burgundy, when Castile no longer retains any of the provinces which belonged to that Principality." For these reasons they begged the King to reform his household and to return to the old forms and usages to which they had been accustomed, and which were distinguished for greater simplicity. This was rational and natural. The King's answer was abrupt and dry: "We have considered about it, and we shall continue to consider."*

The Cortes of 1593 remained in session until 1598, when the King died. A session of five years, to frame ninety-one petitions, out of which only twenty-one were granted! They must have been highly disgusted with this dreary waste of time, and heartily ashamed of their nothingness and impotency. What did Philip mean by having this useless and cumbersome appendage about his person, unless as a body-guard of political eunuchs in imitation of the mutilated attendants kept up by those Eastern Monarchs whose despotism he had emulated to exercise? Nothing, we think, gives a better idea of Philip's character than his deportment toward the Cortes. There was certainly no revolutionary tendency in that body. Their antique fidelity, their chivalrous loyalty, their devotion to himself personally, their traditional conservatism, could not be the object of a doubt, and yet he stood before them as grim and forbidding as the pillars of Hercules beyond which they were not to pass, and he assumed

* Lo hemos visto, y se irá mirando en ello. General acts of the Cortes from 1592 to 1598, promulgated and printed in Valladolid, in 1604.

to be the champion of an immobility which they were not to disturb. He was constitutionally and systematically opposed to progress of any kind, and he wanted them to feel that, if he permitted the slightest movement onward, the impulse was not to come from any other source than himself. Hence his fixed answer: "No innovation," whenever they ventured to propose any reform of any importance. We cannot but fancy that, if Philip had been gifted with omnipotence, he would have delighted in creating a world without motion. Creeping things might, perhaps, have been tolerated, but the wind would certainly have been excluded, and he would have said to the ocean: "Peace, be still."

CHAPTER IX.

We shall now take a brief review of the intellectual condition of Spain under Philip II, and ascertain how far the arts, the sciences and literature were entitled to him for the state in which they were during his long reign. The better to fulfill this task, we must go back to the accession of Isabella to the throne of Castile, for it is impossible to appreciate correctly the intellectual and moral condition of a nation at any fixed period of its existence, without connecting it with the history of the fifty or eighty years, if not more, which preceded it, as the extent, copiousness and capacity of a stream are better known by tracing it up to its source, or at least ascending it to some distance, than by such a limited survey as the eye of the beholder can embrace from the point where he stands. The thoughts of man are not self-created; they have their spiritual ancestry; they are of high or base lineage; and their genealogy, more than any, is entitled to an immortal record. There are epochs when events after events, of an incalculable magnitude, succeed each other in a particular country, which seems then to have been specially chosen by Providence for their development; and they shoot into future ages an influence which is to be felt by unborn generations. Those events come like a Promethean band of giants with torches of sacred fire in their hands, not stolen from but committed to them by Heaven, to light up, as they stalk onward through the long avenue of the human race, those lamps which nature has placed there, awaiting the igniting touch which the course of time is sure to bring. On such occasions, the intellectual fluid darts along those invisible and mysterious wires which bind nations together with sympathetic ties. By the rapidity of its motion it is heated into flame, and a glorious illumination bursts upon the embellished world. The reign of Ferdinand and Isabella in Spain is one of those epochs.

The Monarchy which the Goths had established in that country had been driven into the cave of Covodonga by the invasion of the Arabs. The foot of the followers of Mahomet was planted on the Cross from the Pyrenees to the two seas which bathe the rocky shores of the Iberian Peninsula. The natives, in the extremity of their disasters, which were such as had seldom visited any community, did not despair of their religion and of their country. They came out of the bowels of the earth to fight, until they wrested a portion of the surface of their territory from the grasp of the invaders, and gradually erected petty Kingdoms within frontiers defended by art or by nature, and frequently by both. These petty kingdoms fought against each other; they also fought against the Arabs, and against the Moors, the less polished successors of the Arabs. The races which Africa and Asia had sent to Spain shortly subdivided, like their enemies, into small principalities, and struggled against each other without ceasing their hostilities against the Spaniards. Interminable wars followed—the Christian holding the Infidel by the throat, and only relaxing his deadly efforts for a hostile spring upon his fellow-Christian—the Infidel still hunting incessantly the "Christian dog" with the same undying combination of fanatical contempt and hatred, and only turning from the pursuit to shed Moslem blood with all the merciless fury of sectarian zeal, with the lust of ambition contending for power, and with the insatiable spirit of vengeance entertained by tribe against tribe from the traditional memory of real or fancied wrongs. The heart grows faint, and the head swims with a dizzy sensation, when one looks back at that ocean of blood, whose tumultuous waves yet send the distant echo of their dismal surge reverberating to our ears through the empty halls and porticoes of those centuries which, like imperishable monuments of the past, loom up before us in the hoary twilight which they borrow from time. One wonders how the ordinary avocations which are indispensable to the support of life could have been pursued amidst those eternal massacres ; and yet there is a wonderful fascination in those scenes ; for not only did the peasant run his plow and till the soil ; but even the poet sang, the musician tuned his lyre, the arts bloomed with profuse luxuriance in the lap of danger, and ripened into productions which have hardly been excelled ; the sciences progressed, although with halting steps ; and chivalry, elevating purified love and honor to the level of religion, placed them on the same altar, and descended into the arena with its gorgeous panoply, to defend these three united objects of its worship. The ruthlessness, however, of continued devastations becomes too oppressive to behold, and one would soon turn away in disgust from the appalling sight, if not allured and consoled, amidst those horrors, by frequent glimpses of the better nature of man transfiguring itself into an angel of light. We see deeds so noble that they make us forget aught else ; we hear sentiments which throw a celestial glow into our soul ; we feel subdued by an irresistible sympathy, and we readily grant the honors of an apotheosis to transcendant virtues, which we accept as a compensation for so much baseness and so many atrocities. It was an Iliad of eight hundred years, or rather a myriad of epic poems surpassing each other in the ever diversified magnificence of their poetical details, such as the genius of Homer himself could not have conceived, and teeming with traits of heroism and magnanimity which, in their historical realities, appeal more intensely to the imagination and touch the heart more deeply, than the fabulous exploits of the invulnerable Achilles. At last, the Moslems recede before the advancing step of the soldiers of the Cross, and their possessions are almost confined to the territorial paradise of Granada. The small Christian Kingdoms are fused either into Castile, or Aragon, with the exception of Navarre, which, however, was soon to lose its independence and individual existence. Castile and Aragon remain, bestriding the battle-field and confronting each other like Ajax and Hector, with rival prowess and mutual admiration, whilst the scales of fate hang over them in suspense. Fortunately, instead of engaging in mortal combat, they embrace in a holy union by the marriage of Ferdinand and Isabella. Worldly wisdom in Ferdinand extends the hand of love and protection to genius in Isabella, combined with evangelical piety, and an inflexible rectitude of judgment and purpose.

Providence seems to have been preparing the way for that unity of government which Spain was destined soon to possess. The dynasties which had originally occupied the thrones of Navarre and Aragon had been struck with sterility; they had become extinct, and the sceptres of these two Kingdoms had passed into the hands of members of the Royal Family of Castile. The House of Trastamara therefore ruled the whole of the Peninsula with the exception of Portugal. It was a step in the right direction, although it was not yet visible how it would lead to the desired goal. There was little probability that Ferdinand, at the time he was born, would ever be King of Aragon. There was as little probability, at Isabella's birth, that she was destined to be Queen of Castile, and yet, contrary to all expectations, the brow of each was encircled with the crown which seemed forbidden to their hopes. The glittering prize was secured to them by the commission of crimes in which they had no share, and, as it were through divine mercy, individual wickedness was made instrumental in working out the general good. There appeared also to be insurmountable obstacles to their marriage, and yet those obstacles were overcome. On the other hand, there were ten chances to one that the Sovereigns of two rival and contiguous Kingdoms would quarrel in the exercise of their respective prerogatives. As husband and wife, whom so many temptations surrounded, it was at least an even chance that the course of their wedded life would not run smooth. But they happened to be so wonderfully fitted for each other, that, both in their conjugal and political relations, the utmost harmony prevailed until death put an end to their union. Thus unity existed in duality, which was the more extraordinary, because that duality was composed of two Sovereigns armed with independent power. Providence had certain designs, and we shall see what a concatenation of circumstances brought on their final accomplishment. One of those preliminary designs was that Spain should become powerful, because it was necessary that it should be so for reasons which will soon be discovered. The tool was to be shaped to suit the purpose for which it was to be used.

The Kingdom of Aragon had been impoverished by the foreign and the civil wars in which her two last Sovereigns had been engaged. One of them, Alfonso the Fifth, had conquered, it is true, the Kingdom of Naples, and had filled the world with the fame of his exploits But, by a wise dispensation, military glory, which is so enticing, has its drawbacks, and the Cortes had said to Alfonso: "Sire, this war, of which we have not yet seen the end, has so depopulated your hereditary dominions, that the fields remain uncultivated, and we have been compelled to pay four hundred thousand florins for the ransom alone of prisoners. Industry and commerce are paralyzed. We see no other remedy to those evils than the presence of our King." Seduced however by the meretricious charms of his Italian conquest, which he preferred to the rough loyalty of his Aragonese subjects, he lingered in Naples until his death. Instead of governing from Aragon, his acquired domain, says Lafuente of that Monarch, in his History of Spain, it was from that foreign soil that he governed Aragon. He left his Kingdom of Naples to his bastard son, Don Fernando, and his Spanish dominions to his brother John, King of Navarre. Under this new Monarch, turbulent, self-willed and pugnacious as he was, whom his subjects surnamed the Great, and the

Hercules of Aragon, and who retained to the age of eighty-two all the fire and ambition and almost the bodily strength of which he had given so many proofs in his long career, the Aragonese had not the opportunity to recover from their exhaustion. That exhaustion was such that when John, at the end of his reign, wished to march to the defence of his town of Perpignan in the province of Roussillon, which Louis XI. of France was threatening, he had to borrow money from one of his Barons and to sell his mantle of ermine. When he died shortly after, he was so poor, that, to provide for the expenses of his funeral and the support of those who belonged to his household, it was necessary to sell all the articles of gold and silver which were found in his wardrobe, and to procure ten thousand florins on pledging his jewels and even his decoration of the Golden Fleece. It may be consolatory to those who are suffering from pecuniary distress to know, that he, of whom we write, and who was in the sore predicament which we have described, wore seven crowns—those of Navarre, Aragon, Catalonia, Valencia, Mallorca, Sardinia and Sicily. A wise administrator and a prudent sovereign was clearly required, or Aragon could not have been in a condition to join, a little later, in the accomplishment of those great achievements which were still in the womb of the future. That administrator and that King providentially came forth in the person of the astute, thrifty and politic Ferdinand, the husband of Isabella.

Although the condition of Aragon was not prosperous, yet it was enviable, if compared with that of Castile. When Henry IV., the imbecile predecessor of Isabella, closed his worthless existence, that Kingdom was in such a state of anarchy as almost to amount to a complete dissolution of civilized society. It is hardly possible to express in adequate terms the degradation of the throne, the annihilation of all the resources of the common wealth, the helpless beggary and personal infamy of the Monarch, the insolence and peculations of his favorites, the arrogance and excesses of the nobles, the poverty and demoralization of the inferior classes, the temerity and ferocity of organized bands of depredators, who openly destroyed life and property, the extent and depth of public immorality, and the furious outbreaks of the worst passions, which swept over the land like hurricanes of evils. Few there were who did not live in open violation of the whole decalogue, if full faith is to be given to the chronicles of that age. The Castilians seemed to be a nation of malefactors, although deep in that bed of corruption there lay the seeds of the noblest virtues and of the most dazzling qualities of the head and heart, as will subsequently appear. The castles of the magnates were like caverns of robbers ; travellers were pillaged and murdered on the high roads, and the fruits of such rapines were exposed for sale without concealment on the public squares of the most populous cities.* The officers of the Crown were regardless of the authority which had commissioned them, and were no better than licensed plunderers. The dissoluteness of the Clergy of both sexes was truly frightful. An Archbishop was driven away from his Episcopal See by a popular tumult, for having attempted to do violence to a youthful bride who, before the sacred altars of religion and in his presence, had just pledged her love and fidelity to the husband of her choice. Another Archbishop led an army against his King, whose crown he wished to transfer to that King's brother. That haughty and turbulent prelate, at the head of ambitious nobles followed by their vassals, erected in the field of Avila a platform on which he placed the effigy of the monarch decorated with all the royal insignia. Then the sceptre was wrested from the inanimate hands which held it, the diadem was torn from the brow, the mantle from the shoulders, and the sword from the belt. All this was done amidst the acclamations of the multitude who witnessed the burlesque and extravagant ceremony. At last, the rebellious priest himself stamped his foot on the breast of the prostrated image of his master, whom he proclaimed to be no longer the anointed of the Lord. Castile had reached that state of putrefaction when a nation must be either regenerated by the

* Lafuente's History of Spain, Introduction, vol. I, p. 102.

sword of a foreign conqueror and the infusion of new blood into its veins, or be saved from perishing in the tumultuous chaos of its own creation by the intervention of a native genius, such as Heaven sometimes vouchsafes to earth, to ride the whirlwind and substitute order to confusion. That genius was wanted to operate the resurrection of Castile, and that genius came. It came in the person of Isabella —a woman, so radiant with purity and piety, so free from most of our human imperfections, that she seemed an inspired being, a missionary from above. She said: "Lazarus, come forth, and Lazarus arose from the dead."

Hardly had that illustrious personage ascended the throne, when the scene changed as if under the wand of a magician. A Portuguese army which had penetrated into Castile is driven back in shame and confusion. The French abandon the province of Guipuzcoa, which they had invaded, and the wily Louis XI. is compelled to submit to a peace advantageous to Castile. Evil doers, high or low, poor or rich, are chastised with an impartial hand; the receptacles of crime are swept away, the turbulent prelates sue to be reconciled with the Royal authority which they were in the habit of contemning, the haughty magnates are humbled and curbed, the rebel chiefs implore their pardon, the roads and by-ways are freed from robbers, and the shops teem with merchandise; artisans, peasants and all laborers peacefully pursue their avocations, agriculture flourishes, commerce is encouraged and fills the Kingdom with hitherto unknown wealth, the tribunals of justice are almost as pure as in the fabulous days of Themis, the Cortes legislate in perfect freedom, the revenues of the State are re-established, the empty treasury is replenished, the Crown is radiant with renewed splendor, and its mandates are equally respected in the battlemented mansion, in the modest hut, in the cave of the hermit and in the palace of the Cardinal. The nobles serve their Queen on bended knees with the loyalty of faithful subjects and the high-souled devotion of knights of romance. The commons, prostrated before her with filial reverence and enthusiastic gratitude, worship her like a divinity. Well did she deserve such adoration. The social body had been a corpse ; she made it a thing of life and action, and reanimated its inert limbs with Herculean strength. She had reconstituted into a compact and vigorous nation one which, but lately, had been a jumble of jarring elements. She found the Royal mantle dragging in the mud, and torn into rags by the hand of discord ; she transformed it into a vesture of glory. Under her miraculous influence a corrupt people had suddenly become a moral one.* With prodigious activity and perseverance she had made true the improbable. She had purged the diseased land of its infirmities and restored to it health, vigor, and youth. She had

* Lafuente's History of Spain. See Introduction, vol. I, p. 122.

organized tribunals and presided over them. She had caused the laws to be compiled and arranged into digests. Like St. Louis, she had administered justice herself on more than one occasion. She had overthrown the fortresses of the oppressors, and penetrated into the humblest dwelling to invite shrinking merit to her Court. She had given daily proofs of the most exalted virtue as a Sovereign, a wife and a mother. She had abashed vice, checked immoral habits, and sobered extravagance, not merely by her decrees, but also by her example. That example had been the best of all sumptuary laws. The emanations of her piety and purity had pervaded the social atmosphere and subdued the deleterious miasma with which it was loaded. From the temple where she prayed like a saint, she passed to the battle-field like the goddess of war. The same hand which erected and decorated altars held the reins of the fiery steed who, with distended nostrils and eyes of lightning, swept along the serried ranks of armed battalions. She was, at the same time, the watchful mother of cloistered virgins and of grim-visaged warriors. Where there was a want, there was her ministering care. She built sanctuaries, and took fortresses; she organized armies, and established schools and universities. She reformed the Clergy, restored its ancient discipline, and made them worthy of the consideration which she bestowed upon them. Well did she know how to honor them after having made them honorable.

As a woman and a Christian she bowed meekly before the Holy See, but, as a Sovereign, she was inflexible in resisting the systematic course of Papal invasions and usurpations. Whilst under her keeping, the rights of the Crown of Castile never gave way to the unfounded ones claimed by the Tiara of Rome. She presided over Cortes and tournaments with the same serene majesty; she superintended the education of the people with as much care as the education of her children; she wielded the sceptre and she plyed the needle with equal diligence and skill. Amidst all her overwhelming occupations, and, although she not unfrequently passed whole nights in dictating long dispatches to her secretaries, she found leisure to be a student, and she even learned Latin. She patronized the arts, the sciences and literature with judicious love. She governed Kingdoms in Europe and America with conscientious zeal and scrupulous attention, whilst she did not neglect any of the minute details of the administration of her household. She gave daily some hours to her private devotions, but, in looking up to Heaven, she did not forget the interests which had been intrusted to her on earth. Without the transformation which was due to Isabella, much less than Aragon would Castile have been able to perform the part which she was called upon to act, and, therefore, according to the decrees of Providence, that transformation took place at the right moment. The finger of fate had marked on the horologe of time the hour for the final triumph of Christianity in Spain, for the destruction of what remained there of Moslem domination, and for a unity of government under the not distant reign of Charles V. That hour had struck, and the agents of Divine will had appeared in Ferdinand and Isabella. Under their guidance, Castile and Aragon, linked together by religious faith and conjugal love, well trained and provided for the intended crusade, were ready to march against the last stronghold of the infidels, and to substitute the Cross for the Crescent on the summit of the Alhambra. It had been a wooden cross in the hand of Pelagio, when, issuing from the cave of Covodonga, he began the struggle which was to last eight hundred years. It was of gold, when, under Ferdinand and Isabella, it gleamed resplendent on the towers of Granada.

If the human mind must necessarily become polished, if it must teem with fertility and glow with inspiration, when it is made familiar with the sublime pages of Homer, Virgil and Tasso, and when it is capable of appreciating and assimilating such ambrosial food, what must be the impulse given to its imagination and other faculties of the brain, when, instead of reading, a nation acts epic poems which, in interest and sentiment, in the nature of the subject and in all the attributes of poetry, certainly equal, if they do not surpass, the gorgeous conceptions of the bards we have named? Hence the age of Ferdinand and Isabella was an age of mental development, because the intellect and soul of man were on the stretch to rise up to the grandeur of everything he heard and saw. The war of Granada, like the Trojan, was an epopee of ten years from the fall of Alhama to the fall of the capital of Boabdil, but its episodes were more brilliant and varied, and its consequences far greater. "It is remarkable," says Prescott, in a note to the History of Ferdinand and Isabella,* "that the war of Granada, which is admirably suited in all its circumstances to poetical purposes, should not have been more frequently commemorated by the epic muse." But the immortal historian himself answered, we think, his own remark, although he did not seem conscious of having given that answer, when he said, a few lines after: "Mr. Irving's late publication, the 'Chronicle of the Conquest of Granada,' has superseded all further necessity for poetry, and, unfortunately for me, for history." This is precisely the reason why the epic muse has been silent on the subject. It is because Poetry feels that she is superseded by History, and that the picture which is before her is so illuminated with innate brilliancy, that the most dramatic gorgeousness of coloring which fancy could supply and art could use, would, if applied to it, look like those uncalled-for ornaments which rather shade than set off the attractions of a woman whom nature has made exquisitely beautiful. Hence the

* Prescott's History of Ferdinand and Isabella, p. 109, vol. II.

war of Granada has remained the almost exclusive domain of history—a domain which, inviting as it is, has seldom been approached by the poet, or invaded by the bold step of the novel-writer. It would have been as if Titian had attempted to add more vivid hues to the rainbow. Therefore all those who, be it in verse or in prose, have endeavored to do more than give, like Washington Irving, "a poetical aspect to historical accuracy," have miserably failed, and produced but vapid compositions. If the records of that mighty struggle delight posterity, its stirring incidents, at the time of its existence, absorbed the attention of Europe, because its successful issue was to be an event of the utmost importance to her, as well as to Spain. It was not merely the triumph of a nation resuming its complete entity, recovering its usurped territory, and wiping off the never-to-be-forgotten affront of subjugation. It was the triumph of civilization over barbarism, of a superior religion over an inferior one, of the sanctity of European marriage over the looseness of Eastern polygamy, of chastity over lust, of persuasion over dictation, of freedom over slavery. For Christianity recommends that proselytism shall come from the inspired lips, and not from the strong hand. Its mission is to operate conversions with the tongue of fire. and not with the flashing scimitar. It raises woman to angelical purity, and Islamism degrades her to beastly sensuality. "It breaks," says Lafuente, "whilst Islamism rivets, the chains of man."

For these reasons the whole of Christendom rejoiced at the fall of Granada; but there was one other cause for gratulation which was fully appreciated by Europe. She had not been able to prevent Constantinople from passing, not long before, into the possession of the Infidels, and it was now with undisguised terror that she saw herself threatened from that advanced post by the formidable force of the recently established Ottoman Empire. It was a consolation and an encouragement to her, when she heard of the end of the Moslem domination in Spain. It invigorated the hope of resistance to the new colossus, and added to the resources of attack or defence. If the Crescent had risen to its meridian on the banks of the Bosphorus, it had set forever on the plains of Granada and in the mountain-pass which had echoed the "last sigh" of the Moor. If Christianity wept in the Orient like the captive daughters of Sion, in the Occident she pealed forth her exulting hymns of joy and thanksgiving like Miriam. It is indeed difficult to measure the proportions of an event of such political, moral and religious magnitude, and of such importance not only to Spain, but to mankind.

To the conquest of Granada, and to the triumph of the Cross over the Crescent in battle, and of the dogmas of Christianity over the precepts of Mahometanism succeeded another stupendous event—the discovery of America. There needed an Isabella to understand Columbus and to open to him the paths to the unknown world which he had divined, and there needed a Columbus to complete the glory of Isabella. In both it was piety which illumined their genius and gave it the direction which it followed. It pleases God to create such glorious sympathetic affinities when they are necessary to carry on His designs. The blow given to Islamism, the rise of Spain to the rank of a first-rate power, growing compact and gigantic into an indissoluble unity, and dazzling the other nations with the scintillations of her diadem of newly acquired glory, the discovery of America with the marvellous deeds by which it was accompanied, and the measureless wealth which it brought out of the bowels of an hitherto unknown part of the globe, would have been sufficient to operate, not only in the country which was more directly affected by these events, but also in the rest of the civilized world, a radical revolution in household ideas and domestic economy, in politics and commerce, in the arts, morals, wants and manners of the people. But, as if this was not enough, Spain, who seemed destined to be pent up within herself, like an enchanted giant round whom a magic spell had thrown up mountains and spread oceans, as guards and warders to watch over him, burst loose and poured her invincible battalions over Europe, and particularly into Italy—into that land with which, at that time especially, the mind could not come into contact without being inoculated with its superior civilization ; for by the influence of religion, of the fine arts, the sciences and literature, Rome still ruled the world, when her arms had become effete and powerless. Over the tombs of the Cæsars the chivalry of Spain and France met in deadly opposition and emulous rivalry. Gonsalvo de Cordova, in his Italian campaigns, gained the surname of the "Great Captain," and secured for his country the conquest of Naples and Sicily, with the restoration also of the Roussillon. It looked as if fortune had adopted Spain and made of her a petted child. These events were like meteors which had chased each other, and which, each in its turn, had, within short intervals, irradiated the firmament ; they were also like earthquakes which had shaken Spain and a great portion of Europe ; and if the human mind had been asleep, it would have been awakened by the illumination and the commotion. But it was not asleep. On the contrary, it was on the alert, and the discovery of the compass and of printing, recently made, seems to have been vouchsafed by Providence to facilitate the happening of the events which we have mentioned, the dissemination of their knowledge and the perpetuation of their consequences.

The human mind is like a hive. The dormant mass seems dead ; but shake it and you will find that it is alive. Another shake—and your ears are struck by a low and confused hum—a murmur of discontent perhaps at its repose being disturbed—and then comes out a flight of thoughts, which, like busy bees, scatter far and wide, some distilling honey, and others checking intruders with their sharp stings. It is not astonishing that, in such a reign, during which the mind and soul were so much excited, literature, the arts, and sciences should have acquired such a prodigious development, particularly when fostered by the favor of a Princess who patronized them with fond love and intelligent appreciation. Pompey had boasted that, if he stamped his foot, armies would spring up from the bosom of Italy. At the gentle beckoning of Isabella, there sprang up in Spain a host of men who distinguished themselves as theologians, jurists, historians, physicians, astronomers, naturalists, lyrical and dramatic poets, linguists, musicians, and successful explorers through the whole range of human knowledge. The literary movement extended from the Moorish ballad and the romance of chivalry to the grave studies of the universities; and the most gigantic typographical work of the time, the Polyglot Bible, was, not long after, the production of Spain. With the encouragements of the Queen, the fair sex entered into competition with the other in the cultivation of the arts, in scientific attainments and in literary pursuits. There were, among others, Beatrix de Galindo, surnamed "the Latin," Lucinda Medrano, who held a professorship in Salamanca, Francisco de Lebrija, who gave lessons of rhetoric in the university of Alcala,* Maria de Mendoza, who was

* Lafuente's History of Spain, p. 76, vol. II.

famous for her knowledge of the Greek, Hebrew, Arabic, and other languages, and Maria de Pacheco, of illustrious birth, who shone by her erudition under the reign of Isabella, and who, in the days of Charles V., left an immortal name by the heroism with which she defended the liberties of Castile as the wife and widow of the celebrated and unfortunate Juan de Padilla. The fame of this intellectual development reached even remote climes, and the learned Erasmus expressed his admiration of it from the interior of Holland. This development would probably have been greater under Isabella, Charles V. and Philip II., if it had not been for the establishment of the Inquisition, that thought-killing institution and antagonist of human progress.

The reign of the insane Joana, or rather of her husband, the Count of Flanders, was but a flitting shadow which passed over this brilliant horizon. The reign of Charles V., by its grandeur, was no less favorable than that of Ferdinand and Isabella, to stimulate all the intellectual faculties and energies of the people. That age of battles and religious schisms, was, nevertheless, the golden age of Spanish literature. The wars of Charles had put Spain in frequent and intimate relations with Italy, and Italy had begun to Italianize Spain. The marvellous works of Leonardo da Vinci, Michael Angelo, Raphael, Titian, Correggio, and other artists were not lost upon the grim warriors whose tastes were formed by those masterpieces. It gave rise to those schools which were established in Spain, and which, in their turn, became as famous and as original in their productions as those which at first they had imitated. The Spanish mind could not also but be influenced by the literature of the country of Dante, Ariosto, Tasso and Petrarch ; and many of the Spanish poets adopted the prosody and the forms of composition which met with popular favor in the land which they admired, and in which they had so long sojourned, either as students, or as warriors, or in a diplomatic capacity. Castellejos, Villegas and other partisans of the old Spanish school opposed this innovation and censured the authors who were guilty of it, calling them "Petrarchists." But the new Italian school prevailed, and remained at last a distinct species of Spanish literature. The Didactic style was also cultivated in verse and prose. As to dramatic literature, it progressed with less ease than the lyrical and the didactic, because the Clergy was opposed to it, and prohibited the comedies of Torres Naharro, who had turned his attention to this kind of composition. He was, however, followed with more success by the actor and author, Lope de Rueda, whose comedies were so popular that it was difficult to stop their representations in various cities of Andalusia and Castile. It was art in its infancy, it is true, and the scenic decorations were singularly primitive. Still their effect was new and striking at the time, although they would have seemed ridiculous to us, and Lope de Rueda may be considered as the founder of the Spanish theatre —that theatre which was soon to become the admiration of the world and a school for other nations.

Satirical compositions and light sportive pieces were among the productions which obtained the most success. In both the illustrious Diego Hurtado de Mendoza distinguished himself pre-eminently. He was a lyric poet, the author of satires in prose, an ingenious novel writer, a grave historian, a sagacious and active diplomatist, a loyal, frank and austere member of the Council of the Emperor. His sportive novel, Lazarillo de Tormes, is a faithful and animated delineation of the customs of the epoch, and acquired a reputation which it has retained to this day. Not only has it been translated into several languages, but new and beautiful editions of it have been published even in this century. As to historical literature, it seemed to keep pace with the aggrandizement of the Spanish nation, and to rise in its merits and style in proportion to the importance, fecundity and variety of its materials. Hitherto there had been but mere chronicles; now there were histories. Morales, Garibay and Zurita, made their appearance. Francisco Lope de Gomara, Bernal Diaz del Castillo, Bartolome de las Casas, recorded the discoveries and exploits of their countrymen in the New World, and the erudite Gonzalo de Oviedo published his "Natural and General History of the Indies." As a philosopher and humanist, Luis Vivez gained for himself an European reputation, and it was said that William Budé, Erasmus of Rotterdam, and Luis Vivez of Spain, formed a great triumvirate of learning which could not be matched. In a country so religious as Spain was, and in an age in which the Lutheran schism took place, it is natural that theological studies should have been a subject of special importance and favor, and that profound theologians should have arisen as they did, who were cited as the honor of Spain, and who acted a conspicuous part in the famous and protracted Council of Trent. A peculiarity of the reign of Charles V., which is perhaps no less a peculiarity of the Spanish character, was, that there seemed to be a poetic inspiration in the incessant clash of arms, and that the laurels of Parnassus grew spontaneously in blood-stained fields ; for all those who tuned the lyre, or wielded the pen of authorship, were, with the exception of ecclesiastics, stout warriors whose swords had learned to flash in the van of battles. The chronicler, Perez de Guzman, had distinguished himself as a soldier in the combat of La Higuera ; Lope de Ayala, who figured in the battles of Najeria and Aljubarrota, was made prisoner when fighting stoutly, and wrote of military events in which he had taken an active part. Jorge Manrique commanded armed expeditions, fought at Calatrava and the siege of Velez, whilst he composed elegies as soft as a woman's sigh. Bernal Diaz del Castillo accompanied Cortez to Mexico, and, after being present at one hundred and nineteen battles, this Ajax turned historian and transmitted to posterity a most valuable account of the conquest of New Spain. Boscan, whilst he joins the conquering hosts of his countrymen who subdue Italy, introduces into Spanish poetry the Italian metre of eleven syllables. Hurtado de Mendoza, whilst fulfilling the duties of a general and of an ambassador, finds time to write melodious verses and playful tales with versatile genius, and with the same grave pen with which he records the last war of Granada. Garcilasso follows Charles in all his campaigns, shows the courage of a hero at the taking of the Goleta and of Tunis, and the graceful author of Salicio and Nemoroso dies of a wound received when scaling fortifications.* Thus, during the reigns of Ferdinand and Isabella, and of Charles V., the intellect of Spain, radiant with poetry amidst the turmoils of war, reminds us of the attributes of that beauteous God, who drove the car of the orb of day through clouds and storms, who sped with lofty disdain the unerring shaft at the object of his wrath, and who charmed the immortals with the tunes of his lyre.

* Lafuente's History of Spain. Introduction, p. 164, vol. I.

CHAPTER X.

The reign of Philip was a continuation of that of Charles in literature as well as in politics. There was the same association of martial spirit and love of letters. Lope de Vega, who, as a dramatic writer, astonished the world by his genius and his incomparable fecundity, carried the arquebuse as a simple soldier in the invincible armada. Ercilla met the brave Indians of the Arauco in many an engagement, and wrote on his shield, or on the carriage of a cannon, his epic poem, the "Araucana." Cervantes behaved heroically at the battle of Lepanto, where he lost one of his hands ; and with the other, which had known the weight of the chains of captivity in Algeria, he wrote comedies and novels, and, preeminent among the rest, his immortal and inimitable Don Quixote. The Muses no longer needed the repose and tranquillity of peace to make their voice heard, as the nightingale waits for the calm and silence of a summer evening to exhale its melodious notes. The Nine Sisters had become amazons ; they had assumed the garb of Pallas, and sang as sweetly in the presence of Mars as in that of Apollo.

The works of illustrious writers, which had become classical, served to establish the grammar and prosody of the Spanish language, which acquired at the time all the idiomatic terseness, virility, richness and harmony for which it has ever since been distinguished. Poetry and prose were then marked by a splendor of diction which delights us to this day, when reading the best authors of the epoch. The first difficulties had been surmounted under the preceding reign. The pioneers had opened the way, and the glorious procession of intellectual laborers, provided it kept within certain restrictive bounds, could advance with less obstacles under a Prince who had more fondness than his predecessor for books and for Spanish literature, whose mind had received a considerable degree of cultivation, who liked to write himself, and who had even a mania for acting the pedagogue and correcting the productions of others. It is true that the Inquisition was an incubus on the intellect of Spain, but, although it was far more terrible under Philip than under his father, although it showed itself intolerant, inexorable and harsh beyond description, in relation to all theological or philosophical doctrines, or on any matter which was in the least connected with religion, yet it seemed to be comparatively indulgent to all productions of the imagination, and to understand that it was the political interest of the Sovereign that his subjects should amuse themselves with the nugœ seriæ of polite literature. One could have indited an ode to Apollo or to any other mythological God without peril, but one attempting to write with common sense on government, philosophy or religion, would probably have been burned. Poetry was an Alsatia, or White Friars' privileged ground, where the persecuted mind was permitted to take refuge and avoid the bailiffs of the Holy Tribunal. Hence Castilian poetry was cultivated in all its forms with zealous devotion, and rose to a height beyond which it has never since ascended. It was the crater through which the pent up subterranean fire sent upward its flames.

Beginning * with the class of lyrical compositions, we remark that the example given by Garcilasso was promptly and admirably followed by other choice spirits, who clothed elevated sentiments with elegant language. Among the galaxy of those inspired bards beams the mild and venerable figure of Father Luis de Leon. His poetry has all the moral ingredients of his character, which reproduces itself in his works as accurately as his person would have been reflected in a mirror. There is in him no pomp of thought, no gorgeousness of style, no artistical arrangement, but a simplicity not destitute of elevation, and an amiable modesty in the midst of intellectual grandeur. His writings are impregnated with a subdued tone of pious restraint, which is relieved with sudden strokes of natural sublimity, and which is in perfect harmony with the gentle

* It is with pleasure that we acknowledge how much we are indebted to the recent History of Spain by Lafuente in these observations on Spanish Literature.

virtues adorning the author. He seems, when he takes his pen, to be entering a temple, and purposely to lower his voice. His style is serene like a tropical night, with occasional flashes of the heat lightning gleaming on the distant horizon. His "Ode to country life" implies the existence of a tranquillity of mind which descends on the reader like a refreshing dew. It is worthy and indicative of the man, who, after having passed five years in the dungeons of the Inquisition, returned quietly to his chair in the University of Salamanca, as if nothing had happened, and resumed his lessons with these words: "As I was saying to you yesterday." This allocution is, by the by, a fair specimen of the sublime simplicity which is sometimes to be found in his works. Even in his ode entitled "The Prophecy of the Tagus," in which he affects a more elevated tone than is usual with him, he prefers a pure and simple to a swelling and ambitious diction, and rejects all meretricious ornaments. His verse remains chaste and unpretending like a young virgin, but his thoughts and images move the soul with a sort of mild and self-possessed enthusiasm inspired by his religious and sublime sentiments. Lafuente calls him the Spanish Horace, but we cannot acknowledge the propriety of the expression. We cannot see any resemblance between the two authors. The one was replete with the skeptic and epicurean philosophy of the Augustan age. *Nunc est bibendum*— "Let us drink and be merry, for to-morrow we die."

The empty thunder of Jove has no terrors for him, and he delights in the satyr's dance and in the enticing flight of the laughing nymph. The Spanish poet teaches other lessons, and praises other enjoyments. He glows like the burning bush in the desert, and he draws his inspirations from the commandments of Jehovah, There is as much difference between the two authors, as there is between Paganism and Christianity.

The poetry of the bachelor Francisco de la Torre is full of simplicity and tenderness, like that of Father Luis de Leon. His songs, his elegies, his pastoral compositions are easy and fluent and produce a feeling of pleasant melancholy. He reminds the reader of a gentle stream running with soft murmurs along verdant banks shaded with willows. Even his odes, which are written in verses of unequal metre, are full of harmony, and hardly is the absence of consonance remarked. With less fluency, although he sometimes aspired to it, but with more vigor, and with a sort of austerity not unbecoming his triple character as a distinguished warrior, ambassador and historian, Diego Hurtado de Mendoza, of whom we have already spoken, placed himself by the side of some of the best poets of the epoch.

If the modern doctrine of equality among men is a favorite one in political communities, and soothes that human pride which is so convenient a lever in the hands of demagogues, certain it is that this levelling rod is powerless in the realms of the intellect.

In them there is a hierarchy which cannot be subverted. Wherever the arts flourish, wherever there are men who cultivate them with pride and delight, there is some prominent genius who assumes the first place. It is not an usurpation, but an acknowledged royalty, legitimate in its sway. The diadem which it wears is an irradiation from the brain, and all bow before it as before the sun. This is what took place at this time among the Spanish poets. They had their prince in the person of the Sevillian Fernando de Herrera, surnamed the "Divine." He found the Spanish language as simple and unadorned as a shepherdess, save with natural flowers. He gave it the magnificence of a queen resplendent with barbaric pearls and starlike diamonds. His imagination is always on fire and never gives any sign of refrigeration. His style strikes by its elegance and grandeur; his thoughts soar aloft like uncaged eagles; the images to which he resorts glitter like gold undefiled, and a sort of musical accord, full of vigor and melody, pervades his whole diction. His poetical merits, however, are not wanting in variety, for he is sometimes abrupt, impetuous and bold, and seems to play with a whirlwind; sometimes he stretches himself on a bed of flowers, and his accents become tender and exquisitely sweet. But even when he unbends, he retains the richness and dignity of his style, which has never been equalled in what is called imitative harmony. He is the Pindar of Spain. His "Ode to John of Austria," his "Hymn on the Battle of Lepanto," and his "Elegy on the Death of the King, Don Sebastian," although so different in their beauties, are all sublime, and are masterpieces which will forever remain as models for this kind of composition. Herrera became the founder of a school which may be designated as the "Ornate," and which, unfortunately, soon degenerated into exaggeration of sentiment and extravagance of expression. Some of his imitators, disdaining sobriety, became insupportably affected and turgid, and corrupted the public taste. Among those who followed with most credit in his footsteps were the two brothers, Lupercio and Bartolomé Argensolas, Francisco de Figuerroa, Fernando de Acuña, and the Portuguese Montemayor, Saa de Miraada, and Melo, who attempted with felicity to write Spanish poetry. We must not omit Vicente Espinel, who inaugurated a style of versification called after him, the "Espinela," and Juan de Arguijo, whose florid imagination and virility of thought enabled him to become one of the most successful imitators of Herrera.

Lope de Vega, better known as a dramatic author, although he excelled his countrymen in all styles of poetry, from the short sonnet to the long-winded epopee, did not fail, of course, to establish his preeminence among the lyric poets. As such, he introduced the poetical language into those ballads and popular songs which before had generally been of prosaic simplicity; and into erudite poetry he introduced familiar and unpretending expressions—so as to ennoble the former, and vulgarize as it were the latter. The Spaniards look upon him as the Phenix of geniuses, as a being in whom the faculties of the imagination were such as to be considered truly miraculous.

In didactic poetry, Juan de La Cueva obtained some reputation, but his works are incomplete and destitute of method. He certainly was neither a Horace nor a Boileau, nor a Pope, and seemed not to be disposed or able to practice what he purported to teach. As to the poem entitled: "The New Art to write Comedies," by Lope de Vega, it is rather the vindication of the dramatic style of that author than a didactic work, although it gives valuable lessons. More worthy of the name would have been the poem of the Cordovian, Pablo de Cespedes, on the "Art of Painting," had he left us more than mere fragments of it. If he had finished and polished it, he would have added to his great reputation as a painter, a sculptor and antiquarian, that of a superior poet, for the detached parts which we have of his poem are rich in thought, harmony and coloring.

With regard to epic compositions, that most difficult and elevated branch of poetry, the Spaniards had very little to boast of in that age of intellectual fertility. This may appear somewhat strange, since, several centuries before, when the Spanish language was hardly formed, the admirable although rough-hewn poems of "the Cid," and of "Count Fernan Gonzales," had given room to hope for still more finished and beautiful productions. Such well-founded expectations, however, were not realized. There sprang up a multitude of poems, some of which on subjects worthy of the epic muse, but none ever rose above mediocrity. The epic fecundity of Lope de Vega was as great as his lyric and dramatic abundance, but he never could reach the combination of those qualities which are required in the epopee. It is impossible not to admire the luxuriance of his imagination, the easy flow of his poetic vein, his prodigious facility of versification; but, at the same time, the defects inherent to the precipitation with which he wrote are but too visible. His style is loose, careless, and lacks nerve. His metaphors are frequently offensive to good taste; his frequent playing on words is puerile and out of place; his story is unskillfully jointed and put together, and there is too much improbability in his incidents, episodes and characters. He fails both in the matter and in the form, in the conception and in the ornaments, not only in the "Circe," the "Andromeda," the "Serpentary," the "Beautiful Angelica" and other poems, but also in the "Conquest of Jerusalem," which is the most elaborate of all. Hence it must be concluded that Lope de Vega, notwithstanding the vastness of his genius, had not in him that which constitutes the epic poet. There was a cause of debility in the very excess of his fecundity.

Alonzo de Ercilla, the author of the "Araucana," did not propose to himself, says Lafuente, in his History of Spain, to compose a poem, but to describe in verse the achievements which he had witnessed, and the battles in which he had acted a part. Thus he neither could, nor attempted to, subject his work to the rules and conditions of an epic composition, nor did the object which he had in view permit it. He aimed at being a historian more than a poet, and, if he appealed to poetry, it was more to give precision and brilliancy to his truthful narrations than to soar on its wings into the regions of fiction. But his descriptions of battles are so full of fire, he puts such eloquent and vigorous speeches in the mouths of his personages, and there are such gems of beauty in the mass of his imperfect versification, that the "Araucana" is the poem of that epoch which is the most appreciated by the Spaniards, and the best known among other nations.

Balbuena, with a much larger endowment of the poetical element than Ercilla, with much more richness of imagination, more elevation of ideas, and more facility and flexibility of diction, succeeded not in giving an epopee in his "Bernardo," but only abundant evidence of his possessing happy dispositions for the composition of such a poem. He either seems not to be aware of the difficulties presented by the art which he professes, or he tramples upon them at random and with a heavy foot. Rules and precepts he treats as antagonists in his way, whom he knocks down right and left with the ponderous battle-axe of the lion-hearted Richard. He is so unequal, irregular and incorrect; he is so made up of revolting monstrosities and of incomparable beauties, that, notwithstanding merits which must be acknowledged and admired, it is impossible not to be filled with insupportable disgust in attempting to read his works. It is only with a sweating brow, and with the pickaxe of the miner in hand, that one can reach the pure gold hidden under such heaps of rubbish. In the "Christiad" of Father Diego de Hojeda, in the "Monserrate" of Virues, in the "Conquest of Betica" by Juan de la Cueva, in the "Tears of Angelica" by Luis Baraona de Soto, there are beautiful passages, but nothing which, as a whole, deserves to be mentioned as an epic poem. It is useless to allude to the efforts of many other authors who were still less successful. Spain has never been able to this day to produce a Tasso, or even a Camoens.

As to light and fugitive poetry, Lope de Vega gave to Spanish literature the "Gatomaquia," a poem on cats; and Villaviciosa, the "Mosquea," or the Fly. They are pieces full of wit, grace, and ease, which are a feast for the gravest mind, and which show the rare poetical faculties with which their authors were gifted. The most fastidious taste can hardly refrain from granting an approving smile to these frolics of the imagination, which seems to sport with itself as if intoxicated with glee and fun.

In what may be called sacred, moral and sentimental poetry, there are remarkable compositions due to the pens of Saint Juan de la Cruz, Saint Theresa, Father Melon de la Chaide, Father Jose de Siguenza, who paraphrased many of the Psalms of David; and the universal Lope de Vega, who is to be met in all the fields and paths of literature. But Father Luis de Leon, of whom we have already spoken, surpasses them all. Contemplation of the sacred objects for which he tunes his lyre throws him into ecstatic beatitude. The rapture of his soul breaks out in tender exclamations of reverence and gratitude. He sees and describes the celestial city of the Saints with a sort of poetic mysticism and a harmony of diction which produce ineffable emotions. It sounds like a distant and imperfectly-heard strain from the angelic choirs. Among his works, the "Ode on the Ascension of Our Lord," and another on "Life in Heaven," deserve to be mentioned with special praise. It is worthy of remark that his translation of the songs of Solomon, with commentaries, which he undertook merely to please a friend who did not understand Latin, was the cause of his being detained five years in the execrable dungeons of the Inquisition. He was suspected of heresy on account of his having violated the edict of the Holy Church which prohibited the translation of the sacred books into any of the "vulgar" languages. He went through all the sufferings of his incarceration with the most examplary Christian fortitude, and, when released at last, he contented himself with exhaling a modest complaint in a stanza of ten verses.

Dramatic poetry and scenic representations were much indebted to Torres Naharro and Lope de Rueda for the progress which they made toward a higher order of cultivation. Juan de Timoneda, who collected and published the works of his friend, Lope de Rueda, wrote himself thirteen or fourteen dramatic compositions. They were comedies, farces, interludes, tragi-comedies, and allegorical pieces, which were, as was then the custom, represented in the open air, and in which there were dialogues of much vivacity. Two members of Lope de Rueda's strolling company of players, Alonzo de la Vega and Cisneros, were authors like himself. But he who gave a new tone and physiognomy to the stage was the Sevillian, Juan de la Cueva, who composed pieces divided into four acts or days, and distinguished for their variety of metres. Some were founded on events recorded in the History of Spain, such as the "Infantes de Lara," "Bernardo del Carpio," the "Siege of Zamora;" and others related to ancient history, such as "Ajax," "Virginia," and "Mutius Scævola," or to subjects of pure invention, such as the "Slanderer," or the "Amorous Old Man."

The Valencian, Christoval de Virues produced some extravagant dramas, such as *Cassandra* and *Marcela*, and others remarkable for their atrocities, such as *Attila Furious*, in which the spectator was entertained with the death of no less than fifty persons, and the burning of a ship with her entire crew. His *Dido*, however, is more sparing of absurdities and horrors, and in it the unities are observed, probably by accident, and without any design on the part of the author to be guided by any of the acknowledged rules of art. At about the same time, the Galician, Geronimo Bermudez, wrote certain dramatic pieces, which, with considerable boasting, he pretended to be the first that deserved in Spain the name of tragedies. They turned on well-known events of the life of Ines de Castro, whose name, by a strange conceit, the author transformed into Nise, the anagram of Ines. But, notwithstanding the pretensions of the vainglorious Geronimo Bermudez, he was eclipsed by the Aragonese, Lupercio de Argensola, whose three tragedies, *Isabella*, *Filis*, and *Alexander*, attracted more attention than any other compositions of the same kind. Cervantes says that they surprised and delighted all those who saw them acted—both the rabble and the higher ranks of society. If true, it shows how vitiated was the public taste at the epoch, for not only did all the personages in those tragedies meet a frightful death in sight of the spectator, but he was regaled also with other scenes so disgusting, that no modern audience could tolerate them for a moment.

The fact is, that theatrical art and dramatic poetry had been in a state of infancy for several centuries. The representations were given by strolling actors and in the open air, with costumes of the poorest, and scenic decorations of the roughest. Under Philip II. all this rudeness began to peel off, and was succeeded by the splendor which was due to the genius of Cervantes and Lope de Vega. It was a sudden transition from twilight to the glories of the meridian. The thirty or forty comedies written by Cervantes were not, it is true, such as might have been expected from him, and, although they are but little remembered, still they contributed greatly to the progress of the dramatic art and to the introduction of a purer taste. In a play which was intended to portray the misery of captivity in Algiers, he represented himself in the character of the slave Saavedra. His *Numancia*, although deficient in its plot and other requisites, is full of originality and beautiful scenes. The *Confusa*, which he considered his best piece, seems to be the one which obtained the most vogue at the time. It was not, however, to his dramatic genius that Cervantes was to be indebted for the universal and immortal fame which he was to acquire.

But all dramatic authors were thrown into the background as soon as Lope de Vega made his appearance. Such was his fecundity, that he was looked upon as one of the greatest prodigies of nature. It can hardly be comprehended how he found time to write eighteen hundred comedies and four hundred allegorical plays, besides innumerable poems, and epic, didactic, lyric, and burlesque compositions. He was a literary Briareus, with a hundred arms. He frequently, it is said, wrote in the morning the piece which was to be acted in the evening; although it is difficult to understand how the actors managed to learn their parts. He went to work on the inspiration of the moment, took up the conception which suddenly presented itself to his mind, and, trusting to his prolific imagination, he added scene to scene without caring for the appropriateness of their connection, until he filled up the outlines of his subject. In all these improvisations it is impossible not to admire the richness of Lope de Vega's fancy, and not to be amazed at his inexhaustible vein of invention. At the same time, it is evident that he rushes onward without knowing where he goes. Therefore he is the author of many very admirable scenes, but only of few good comedies. Hence, with his varied talents and his boundless imagination, he failed to raise the stage to that state of perfection which it was in his power to invest it with, if he had subjected himself to patient labor, and checked with the hand of sobriety the headlong flight of his muse. As it is, his voluminous works are an immense chaos, where precious gems and rubbish, and all the elements of nature, occasionally brought together into harmonious arrangements, and with transient glimpses of accidental fitness and adaptation, are nevertheless whirled along in inextricable confusion.

Lope de Vega, however, greatly ameliorated the dramatic art in Spain, by driving from the stage those coarse farces and repugnant monstrosities to which it had been exclusively surrendered. He gave more decency and decorum to the language and sentiments ; he felicitously united together the popular and erudite expressions of the Spanish idiom ; he introduced personages more polished, more tender-hearted, more interesting, and more within the range of probable existence. Thus he inaugurated a new era for dramatic representations, and it may be said that he was the inventor of the Spanish drama, which shortly after became the admiration of the civilized world, and a model for all the theatres of Europe.

Lope de Vega's fecundity has remained a unique phenomenon in the annals of mankind. He lived seventy years, and it is calculated that, during that lapse of time, he wrote poetry to the average of eight pages a day. It was an intellectual cataclysm, which could no more be stopped than the rush of waters over the Falls of Niagara. He monopolized the theatres of Spain ; there was no room for anybody else. His was the only name which, for many years, figured on the play-bills — so much so, that whenever a production of peculiar merit appeared on the stage, the people would obstinately attribute it to Lope de Vega. The multitude followed him in the streets; strangers inquired for him as an object of extraordinary curiosity; Monarchs gazed at him with complacency, and admitted him into their presence to shower honors upon their admired poet. Even the Pontiffs of Rome wished to reward so wonderful a genius; Urban VII. sent him the decorations of the Order of St. John, and conferred upon him the strange and unexpected honor of Doctor of Theology, forwarding to him the diploma with an autograph letter under the Pontifical hand and seal. Never was a writer more in danger of being smothered under his laurels, so profusely were they heaped upon the fortunate Spaniard.

Passing from poetical to prose productions, and beginning, on account of their analogy with the former, with those which are mere works of the imagination and only intended to amuse the reader, we find, in relation to the kind of compositions which were known under the general name of novels, and which, in our days, have come to exercise so marked an influence on the morals of nations, that the Spaniards cultivated with success this branch of literature under Philip II. In preceding years, Spain had teemed with those romances of chivalry which seemed so peculiarly adapted to the genius of her people, and some of which had been enumerated by Cervantes in his Don Quixote. After them, *pastoral* novels became the fashion, and, in our opinion, had not the merit of their predecessors. The adventures of Amadis, Palmerin, and Belianis, were full of marvellous extravagances and monstrosities, it is true; but they maintained alive that antique warlike spirit, those notions of honor, those sentiments of refined love, courtly gallantry, and deep-seated religious tendencies, which had always characterized the Spanish nation. Such works were like the sound of the trumpet which used to call on the Christian standard to unfurl itself, and on the stout knight to spring on his war-horse. But these pastoral novels, which were neither more probable in their inventions, nor more regular in their forms of composition, made no stirring appeal to the soul, in which they awoke no sentiment of grandeur or generosity. They did not even represent truthfully the manners, usages, customs and feelings of the shepherds and shepherdesses whose milk-and-water amours they languidly pretended to portray, in a language little in harmony with the humble condition of keepers of goats and sheep. The ear rebels against the monotonous melody of the love-sick flute which eternally pipes the same tune, and the cloyed stomach rises up to the gorge in disgust at the excessive sweetness of those literary condiments. Of this kind of compositions were the *Golden Age*, by Balbuena, the *Diana* of Montemayor, the *Arcadia* of Lope de Vega, the *Galatea* of Cervantes, with innumerable others of these water-melon productions.

The mind delights like nature in variety, and the pastoral novels were followed by those light and playful stories of which Don Diego de Hurtado had given us so felicitous a sample in his Lazarillo de Tormes, which formed so remarkable a contrast with the austere character of the author. The compositions of this class which obtained the greatest reputation were the *Adventures of Squire Marcos de D'Oregon*, by Vicente Espinel ; the life and achievements of the roguish *Guzman de Alfarache*, by Mateo Aleman ; the *Lame Devil*, by Luis Velez de Guevara ; and the life of *the Great Tacaño*, by Quevedo. The chief merit of these works consists in the more or less piquancy and graces of the style, and in the more or less exact delineation of the morals and customs of a certain class of society. But as the heroes of these novels were always personages of the most abject description, such as servants, thieves, adventurers, swindlers, and other characters of the same black stamp, who delighted in making a parade of their vices and infamy, and who ended by being the permanent tenants of a jail, the reader, notwithstanding the amusement which he derives from the perusal of these witty and loose compositions, cannot but be aware that he has stooped to very low company, and that he has indulged in a sort of debauch which it would not be proper to repeat with too much frequency. These works, in which the humorous knaveries of a valet are recited *con amore*, seem almost to be the parody of those nobler compositions in which the superhuman exploits and virtues of a knight are related in language equally extravagant and appropriately bombastic. It reminds us of Homer singing the Battle of the Frogs after that of the gods and heroes of the Iliad.

Of a different nature were the *Moral Tales* of Cervantes (Novelas Ejemplares), to which he gave this title, because he said there was nothing in them from which useful lessons could not be drawn. He went so far as to declare, that his object was to instruct as well as to amuse, and that he would rather cut off his hand than publish anything in his novels which might inspire a criminal thought. A most worthy determination, which should be common to all the authors of works of this kind! His style and tone correspond in these moral tales with his delineations of real life, and are neither too low nor too elevated. But he soon surpassed himself in his *Don Quixote de la Mancha.* This work, which has never been equalled, which retains its indescribable charms in all the languages of the civilized world into which it has been translated, which is a favorite book with the young as well as with the aged, with the frivolous as well as with the austere, which has been and will be the delight of every successive century to the end of time, is too well known and appreciated to require that anything should be said on its transcendent excellence.

Under the reign of Philip II., there could, of course, be no political writer. But one exception is afforded by his celebrated minister, Antonio Perez, who, in his exile in a foreign land, wrote to vindicate himself from the cruel persecution of his master. The pamphlets in which he speaks of his official career, his fall, his numerous trials before different tribunals, his various imprisonments and his flight, although disfigured at times by an affected display of erudition, are written with energy and vivacity. In his letters there is more elegance, more sprightliness, a more natural style, and a greater appearance of candor and frankness. They are not free from defects, but they are, on the whole, a good model of epistolary composition. He owes his literary reputation to persecution and exile.

Historical literature was more progressive. There was an abundance of histories of particular events, of the several kingdoms and provinces which composed the Spanish monarchy, of cities, towns, localities, institutions and men. It would be useless to look into any one of them for much criticism and philosophy. Philosophy was then an exotic in the land of the Inquisition, and circumstances were evidently not favorable to its growth. In some of those productions the language is ornate and florid; in others chaste, correct and pure; in many heavy and uncouth; and in most is to be observed the prevailing taste of the epoch for pompous harangues, long descriptions of sieges and battles, and a minuteness of details which makes those narrations insupportably tedious. All those historians are either military men or ecclesiastics, and their works bear the impress of those predilections and ideas which were natural and inherent in their respective professions. There is in them too much of the priest, or of the warrior; too much of the incense of the altar, or of the smoke, dust and clang of the battle-field. Such were, for instance, the *History of the Rebellion and Chastisement of the Moors*, by Marmol; the *War of Granada*, by Diego Hurtado de Mendoza; the *Commentaries* of Luis de Avila on the *War waged in Germany by Charles V.;* the *Wars in the Low Countries*, by Carlos Colomar, Marquis de Espinar; the *Commentaries on the Wars in Flanders*, by Bernardino de Mendoza; the *History of the Civil Wars of Granada*, by Diego Perez de Hita; and other works of the like nature, of more or less merit, composed by actors in the scenes which they described. These historians had bled in the battles which they narrated, and wielded the pen with a hand used to the grasp of the sword. If the military men cared little about recording anything else than deeds of arms, on the other side, the ecclesiastics, who became historians, neglected facts of importance to fall into ecstasy over the virtues of a saint, or the merits of a religious institution, or the happening of a miracle, and briefly mentioned worldly events, merely, as it were, to have the opportunity of appending to them moral reflections and Christian advice intended for the edification of the reader. Such is the *Life of St. Teresa de Jesus*, by Father Diego de Yepes, the Confessor of Philip. Father Jose de Siguenza, who wrote the *Life of St. Jerome*, and the *General History of the Order of that name*, with admirable elegance and an easy flow of style, and at the same time with great dignity of tone, elevation of ideas, and profound erudition, had all the qualities of a historian, and it is to be regretted that he did not employ his eminent talents in transmitting to posterity the annals of the Kingdom.

Among the various histories which deserve to be mentioned, notwithstanding the imperfections of which they are full, and which appertained to the epoch, are the *General History of the World*, by Antonio de Herrera; the *First Part of the History of Philip II.*, by Cabrera; the *Historical Annals of the Kingdom of Aragon*, by Argensola, the author of the *Conquest of the Molucca Islands;* and, above all, the *Annals of the same Kingdom*, by Geronimo de Zurita, the most conscientious, correct and searching of all the historians who wrote on the subject, and the one who demonstrates with the greatest lucidity and precision the manner in which the Constitution of Aragon grew and established itself. Estevan de Garibay published a *Summary of the Chronicles and Universal History of all the Kingdoms of Spain*, and the *Genealogies of the*

Catholic Kings,* for which he was handsomely rewarded by Philip. This author was a most diligent investigator of facts, but his style is so dry and disagreeable, that, although his work may be consulted with advantage as a valuable source of information, it cannot be read with pleasure.

Nothing which deserved the name of a General History of Spain had yet made its appearance. The glory of such a composition was reserved to Father Juan de Mariana. The Spaniards have compared him to Titus Livius, whom he imitates so far as to put in the mouths of illustrious personages the most prolix harangues or orations; thus sacrificing historical truth to the desire of making a display of eloquence. Like his Roman predecessor, he gathered into a body materials which were dispersed and isolated in disjointed ancient chronicles, but his work could not now be properly called a history. His style is clear, pure and dignified. His ideas and sentiments are noble, his judgment correct, his erudition extensive, and his talents of a high order. He did, probably, all that could be done at the time. Had he lived in this century, his work would, no doubt, have answered better all the requisites of history. It must be remembered that he could not but be under the influence of the age in which he wrote. To this must be attributed, be it from credulity, timidity, or respect for prevailing opinions and

* Ferdinand and Isabella are emphatically called, in Spain, "The Catholic Kings."

prejudices, his having admitted in his pages so many absurd fables, popular errors and ridiculous traditions, of which some were so strikingly exceptionable that he himself was obliged to say: "I transcribe more things than I believe." In relation to the domination of the Arabs in Spain, which is one of the most important and most brilliant parts of the history of that country, he is particularly defective and meagre. He so invariably disfigures their names, that they can hardly be recognized, and he is so prejudiced, that he never fails to designate as "barbarians" a people who, in civilization and knowledge of the arts and sciences, had long been superior to his own countrymen. His work, however, is of considerable merit; but it is not in its pages that the philosophic reader can expect to trace with lucidity and method the march of those successive events, and the gradual influence of those causes, which had produced at last the political and social organization of Spain, such as it existed in the days of the author.

The learned humanist, Francisco Sancho de Brozas, who was surnamed the "Apollo and Mercury of Spain," published several works on the Latin and Greek Grammar, on rhetoric and dialectics, and became so much pleased with his own attainments and performances, that too much learning, assisted by too much vanity, may be said to have "made him mad;" for he boasted that he could teach Latin in eight months, Greek in twenty days, spherical geometry in eight, dialectics and rhetoric in two months, and philosophy, with mystic theology, within even a shorter allowance of time.

But it is in the writers on sacred subjects that the richness and perfection at which the Spanish language had arrived are to be seen. Their fecundity and eloquence seem to have been unsurpassed. Juan de Avila, surnamed the "Apostle of Andalusia," had astonished and edified Spain by the fervor of his sermons, glowing with force and fluency of diction, like a fiery stream of fused gold. He was succeeded, under Philip, by his friend and disciple, Father Luis de Grenada, who was called the "Prince of Sacred Eloquence in Spain." His style is so pure and vernacular, that in all his writings there is not to be found, it is said, one word which is obsolete, or disused, or affected, or Latinized, or which is borrowed from any foreign idiom. This must have been a difficult task, considering how largely the Latin element enters into the composition of the Spanish language. He had the rare faculty of producing grand effects by the felicitous way in which he introduced the simplest and most commonly used expressions, and, although there is hardly one of his periods in which there is not the most consummate art, it is so concealed as not to appear, except on minute examination. It was said of him that no theological writer spoke of God with more dignity and awe-inspiring force, and that he opened to his readers the "very entrails of the Deity." It must be admitted, however, that his extreme facility of composition tempts him sometimes into verbosity and redundancy.

There was living at that time an admirable woman, a saint, who, with the meekness of the dove, had a heart glowing with passion—such passion as angels are gifted with—passion for all that is noble and divine, and a soul as ardent as those seraphic lamps which burn in the presence of the Most High. Her name was Saint Teresa de Jesus, and her whole existence was a sort of celestial ecstasy. Her works were written with talent and discrimination, and in a style chaste and simple, which not unfrequently rises to the sublime. She is so transported herself with poetical and religious frenzy, that the reader, catching her enthusiasm, feels as if carried with her to the mansions of eternal glory. "She seems," says Lafuente, whom I have so often quoted, "to have inherited the soul of Isabella the Catholic, and we feel justified in believing that Teresa, on the throne, would have been an Isabella, and that Isabella, in the cloister, would have been a Saint Teresa."

One of the most eminent sacred writers of the epoch is Father Luis de Leon, whom we have already mentioned as a distinguished poet. He is less oratorical, less abundant and harmonious than Father Luis de Granada, but more philosophical, more profound and energetic. Both were eloquent, and both were skillful dialecticians; both were models of meekness, virtue, and Christian piety. The one has been compared to Massillon, and the other to Bourdaloue. These ascetic writers, with many others equally meritorious, who obtained distinction in the same field of literature, and whom we are compelled to pass over in silence, on account of the limits which we have assigned to this disquisition, were also celebrated for the suavity of their temper, their benevolence, their indulgent and compassionate virtues, and their forbearance to treat harshly the frailties of humanity. They never attempted to make proselytes except by persuasion, and the sweet influence of instruction given in the blandest form. They look like a luminous constellation in the midst of the darkness of that firmament which the Inquisition had spread over Spain, and they present a singular contrast with the unmerciful ministers and agents of the Holy Office, whose catechism was the gag, the dungeon and the stake. Some of them were even brought before that terrible tribunal, and barely escaped the most cruel punishment.

With regard to theology and jurisprudence, it would require page after page to do justice to those who have acquired an illustrious name in these two branches of human knowledge under the reign of Philip II. We shall only mention a few. Diego de Lainez, the companion of Loyola in his apostleship, and his successor as General of the Order of Jesus, first obtained notoriety by his discourses in the celebrated Conference of Poissy near Paris, and rose to celebrity in the third meeting of the Council of Trent, by the oration in which he advocated the necessity of having a supreme and infallible head of the Church, immeasurably superior to the Bishops, who were to be the mere delegates of his pontifical authority. The 11th volume of the "General History of the Jesuits" bears his name. His contemporary, Alfonso de Salmeron, one of the seven first disciples of Loyola, was an enthusiastic propagator of the doctrines of his Master in Germany, Poland, Flanders, France and Italy, a professor in the University of Ingoldstadt, a distinguished orator in the Council of Trent, a learned commentator of the Epistles of St. Paul and of the Scriptural Books. Two other Jesuits, Father Thomas Sanchez and Luis de Molina, produced a sensation by their works. The first wrote a celebrated treatise on "Marriage," and compiled a "Digest of Laws." The second threw before the public, like an apple of discord, his famous book on the "Accord of Grace with free will." It gave rise to interminable disputes on grace and predestination between the Jesuits and Dominicans, by which the religious world was long agitated. Melchior Cano, who acted a conspicuous part in the Council of Trent, and who denounced in his writings the institution, the morals, and the plans of the Jesuits, composed a work on theology which is said to be incomparable. It is retained to this day as a text-book in the Spanish Universities. Bartolome de Carranza, Archbishop of Toledo, also famous among the members of the Council of Trent, and the last Confessor of the Emperor Charles V., was the author of an "Abbreviated History of the Councils and the Popes, from St. Peter to Julius III," of a treatise on "the Residence of Bishops in their Dioceses," and of a "Spanish Catechism." For this last production he was accused before the Inquisition, which persecuted him with incredible tenacity, although the people persisted in venerating him as an eminent and orthodox Prelate. Notwithstanding his being suspected of Lutheranism by the Holy Office, when he died at Rome, where he had taken refuge, the whole population went into mourning, all the shops were closed, and to his corpse were paid all the honors due to a saint.

No less famous than the theologians were the men present at the Council of Trent as jurisconsults. Azpelcueta, the two Covarrubias (Diego and Antonio), the Archbishop of Tarragona, Antonio Augustin, and other profound jurists who, in that age, came out of the Universities of Alcalá and Salamanca, who afterwards did honor to the schools of Bolonia and Paris, and who shone brilliantly in the ecclesiastical assemblies of Rome, or Trent, or in the courts of England, France and Germany, raised to the highest pitch the fame of Spanish jurisprudence, civil and canonical. Many foreign critics have paid due homage to their prodigious erudition, and have left on record appropriate eulogies of their works.

It is impossible to speak of the intellectual movement which took place toward the middle and the end of the 16th century, without mentioning one of the most eminent literary characters, and one of the most learned men of the epoch, Benito Arias Montano, who, with many others, reflected so much honor upon Spain in the Council of Trent, which was so grand an assemblage of the most exalted talents, virtues and erudition of Europe. He is well known in the Republic of Letters for his "Jewish Antiquities," his "Monuments of Human Salvation," his "Translation in Verse of the Psalms of David," his "History of Nature," and his work on "Rhetoric." But he is more indebted for his fame to his edition of the Polyglot Bible, which was especially intrusted to his care by Philip, and which was published at Antwerp. To no other man could the charge of so difficult and delicate a task have been given with more justice, for not only was he a profound theologian, and versed in the Belles Lettres and sciences, but he was also an extraordinary linguist. Besides his native language, he was a complete master of the Hebrew, the Chaldean, the Syriac, the Arabic, the Greek, the Latin, the French, Italian, Flemish and German. This magnificent edition of the Polyglot Bible honored equally the Monarch who had ordered it and the age which had seen its execution. As a reward, Philip offered a Bishopric to Montano, who modestly refused. Unfortunately, he had not consulted the Jesuits in the preparation of his great work. They became envious, and, at their instigation, Montano was denounced to the Inquisition as suspected of Judaism, because he had given the Hebrew text as adopted by the Rabbins. This compelled him to publish a book in self-defence, the title of which was, "My Vindication." The accusation was referred by the Grand Inquisitor to the investigations and judgment of the Jesuit, Juan de Mariana, who, contrary to the expectations, and much to the mortification of the members of his company, reported favorably to Montano. He must have been a bold man, that Jesuit Mariana, thus to resist, for the sake of justice, the pressure brought to bear upon him. In consequence of it he fell himself under the displeasure of the Inquisition, which persecuted him, and punished him severely for his work on the "Alteration of Coin," for another on "Death and Immortality," and particularly for his treatise on "Kings and the Institution of Royalty," which was condemned as seditious by the Parliament of Paris, and burned by the hand of the public executioner, because it contained a defense of regicide under the name of tyrannicide. He did not forgive his brother Jesuits for their ill-will toward him, and he wrote a book, which was brought to light only after his death, and the title of which is: "Infirmities of the Company of Jesus."

In this short literay sketch, we could not but omit to mention a crowd of men who contributed their mite to the intellectual wealth of Spain under the long reign of Philip. The reader who may have followed us in our course must have come to the conclusion that, in those days, there were two sciences which must necessarily have been excluded from cultivation and progress—politics and philosophy. The reason is apparent under such a monarch as Philip, and such an institution as the Inquisition, from whose terrible grasp the most eminent and holiest members of the Church, such as Archbishops, Bishops, and even Saints, were not free, whenever they indulged in what was deemed a liberty of thought. For instance, eight venerable prelates and nine doctors of theology who had participated in that Council of Trent which had established forever all the articles of faith of the Catholic Church, were tried by the Inquisition as suspected of Lutheranism. What philosopher could have escaped being roasted alive, when Loyola himself, the founder of the Order of Jesus, St. Francis de Borgia, his intimate friend and disciple, when St. Teresa, and a legion of others whom one could hardly have fancied within the reach of a suspicion of heresy, had to appear like supposed culprits before that redoubtable tribunal, and when the same fate awaited Martin Martinez de Cuntalapiedra, the author of the Hippoteposeon, merely for his having recommended to consult the original text of the sacred writings? The wonder is that anybody presumed to think at all, on any subject, with the fear of the Inquisition hanging over one's head like the sword of Damocles. Fortunately, as we have seen, there is no prison of iron, be it built by man, or devil, which can entirely prevent the irruption of mind into that boundless space of free air which is its natural element.

We do not see how the intellectual movement which unfolded itself in Spain under the reign of Philip, can be attributed to the patronage or influence of that Monarch. It was the result of other causes, as we have said before. Philip was not a protector of the arts and literature after the fashion of a Mæcenas, an Augustus, a Medici, a Francis, or a Louis the Fourteenth of France. He would not have chatted familiarly over a bottle of wine with Horace, or Virgil, as with a friend and equal. Although not deficient in taste, he was too cold, too phlegmatic, too distant and methodic, too systematically a thing of starch and buckram, to be in sympathizing harmony with the wayward, enthusiastic, warm-hearted, hot-headed race of artists and poets. The patron of the arts must be like Apollo, who guided the car of the Sun, and must surround himself with an atmosphere of genial heat. He must shower gold, rewards, honors, smiles, caresses, and, above all, those felicitous words, which are the gift of Heaven to certain men, by which they create heroes, and bind forever contented the priests of the mind to the altar where they worship with so much toil and love. Such was not Philip. There must have been something freezing in his very encouragements. It was such a warming as is imparted to the earth by the mantle of snow which covers it, and not by the rays of the great celestial luminary. Philip would not have picked up the dropped pencil of Titian, and would not have said, when presenting it to him: "You are worthy of being waited upon by an Emperor." Thus spoke Charles. Let us see how Philip, in his turn, treated a painter. In 1581, he was on his way to Lisbon, and passed through Badajoz, where the famous Morales, surnamed the "Divine," was living. He sent for the artist. We do not presume to imagine what a Francis the First, or a Louis the Fourteenth, would have said on such an occasion, but we are sure that it would have been something worthy of royalty, and of the majesty of genius which bent, like a humble vassal, before the majesty of the throne. What were the most gracious words which Philip's heart suggested to Philip's mind? He looked with his cold gray eyes at the great painter whom he had summoned to his presence, and found nothing better to say than: "You are very old, Morales." "Aye, and very poor, sire," was the emphatic reply. Philip could not but take the hint which he had provoked, and granted the artist an annual pension of 300 ducats, which his advanced age prevented him from enjoying long. Out with such a man! We have no patience with him. He, forsooth, a patron of the arts! He may at times have paid well, perhaps, and that is all. But is genius a base born varlet, that he is to be satisfied with mere wages? Is he not entitled to something else? We have lived, thank God, to see Royalty make way for Humboldt to pass. That is the something more which was wanted. It is to the praise of our age that the sceptres of the Kingdoms of the earth have learned not to treat, like an intrusive upstart, the sceptre of the intellectual world.

Philip, on his death-bed, had complained that "Heaven, which had granted him so many Kingdoms, had refused him a son capable of governing them." He does not seem to have thought of asking himself what he had done with the rich inheritance which had been bequeathed to him by his father. The judgment of history must be, that he did very little for the welfare and progressive improvement of the condition of those whom Providence had intrusted to his care. "If I live long enough," had said his contemporary, Henry IV, "every peasant in France shall have a chicken in his pot every Sunday." Philip lived long, and yet no peasant's home in his dominions was made more cheerful or comfortable by his exertions. On the contrary, what was bad when he ascended the throne, had grown worse, when he descended into the tomb. He left Spain in a state of rapid and hopeless decadence, which he had never attempted to arrest. He had torpified her and everything else which had come within the reach of his fatal influence. His own son and heir had grown by his side hardly with the capacity of generating a thought and the faculty of having a will of his own. Philip the Third became a crowned slave—a being who was as anxious to forego power as his father had been not to delegate a particle of it. Philip IV., was, if possible, a still greater imbecile as a King, although a good-natured individual, amiably fond of dramatic poetry, in the innocuous composition of which he loved to indulge, and could not have lived without a master. Charles II., the last of his race, was an idiotic maniac, who thought himself bewitched ; and when his wretched existence ceased, the Crown was transferred to one of the descendants of that Henry whom Philip II. had done so much to exclude from the throne of France. The Austrian dynasty had lasted about one hundred and eighty-five years. It began in a blaze of glory which, for a while, concealed the deleterious effects of tyranny and maladministration, and, having destroyed the antique liberties of Spain, it ended, as it were, by a decree of stern justice, in premature decrepitude, in inconcealable humiliation and abject lunacy. It is well. Let the judgments of God be recorded in the high court of history.

THE END.

www.ingramcontent.com/pod-product-compliance
Lightning Source LLC
LaVergne TN
LVHW020127110826
845151LV00001B/301

* 9 7 8 1 4 2 5 5 4 0 8 8 3 *